D0326114

FREEDOM
Human Rights Education Pack

Caroline Adams, Marietta Harrow and Dan Jones

AMNESTY
INTERNATIONAL
UNITED KINGDOM

Hodder & Stoughton
A MEMBER OF THE HODDER HEADLINE GROUP

Acknowledgements

The front cover illustration is reproduced courtesy of © Frank Fournier/Contact Press Images.
The publishers would like to thank the following individuals, institutions and companies for permission to reproduce copyright illustrations in this book: © Amnesty International, pages i, v, 44, 45, 46, 47, 49, 52, 63, 64, 66, 67, 70 bottom, 71, 74, 93, 104 top, 104 bottom, 117, 118, 121 middle, 122, 124 top, 124 bottom, 128 top, 128 bottom, 136, 148, 149, 155, 163, 183, 188, 193, 195, 244 (seventh logo), 250; Amnesty International USA, page 133; © AP, pages 32, 70 top, 166; © The Campaign for Nuclear Disarmament, page 244 (first logo); © Christian Aid, page 244 (fourth logo); © Corinne Dufka/Reuters, page 224; David Turnley/CORBIS, pages 216, 218; © Gamma/Frank Spooner, page 75; © Helen Stone, page 130; Hulton-Deutsch Collection/Tony Stone Images, page 98 bottom; © Hulton Getty, pages 160, 220; The Birmingham Post and Mail, p.115; © John Garrett/CORBIS, page 170; © Jon Bjornsen, page 185; © Liu Heung Shung, Contact Press Images/Colorific, page 34; Mary Evans Picture Library, pages 98 top, 210; © MENCAP, page 244 (fifth logo); © Museum of London, pages 100, 101; © National Concord, page 158; Newham Monitoring Project, page 231; © Oxfam, page 244 (third logo); Popperfoto, pages 55 bottom left; © Popperfoto/Bob Thomas Sports Photography, pages 55 top left, 55 middle right; © Popperfoto/PPP, page 226; Popperfoto/Reuters, pages 28, 121 bottom, 223; © Radio Times Hulton Picture Library, pages 169, 179; © Reuters, page 91; © Reuters/ Popperfoto, pages 105, 121 top; © Rex, page 162; © Royal Society for the Protection of Birds, page 244 (sixth logo); © Santiago Llanquin/AP, page 127; © Save the Children Fund, page 244 (second logo); Sophia Smith Collection, page 99; © UN, pages vi, 20, 25.

The publishers would also like to thank the following for permission to reproduce material in this book: Cambridge University Press for the extract from *A Vindication of the Rights of Man and A Vindication of the Rights of Woman and Hint* by Mary Wollstonecraft (Cambridge University Press, 1995); extracts from *Youth Lifestyle Survey* Crown Copyright 1993 is reproduced with permission of Her Majesty's Stationery Office; Ariel Dorfman for the extract from 'Last Will and Testament', *Missing: Poems by Ariel Dorfman* (Amnesty International); *Guardian* for the extracts from 'It would diminish the importance' by Esther Addley, © *Guardian* (26 July 1999), 'Silence is death' by John Gittings, © *Guardian* (21 January 1999), 'Innocent after 23 years in jail' by Duncan Campbell, © *Guardian* (13 June 1998); the extract from *Collected Essays, Journalism and Letters* by George Orwell (Penguin, 1968), copyright © George Orwell, 1931, by permission of Bill Hamilton as the Literary Executor of the Estate of the Late Sonia Brownell Orwell and Martin Secker & Warburg Ltd; the extract from *1984* by George Orwell (Penguin, 1949) (Copyright © George Orwell, 1949), by permission of Bill Hamilton as the Literary Executor of the Estate of the Late Sonia Brownell Orwell and Martin Secker & Warburg Ltd; the extract from *Talking Points: Genocide* by R.G. Grant (Wayland, 1998), reproduced by permission of Hodder & Stoughton Limited; Human Rights Watch for the extract from 'Leave none to tell the story: genocide in Rwanda' (Human Rights Watch, 1999), used with the permission of Human Rights Watch. Not to be republished or reprinted without the expressed written consent of Human Rights Watch; *The Independent*/Syndication for the extracts from 'Indonesian military gives students a lesson in torture' by Stephen Vines, *Independent* (30 March 1998) and 'When the pen is the key to the gaol door' by Mark Lattimer, *Independent* (23 June 1998); Index on Censorship for the extract from 'Hate speech: the speech that kills' by Ursula Owen (1 August 1999) from *Index on Censorship*, the magazine for free expression (**www.indexoncensorship.org**); Sue Lees, Professor of Women's Studies, University of North London and author of *Carnal Knowledge: Rape on Trial* (Women's Press, forthcoming 2002), for the extract from 'When in Rome' by Sue Lees, *Guardian* (16 February 1999); Hugh Lewin for the extracts from 'Hang' and 'Touch' in *Poets to the People* ed. Barry Feinberg (Heinemann AWS, 1980), © Hugh Lewin; Little, Brown and Co. for the extract from *A Long Walk to Freedom* by Nelson Mandela, Abacus, 1994; Macmillan, London, UK for the extract from *We Wish to Inform You that Tomorrow We Will be Killed with our Families* by Philip Gourevitch (Picador, 1999); New Internationalist for the extracts from Womankind Worldwide Factsheet, *New Internationalist*, Jan/Feb 1998, **www.newint.org**; by permission of Oxford University Press the extract from *The Death Penalty: A World-wide Perspective* by Roger Hood (Clarendon Press, 1996); the extract from *Witness to War* by Michael Leapman (Viking, London,1998), copyright © Michael Leapman, 1998, reproduced by permission of Penguin Books Ltd; the extract from pp.153–4 of *London: A Social History* by Roy Porter (Hamish Hamilton, London, 1994) copyright © Roy Porter, 1994, reproduced by permission of Penguin Books Ltd; the extract from *A Sense of Freedom* by Jimmy Boyle (Pan Macmillan, 1977), reprinted by permission of PFD on behalf of Jimmy Boyle; the extract from *Out of Danger* by James Fenton (Penguin, 1993), reproduced by permission of PFD on behalf of James Fenton; Cecil Rajendra for the extract from 'The Animal and Insect Act' in *Refugees and Other Depairs* (CHOICE Books, 1980); Irina Ratushinskaya for the extract from 'I will live and survive' in *Pencil Letter*, trans. David McDuff (Bloodaxe Books, 1998); Reuters for the extract from *12/04/97 Turkey: Turkey's Mothers Demand Word of the Missing* by Jonathan Lyons, © Reuters Limited 1997; © Nick Ryan for the extract from 'Truth under attack' by Nick Ryan in *Guardian* (20th July 1998); Simon & Schuster UK for the extract from *Survival in Auschwitz* by Primo Levi (Touchstone, 1993), copyright © Primo Levi, 1958; the extract from *Styles of Radical Will* by Susan Sontag (Vintage, 1994), copyright © Susan Sontag 1966; Stonewall for the extracts from the Queerbashing surveys, a part of the Stonewall Equality 2000 Campaign; University of Illinois Press for the extracts from pages 87–96 *Women in Revolutionary Paris, 1789–1795: Selected Documents Translated With Notes and Commentary*, edited and translated by Darline Gay Levy, Harriet Branson Applewhite and Mary Durham Johnson (University of Illinois, 1979); Wordsworth Editions Limited for the extract from 'The Ballad of Reading Gaol' in *'De Profundis', 'The Ballad of Reading Gaol' & Other Writings* by Oscar Wilde, ISBN: 1840224010 (Wordsworth Editions Limited, 1999).

Every effort has been made to trace and acknowledge ownership of copyright. The publishers will be glad to make suitable arrangements with any copyright holders whom it has not been possible to contact.

Sutton Coldfield
College LRC
Sutton Campus

Accession

1 1 4 9 8 6

Class

323·4
AOA

Orders: please contact Bookpoint Ltd, 130 Milton Park, Abingdon, Oxon OX14 4SB. Telephone: (44) 01235 827729, Fax: (44) 01235 400454. Lines are open from 9.00–6.00, Monday to Saturday, with a 24 hour message answering service. Email address: orders@bookpoint.co.uk

British Library Cataloguing in Publication Data
A catalogue record for this title is available from The British Library

ISBN 0 340 73058 7

First published 2001
Impression number   10 9 8 7 6 5 4 3 2 1
Year   2007 2006 2005 2004 2003 2002 2001

Copyright © 2001 Amnesty International UK

Amnesty International UK
99–119 Rosebery Avenue
London EC1R 4RE

Amnesty International product code: PB210

All rights reserved. This work is copyright. Permission is given for copies to be made of pages provided they are used exclusively within the institution for which this work has been purchased. For reproduction for any other purpose, permission must first be obtained in writing from the publishers.

The text of *Freedom!* covers a very wide range of topics and areas of work that fall outside the scope and mandate of Amnesty International. It has been published in order to stimulate and raise awareness of human rights issues and to encourage a broad approach to human rights education. It does not necessarily represent the views of Amnesty International United Kingdom.

Typeset by Fakenham Photosetting Ltd
Printed in Great Britain for Hodder & Stoughton Educational, a division of Hodder Headline Plc, 338 Euston Road, London NW1 3BH by Hobbs the Printers Ltd.

Contents

Foreword

The United Nations Decade for Human Rights Education (1995–2004) provides Governments, international bodies, non-governmental organisations, professional associations, all sectors of civil society and individuals with a common framework in which to concentrate efforts for human rights education, training and public information, and to establish partnerships to this end. The publication by Amnesty International of this handbook will serve as a valuable contribution to the global effort to promote greater understanding of human rights.

Human rights education is empowering. It ranges from the provision of information about human rights standards and protection mechanisms to the development of values and attitudes which uphold human rights, to the encouragement to take action to defend one's rights and the rights of others. Human rights education makes a critical contribution to the prevention of human rights violations and constitutes an investment for the future in the long struggle to achieve a world where everyone's rights are valued and respected.

Human rights education is particularly important in schools. All concerned should involve themselves – students, teachers, parents, administrators. The atmosphere should be one of participation and mutual respect, the goal that of developing together an understanding of our common responsibility to make human rights a reality in our communities. Human rights education is not just about lessons for school, it is about lessons for life.

Mary Robinson
United Nations High Commissioner for Human Rights

Mary Robinson

Introduction

Eleanor Roosevelt

When the United Nations General Assembly adopted and proclaimed the Universal Declaration of Human Rights on 10 December 1948, it saw education as the vehicle to develop human rights understanding and skills and avoid the horrors and 'barbarous acts which have outraged the conscience of mankind'. There were visions of 'a world in which human beings shall enjoy freedom of speech and belief and freedom from fear and want' – a world in which the fundamental rights of people would be protected by the rule of law. The world's governments promised to take action to promote 'universal respect for and observance of human rights and fundamental freedoms for all without distinction as to race, sex, language or religion'. The upholding of these rights and freedoms of all members of the human family, and their right to a social and international order in which they can be enjoyed, was made obligatory on UN member states.

However the Universal Declaration of Human Rights has been called 'the world's best kept secret'. Few know what it contains. Fewer have seen a copy. Yet it is meant to be 'disseminated, displayed and expounded, principally in schools and other educational institutions'. Every individual and every organ of society is meant to 'strive by teaching and education to promote respect for the rights and freedoms in the Declaration and to secure their universal and effective recognition and observance'.

Amnesty International, which for 40 years has campaigned against the violations of human rights round the world, believes that human rights education and awareness is a key and essential defence against the abuse of human rights. In the United States, the magazine of the Human Rights Educators Network is called *The Fourth R*, suggesting teaching and learning about human rights should be placed alongside reading, writing and arithmetic as essential skills and knowledge to be learned in school.

Teaching human rights has a knowledge content – young people should know what human rights are and how they developed. But they should also be able to detect and recognise a human rights issue, and know how to act on it.

Freedom! is published at the start of the new millennium. In the UK citizenship education is to be a new and important part of the National Curriculum for England and Wales from September 2002. It will include an emphasis on democracy and human rights, understanding right and wrong, and appreciating obligations as well as rights to enable young people to play a full role in the life of their communities. 'Education should not attempt to shelter our nation's children from the harsher controversies of adult life, but should prepare them to deal with such controversies knowledgeably, sensibly, tolerantly and morally', writes Professor Bernard Crick. Professor Sir Bernard Crick was the Chair of the Advisory Group on Education for Citizenship and the teaching of Democracy in Schools (1998).

In its Initial Guidance for Schools on teaching Citizenship at Key Stages 3 and 4 the Qualifications and Curriculum Authority (QCA) states that 'learning from real life experience is central to Citizenship'.

It lays down guidelines on the teaching of controversial issues: 'The Education Act of 1966 aims to ensure that children are not presented with only one side of political or controversial issues by their teacher.

'Sensitive and controversial issues are certain to arise. Pupils should not be sheltered from them. Through them pupils can develop an important range of skills including listening, accepting another point of view, arguing a case, dealing with conflict and distinguishing between fact and opinion.

'In the teaching of controversial issues there is always the risk of bias whether unwitting or otherwise. Teachers should adopt strategies that will teach pupils how to recognise bias, how to evaluate evidence put before them, how to look for different interpretations, views and sources of evidence, and how to give reasons for what they say and do.

'The need for balance should not be regarded as inhibiting a clear stand against racism and other forms of discrimination. Our common values require that there are behaviours that we should not tolerate. For example racism, bullying, and cruelty in all its forms are never acceptable.'

Amnesty International UK has been producing valuable education materials on human rights for use in schools over the past 15 years. **Freedom!** is the latest of these, a practical set of ideas and information exploring a wide range of human rights topics across different subject areas in a creative and dynamic way that will be welcomed in schools across the country and overseas.

Dan Jones, AIUK Education Officer

How to use this Education Pack

Human rights education is not to be considered a subject area in its own right to be isolated from the mainstream of education, shoehorned into the corner of an RE or PSHE lesson. Human rights education should be introduced across the curriculum from Geography and Art to English and Mathematics. **Freedom!** looks at how the concept of human rights began and how it became embodied in national and international law. It points out opportunities to introduce human rights topics into different subject areas, and is designed for teachers of students from 14 to 18, (Key Stages 3 and 4 and post GCSE) and for educators working in informal youth education.

In each Unit in **Freedom!** a chart is provided for the teacher suggesting the suitability of the material for inclusion in different curriculum subject areas. In the Topic Summaries we refer to the National Curriculum for England and Wales and to the Guidance Notes on Citizenship and suggestions for Key Skills for England and Wales. In Scotland and Northern Ireland we recognise that there are significant differences in subject areas, curricula and in the detailed requirements of the Citizenship curriculum.

Freedom! is a practical, hands-on educational tool designed to provide accessible materials and ideas for active teaching and learning about a range of human rights issues. In recognition of the increasing pressure of time on teachers, and the lack of hours and space to prepare new materials for classroom work, each unit of **Freedom!** is laid out with a set of teachers' notes for lessons and activities followed by a set of teaching materials for students that can be taken straight from the page and used as they stand. Teachers are encouraged to photocopy the exercises, activities and information in the workbook. **Freedom!** offers scope for teachers to adapt the approach and topics to their current work and interests.

Freedom! contains:

- Ideas for interactive approaches and participative classroom activity
- Information sheets and background material
- Suggestions for follow-up work
- Sources of further information, including relevant Internet addresses.

Apart from Unit 1 on Understanding human rights, the units need not be taken in any particular sequence. Teachers may 'dip' into different parts of the workpack to suit their needs.

Professor Ian Lister of the School of Education, University of York, has defined three essential components of human rights learning:

- learning *about* human rights (**knowledge** about rights, responsibilities, laws, documents, information, and the people and movements involved in the struggle for rights);
- learning *for* human rights (developing the political, social and interpersonal **skills** necessary to understand what human rights and responsibilities are, and how to exercise them);
- learning *through* human rights (students **experience** respect, freedom and human rights values through the way that their learning takes place).

The exercises in **Freedom!** are participative. They aim to stimulate the student's awareness of human rights issues, starting with their own knowledge and experience. A pair of participating students, the group, the class or the school itself become the sounding board against which ideas of justice are tested, and human rights skills are developed and honed. Skills for human rights include collaborative learning, discussion and debate, role play, visualisation, empathy exercises, creative work, research and analysis, developing social skills, respecting opinions, listening to each other, interpreting and making judgements, and taking action. In the exercises, students also develop the knowledge-based skills of collecting, analysing and presenting information.

In its approach, **Freedom!** has attempted to avoid any stereotypical implication that human rights abuses are concentrated 'somewhere else', far away in one particular part of the world or another. Examples and concerns about human rights abuses and about the positive struggle for justice are taken from all over the world, including the UK.

The authors
Caroline Adams: youth and community worker in Tower Hamlets, trainer, lecturer, writer and historian. (Sadly Caroline died shortly before the publication of this book.)
Marietta Farrow: further education teacher in East London and writer on race and social issues.
Dan Jones: education officer of Amnesty International UK, writer and artist.

Amnesty International Educational Resources
Education work that is based on current events tends to date rapidly. Teachers are strongly recommended always to check Amnesty International's website **www.amnesty.org.uk** or other sources of information mentioned in the text for the latest news.

Amnesty International's Human Rights Education website **www.amnesty.org.uk/education/index.shtml** includes the full text of the Universal Declaration of Human Rights, an animated cartoon version of the UDHR, other international human rights treaties, Amnesty International's illustrated human rights history, 'The Long March to Freedom' and the human rights story 'A Long Way to Cherry Time' and other materials and exercises in this book.

'Amnesty Interactive' is the Youth Action section of the Amnesty International website, with information on the 400 Amnesty International school groups plus news of the latest campaigns and events on **www.amnesty.org.uk/student/**.

Just Right is a companion volume to **Freedom!** with a CD Rom which explores aspects of the Convention on the Rights of the Child. (Product Code: CC 005. Order from Amnesty International 01788 545553 – £10.00 inc. postage.)

Understanding human rights

UNIT AIMS

This unit aims to enable pupils to:

- unpack the complex web of ideas called human rights
- explore their ideas about human needs, rights, claims and responsibilities
- learn about the Universal Declaration of Human Rights (UDHR)
- consider how conflicting human rights claims should be resolved
- think about how human rights are denied
- understand how human rights are developed and protected
- explore the role of democratic systems in protecting human rights
- consider personal responsibilities in maintaining and promoting human rights

INTRODUCTION

This unit explores the links between needs, rights and responsibilities and how these are claimed, met, denied or enacted at a variety of levels. Students can consider their own needs, rights and responsibilities and relate their experiences to wider society, world events and international legal human rights frameworks.

Some students may have painful experiences of their basic needs or rights being denied – for example, as refugees fleeing from oppressive regimes, and teachers will need to use their judgement in selecting appropriate activities.

Several of the activities explore how rights often conflict. They are designed to encourage students to think about what can happen in such situations; to consider how such conflicting rights might be prioritised and resolved; and to look at serious problems and consequences that emerge when the conflicts are not resolved.

This unit describes and explores the historical context in which the Universal Declaration of Human Rights was agreed, and introduces the other major human rights conventions and instruments drawn up in the 20th century. It asks students to think about why there is such a need for agreed international standards and frameworks for the protection and promotion of human rights.

Activities on the right to participate look at the concept of democracy, struggles to achieve it, and its practice. The limitations and strengths of democratic systems in protecting and promoting human rights are explored, as is the denial and abuse of human rights in crackdowns on democratic movements. Activities on the struggle for the vote for women in the UK can be found in Unit 3 on Women's Rights.

Throughout Unit 1, students are encouraged to develop self-awareness and an understanding of human behaviour and actions that can deny or promote human rights. The activities are designed to highlight the importance of individual

2

FREEDOM!

responsibility and collective action in
protecting and promoting human rights,

demonstrating why this is relevant to
students' own lives and futures.

SUMMARY OF TOPICS

TITLE	CURRICULUM LINKS	PAGE
1. What do we need?	13+: PSHE/RE/Geography/English/Sociology/History	3/10
Citizenship	**Knowledge and Understanding:** *human rights and responsibilities, democracy, justice systems* **Key Skills:** *communication, problem-solving*	
2. Esperanza: the Island of Hope	13+: PSHE/General Studies/RE/Geography/History/English/Sociology	3/11
Citizenship	**Knowledge and Understanding:** *legal and human rights, democracy, justice systems* **Key Skills:** *communication, problem-solving, working with others*	
3. Esperanza settlers meet the Rakyat	14+: PSHE/General Studies/RE/History/Geography/English/Sociology	5/12
Citizenship	**Knowledge and Understanding:** *diversity, resolving conflict fairly, legal and moral rights, responsibilities* **Key Skills:** *communication* **Participation Skills:** *negotiation, considering others' experience*	
4. Rights and responsibilities	14+: Drama/PSHE/General Studies/RE/Geography/English/Sociology	5/15
Citizenship	**Knowledge and Understanding:** *legal and human rights and responsibilities* **Enquiry Skills:** *researching social issues*	
5. History and human rights	13+: History/RE/Law/English/PSHE/General Studies	5/16
Citizenship	**Knowledge and Understanding:** *legal and human rights and responsibilities underpinning society* **Enquiry Skills:** *researching and analysing information* **Key Skills.** *Application of number*	
6. The UDHR	14+: History/English/Law/PSHE/General Studies/Art and Design/Drama	6/20
Citizenship	**Knowledge and Understanding:** *legal and human rights underpinning society, the work of the UN* **Key Skills:** *communication, working with others*	
7. Human rights in the news	14+: Media Studies/Maths/English/PSHE/General Studies/RE	6/23
Citizenship	**Knowledge and Understanding:** *the media's role in society* **Key Skills:** *communication* **Participation Skills:** *critically evaluating views*	
8. Can rights justifiably be curtailed?	14+: PSHE/General Studies/English/Law/RE	6/24
Citizenship	**Knowledge and Understanding:** *legal and human rights, conflict resolution* **Key Skills:** *communication* **Enquiry Skills:** *researching a topical issue*	
9. Conflicting rights	16+: English/Law/RE/PSHE/General Studies	6/25
Citizenship	**Knowledge and Understanding:** *legal and human rights, conflict resolution* **Key Skills:** *communication* **Enquiry Skills:** *researching and analysing topical issues*	

TITLE	CURRICULUM LINKS	PAGE
10. Claiming rights	14+: English/Drama/PSHE/General Studies	7/26
Citizenship	**Knowledge and Understanding:** *legal and human rights* **Participation and Enquiry Skills:** *considering others' experiences, analysing information*	
11. The Great Escape	14+: PSHE/General Studies/RE/Law	7/—
Citizenship	**Knowledge and Understanding:** *conflict resolution, democracy* **Key Skills:** *IT, communication, application of number, problem-solving, working with others*	
12. How the human rights machinery of the United Nations works	16+: English/Drama/Law/PSHE/General Studies	7/—
Citizenship	**Knowledge and Understanding:** *legal and human rights, democratic process* **Key Skills:** *IT, communication, application of number, problem-solving, working with others* **Enquiry Skills:** *researching topical political/moral issues* **Participation Skills:** *expressing/thinking about views not their own*	
13. The right to take part in government	14+: PSHE/General Studies/English/Law	7/—
Citizenship	**Knowledge and Understanding:** *democracy* **Key Skills:** *communication* **Participation Skills:** *Reflect on participation*	
14. The struggles for Democracy – South Africa and the UK	14+: English/PSHE/General Studies/History/Drama/Theatre Studies/Law/Mathematics	8/28
Citizenship	**Knowledge and Understanding:** *democratic process, bringing about social change* **Key Skills:** *communication, IT*	
15. Tiananmen	14+: English/History/PSHE/General Studies	9/32
Citizenship	**Knowledge and Understanding:** *democratic process* **Participatory Skills:** *empathising with others, experience*	

ACTIVITIES: NOTES FOR TEACHERS

Activity 1: What do we need?

Photocopy the exercise sheet. Get the students to cut out each of the rectangles.

Ask small groups to do a diamond ranking of the needs and wants written on the rectangles in order of importance to them.

Then ask:

- Were there areas of disagreement?
- How did you agree an order?
- Did the order change when you imagined the needs of a baby, adult with a medical condition, pensioner?
- Which needs are essential to keeping us alive?
- Which needs are to do with making our lives more pleasant or fulfilling?

Activity 2: Esperanza: the Island of Hope

You will need:

- felt-tip pens
- flip charts
- coloured stick-on labels – three per student

- a copy of the Universal Declaration of Human Rights (summary version, in Activity 6, full text on the website: www.amnesty.org.uk/education/index)
- Blue-Tac
- if possible, a video player and the animated cartoon film of the UDHR. Order from Amnesty International 01788 545553. Quote Product Code ED071 (£10.00 inc. postage).

Students imagine they are on a luxury passenger liner with thousands of others sailing across a southern ocean. One day the ship sails into a severe typhoon and sinks. Thankfully almost all the passengers and crew escape in lifeboats. After some days at sea they see a strange land mass, unknown on any map, emerging from the mist. They discover a large, and apparently uninhabited island. They name it 'Esperanza', the Island of Hope. It is a beautiful place with plenty of clean fresh water, building materials, rich soil, plants, birds, flowers, fish and lots of things to eat. The passengers soon establish a whole community on the island, working together to build new homes, grow crops, keep warm and organise the basic necessities of life.

People's Charter

One day, representatives of the new community meet together to draw up an Esperanza People's Human Rights Charter.

Get students in pairs to try and define a human right. Share as a whole class.

Groups *brainstorm* about all their basic needs and rights on Esperanza. In brainstorms:

- only one person speaks at a time;
- all ideas are received without criticism or praise;
- someone from each group writes up all the different suggestions on a flipchart

What are the fundamental rights, responsibilities and freedoms that all citizens of the island should enjoy? These may be rights to have good things, rights that require mutual support and responsibilities and rights not to be treated unfairly or bullied. Who will make the decisions? Who should work? Will there be formal education? Will there be a system of justice? Each group should write down as many ideas as possible, producing at least a dozen suggestions. The group's ideas should then be ranked in order of importance.

Groups call out their list of suggestions one by one in turn. Write them clearly on a flipchart. Try and put similar ideas together.

Each citizen of Esperanza is now given three small stick-on coloured voting slips from the rights listed on the flipchart, everyone selects the three rights they consider most important and casts their votes by sticking them on the chart. The votes are anonymous. A Registrar is chosen to count the votes. The results are announced.

The UDHR

Give each student their own copy of the Universal Declaration of Human Rights (UDHR). If possible, show them the Amnesty International animated video of the UDHR. They compare the UDHR with their Esperanza Charter.

What rights has the UN listed that they did not include?

What rights have they listed that the UN did not include?

FURTHER ACTIVITY

Give out the exercise sheet 'What are human rights?'

Ask each student to list rights they have at home, in the school and in the community. Groups draw up a list of rights for young people.

Ask:

- Can you think of an example where the rights of a teacher, a parent/carer, or another student conflicts with your rights? (For example, students have a right as well as a responsibility to involve themselves in learning; teachers have a right to choose appropriate learning materials and a responsibility to prepare lessons properly.)

Pairs share and discuss examples of the following experiences:

- a time when they have participated in denying someone else's rights, such as bullying, or discriminating against someone on the basis of age, race, gender, disability, etc.

- a time when they have challenged the denial of their own or someone else's rights. What happened? How do they feel about it now? What would they do in similar situations?

Activity 3: Esperanza settlers meet the Rakyat

It turns out that the beautiful island of Esperanza is not uninhabited as the new settlers had thought. In fact, there is quite a large indigenous community, the Rakyat, which means 'people' in their language. They have lived in the southern part of the island for centuries. There are about a thousand of them. They are very religious and democratic people. They work cooperatively, and share responsibilities, living mostly by hunting and fishing. They call the island 'Harap', which means 'hope' in their language.

Divide the class into two groups: the new Esperanza settlers and the Rakyat people. Give each group their briefing sheet.

PART 1: NEGOTIATING WITH A DIFFERENT COMMUNITY

Give each group time to discuss their briefing sheet and decide what approach they will take to the other community.

Will everyone speak at the meeting or will they choose delegates to be spokespeople? Are there any 'preconditions' on which they insist before the meeting starts?

PART 2: THE MEETING

The meeting takes place. Intervene if things get heated.

PART 3: DEBRIEFING AND DISCUSSION

Make sure that everyone comes out of the roles they have been playing. Discuss how they felt about the situations they were in.

Give each group the opportunity to answer these following questions:

- How did they make their decisions before the meeting?
- Did one/a few people influence the rest of the group? How?
- Did everyone feel happy about what was decided? Why/why not?
- How did they feel during the meeting?
- Did one group have more power than the other? If so, was the power used well or badly?
- What did they feel about the other community and their proposals?
- What did they feel most angry or pleased about?
- Were any agreements reached? – why/why not?
- Did either group deny the rights of the other group?
- What could happen in the future?
- Which community would they choose to live in if they had a choice and why?

Small groups can then be asked to suggest real situations that the simulation reminds them of.

Activity 4: Rights and responsibilities

Cut up the statements on the exercise sheet. Give one to each pair.

Ask them to consider the statement carefully. They can do some research and then make a short presentation about what their statement means in practice. (For example, should public buildings which do not have access for wheelchair users be closed down? Should authorities be forced to make them accessible? How should the change be paid for? What buildings do they know in their area which are not accessible?)

Pairs report back on their findings to the whole group.

Activity 5: History and human rights

THE LONG MARCH TO FREEDOM

Give the students the two briefing sheets.

Invite individual students or pairs to choose characters from the human rights defenders featured in the Time Line 'The Long March to Freedom' in briefing sheet 1. Ask them to find out information about them, a picture (if possible), brief life story, dates, birthplace, their work for human rights, books they wrote (if any), a quote from their actual words (if available). They record the information on their human rights defender on an A4 sheet. Are they surprised by the presence or absence of names on this list? If there are human rights defenders in the UK or elsewhere they want to add to the timeline, encourage this.

Students present their findings to the class. The defenders' cards are posted in date order on a Time Line which might go right round the classroom.

Underneath the Time Line, students add key human rights events and important human rights laws with their dates. 'The Long March to Freedom' is available on the Amnesty International Human Rights Education website **www.amnesty.org.uk/education/index.shtml**. A 14 ft long illustrated wall chart is available from Amnesty International on 01788 545553 Quote Product Code ED074 (£5.50 inc. postage).

FURTHER ACTIVITIES

Create a blank display space next to the Time Line. Invite students to describe, in images or words, what human rights developments they hope will happen, and what human rights disasters they fear may occur, and where and when they will take place in the world over the next 50 years.

Activity 6: The Universal Declaration of Human Rights (UDHR)

Give students the information sheet on the UDHR. Encourage them to read the actual text and its magnificent preamble on **www.amnesty.org.uk/education/index.shtml**. We feature a shortened version of the UDHR in the information sheet.

- When the UDHR was written, the words 'he' and 'his' were assumed to include 'she' and 'her'. How might these sentences be written now?
- Why has the UDHR been described as 'the world's best kept secret'? What difference would it make if everybody knew about and understood the UDHR? What could be done to make this happen?
- Draw up a plan to publicise the UDHR in your school and local community.

FURTHER ACTIVITIES

- Small groups choose an Article from the UDHR. Make sure they understand it. They are to plan, rehearse and produce a TV advert to promote their chosen Article. They should make a poster with the number of the Article, which may be illustrated with pictures of the rights the Article defends. When ready each advertisement is presented to the class. At the end of each sketch someone in the group reads out the actual text of the Article chosen.
- Create a UDHR 'quilt'. Each square illustrates the meaning of one of the Articles of the UDHR and its number. It could be made with collage; prints; embroidery; appliqué; found objects; painting; fabric crayon; batik.

Activity 7: Human rights in the news

Buy two copies of each of the day's newspapers, tabloid and broadsheet, and hand them out to small groups with scissors, tape, a large sheet of sugar paper, a magic marker, a summary of the UDHR (from Activity 6) and the exercise sheet.

Each group needs to read right through the paper carefully and prepare a report on the newspaper and the coverage it gives to human rights, cutting out anything that they consider deals with a human rights issue. What Article in the UDHR applies to each cutting? In each case decide if this is a right won, a right demanded or a right denied?

When they have answered the questions in the exercise sheet, each group presents its findings to the rest of the class. The class should then decide which paper wins today's human rights award and which paper gets the human rights wooden spoon.

Activity 8: Can rights justifiably be curtailed?

Give small groups the exercise sheet to debate. Ask them to decide whether each example can be justified. (**Note:** in 2001 the following examples applied in the UK – A5; B3, B4; C2, C6; D3, D4, D5.)

Activity 9: Conflicting rights

Give the students a copy of the UDHR (See Activity 6) and a copy of the information sheet 'Drafting disagreements'.

Get pairs to look at the information sheet and the UDHR and decide:

- Why were the objections made?
- How were they resolved?
- What other objections might have arisen?

Pairs/small groups make a list of examples of conflicting rights at local and global levels, like disputes between neighbours or road building versus environmental protection. They should decide how the conflicts might be resolved.

Students could explore how mediation and compromise work through role-playing their examples of conflicting rights, where different 'sides' have just, but opposing claims. Different students can take the role of mediator. The whole class can then analyse what is needed to enable a 'win–win' outcome rather than a 'win–lose' or 'lose–lose' situation.

Activity 10: Claiming rights

Give small groups a case study to research from the exercise sheet 'Claiming rights'. After groups have presented their cases, they can question each other about their research and discuss discrimination and rights in the UK.

FURTHER ACTIVITIES

- Write a report on the process of claiming rights, how discrimination operates and how it can be challenged
- Find out about anti-discrimination legislation in the UK
  Commission for Racial Equality, 0207 828 7022 **www.cre.gov.uk**
  Equal Opportunities Commission, 0161 833 9244 **www.eoc.org.uk**
  Trade Union Congress, 0207 636 4030 **www.tuc.org.uk**
- Design stickers and posters to campaign on a UK equal rights issue

Activity 11: The Great Escape

Visit Amnesty International's website **www.amnesty.org.uk/education/index.shtml** for an exciting 45 minute exercise exploring human rights in conflict. Teams of students role play a group of refugees fleeing to safety, and confronting issues of morality, rights, safety, justice, life and death, on their journey.

Activity 12: How the human rights machinery of the UN works

Visit Amnesty International's website **www.amnesty.org.uk/education/index.shtml** for a 45 minute role play for up to 30 students on how the UN Commission on Human Rights works. The exercise is loosely based on a 1997 Commission debate on the death penalty. Students take the positions of different countries. This activity can be used with Unit 5.

Activity 13: The right to take part in government

HAVING A SAY

Ask pairs to list choices they have to make in everyday life. How do they make them? What information do they need? What important decisions will they have to make in the future?
   Groups discuss and agree:

- Three things they think everybody should have to decide.
- Three things it makes sense for others to decide for us (who, why, how).
- Different ways in which they could influence society, ticking those which they would be prepared to do.

Ask groups to investigate different systems of government they can think of; monarchy, theocracy, direct and representative democracy, dictatorship, military rule, one-party state, 'people's democracy'.

   List advantages and problems with each system. Name a country where such a system of government operates. Using information from Amnesty International investigate the human rights record of a country in which each system of government is practised.

FURTHER ACTIVITIES

- Find out about the work of Parliament from the House of Commons and House of Lords

Public Information Offices, 1 Derby Gate, London SW1 2DG, or **www.parliament.uk** or the Education Unit: **EdUnit@parliament.uk**

- Find out about the European Parliament from: European Parliament Information Office, 2 Queen Anne's Gate, London SW1H 9AA (0207 227 4300).
- Find out who your local Member of Parliament (MP) and your Member of the European Parliament (MEP) are. Write to them about a human rights issue that concerns you.
- Find out about the work of your local Council. Telephone or visit their website: www.tagish.co.uk/links/localgov.htm.
- Find out who your local councillors are. You might contact them about any local issues which concern you.
- Encourage the development of a student council at your local school/college if one does not already exist.
- Find out about your local Youth Council. Find details on the web: www.byc.org.uk.
- To learn more about how you can participate in the running of the country, contact The Citizenship Foundation or get a copy of the students' workbook, *Active Citizenship Today*, from the Institute for Citizenship.

Activity 14: The struggles for democracy – South Africa and the UK

Give out the case study 'Mandela on Democracy'.

Ask pairs to note:

- the major differences between direct and representative democracy
- two things Mandela learned from his experience at the Great Place
- the judge's view on why not everyone should have a right to vote
- Mandela's view on why everyone should have a right to vote
- whose argument they find most convincing and why

FURTHER ACTIVITIES

- Read more extracts from *Long Walk to Freedom* and create a play based on a part of Nelson Mandela's life.

Give out the fact sheet 'Votes for all'. Ask pairs to note:
- differences and similarities they can find in the two histories
- why they think it takes so long for full democracy to be won

FURTHER ACTIVITIES

- Find out what percentage of the electorate voted in your local ward/constituency in the last local/national elections, compare with the national average, and consider the reasons.
- Research the struggles which led to each widening of the franchise in the UK – find out about some of the dramatic events and the people involved in them. Make a wall chart showing the different groups of people who gained the vote in each reform.
- Find out which groups of people still cannot vote in the UK and why.
- Research the different systems used to elect representatives in the UK. List the advantages and disadvantages of 'first past the post' and 'proportional representation'.
- Devise a questionnaire and conduct a survey of a sample of adults. Find out: whether they voted in the last election, whether they usually vote, why/why not, how they decide who to vote for, etc. Present your data graphically.
- Interview someone about the first time they voted.
- Create a mural, a banner or a song to celebrate the new South Africa.
- Write a letter to a friend from someone voting for the first time in South Africa in 1994.
- Hold a debate on whether voting should be compulsory.

OPINIONS

Give out the exercise sheet 'Voting: right or duty?'

Ask small groups to cut out the statements and place them in a diamond shape, with the statement they most agree with at the top and the one they least agree with at the bottom. Groups can then compare their rankings and the reasons for them.

Activity 15: Tiananmen

Read the poem 'Tiananmen' as a class. Ask students if they know what event the poem refers to, and if not, briefly explain the background.

Pairs can then discuss:

- What do you learn about the place from the poem – if you had to paint a picture of 'Tiananmen' what would it show?
- What do you learn about the massacre, the aftermath, and those responsible for it?
- Find examples of: repetition, double meanings of words/phrases, irony, ambiguity; why do you think the writer uses these devices? Do you think they are effective?
- What do you think the last three lines mean?
- Do you think the poem is optimistic or pessimistic? Why?

Give out the fact sheet 'Ten years after Tiananmen'.

Pairs can then make notes on:

- why do they think Liu Baiqiang sent the messages on the locusts?
- what they think were the ideals for which Jiang Jielian was prepared to die?
- what do they think of the words of comfort from Ding Zilin's friend?
- what does Ding Zilin mean by the last paragraph?

FURTHER ACTIVITIES

- Find out more about the massacre in Tiananmen Square and the democracy movement in China from Amnesty International or Human Rights Watch (**www.hrw.org**). Read the full text of the interview with Ding Zilin by downloading the full report on: **www.amnesty.org.uk**
- Create a poem, a song or a picture for Liu Baiqiang, Ding Zilin or Jiang Jielian.
- Find out about pro-democracy movements in other countries. Choose one country to research and design a 20 minute lesson to enable your class to learn about your research.

ACTIVITY 1 EXERCISE SHEET

What do we need?

In small groups, cut up the items below into rectangles. Now rank the rectangles in an agreed order of importance to the members in your group, with the most important on the top, the least important on the bottom. You may find a diamond shape a useful way of ranking.

Now decide whether you would need to change the ranking of the rectangles if you were:

- a baby
- an adult with a medical condition such as multiple sclerosis
- a pensioner

A summer holiday	Prayers
A doctor	An Umbro or Fila jacket
Warmth	A mobile telephone
Going to the cinema	Pocket money every week
A vote	Friendship and love
A passport	Spectacles
A pet	Buffalo or Nike trainers
School	Enough to eat
A home and a bed	A car
A bus pass	A book
A strong walking stick and a bottle of pills	A dry nappy and a dummy
A CD player and cool sounds	A television and video
A family	A job

Photocopy Original © Hodder & Stoughton 2001

ACTIVITY 2 EXERCISE SHEET
What are human rights?

As individuals, list five rights you have at home, five rights you have at school and five rights you have in the community where you live.

These could be:

the right to do things; the right to protection from something; the right to be provided with something.

	Home	School	Community
1.			
2.			
3.			
4.			
5.			

Then in small groups make a list of rights for young people, choosing the best ideas from your individual lists. Decide on the ten most important rights each for school, home and community.

Photocopy Original © Hodder & Stoughton 2001

ACTIVITY 3 BRIEFING SHEET 1
Esperanza settlers

It is now a year since you drew up your Esperanza People's Human Rights Charter. The community is having a meeting to decide what to do in the current situation.

There is a serious food crisis. You should have plentiful supplies of food from all the crops that you have grown since you arrived, but there are not enough of you to harvest the crops, and you don't know how to do it. As a result, you are running short of food. The goats that you brought from the ship have bred in large numbers all over the island. Your water supply is just outside the main village and is beginning to run dry because of the drought.

It turns out that Esperanza is not an uninhabited island after all. On the southern shore is a community of tribal fishermen and hunters. You do not understand their language much. They call themselves Rakyat, 'people' in their language. They call Esperanza 'Harap' which means 'hope' in their language. Their women are very strong and skilled farmers. There seem to be about 1,000 of them. The drought has affected the south of the island very badly. Streams there have dried up. Your dwindling water supply in the north of the island is now being used by the Rakyat too. Most of their crops and many trees have either died or been eaten by the goats. Game in their part of the island has become scarce. They seem to be short of food. Their babies look sick.

You are concerned because there have been several 'incidents' around the water supply, which the Rakyat community seem to think belongs to them. Their girls even wash their hair in the stream, and their hunters have been killing your goats with their bamboo spears.

You think you might be able to do a deal with them.

When the ship was sinking you rescued this special sort of gatling gun. This might be useful in case of trouble, but nobody knows exactly how to use it. An experimental volley produced a very loud explosion, a lot of black choking gas, and killed several goats 100 yards away. You don't know what kind of effect it might have if used. Perhaps it could contaminate your water and food supplies.

Now make some decisions about the serious food and water situation. How are you going to get the harvest in?

Do the Rakyat who lived on the south of Esperanza before you arrived have the same rights as you? They are taking your water and killing your animals.

What are you going to do if there is trouble?

Appoint one person in your group to note your decisions.

Photocopy Original © Hodder & Stoughton 2001

continued

Esperanza settlers

YOU NEED TO THINK ABOUT THE FOLLOWING AREAS:

- What do they have that you want? What do you have that they want?
- What are your views about the water supply and the 'incidents'?
- What are the possible ways in which you might get what you want from them?
- What are the possible ways in which they might get what they want from you?
- How might you persuade the Rakyat to do a deal with you?
- What could you do if you don't like the proposals that the Rakyat put to you?

YOU AGREE TO MEET WITH THE RAKYAT TO DISCUSS THESE THINGS, SO YOU NEED TO DECIDE:

- Are there conditions you wish to agree with them before you meet? E.g. each community should have an equal amount of time to put across their views.
- Will you choose one or two people to put forward your ideas and negotiate for you or will you all speak when you feel like it?
- Decide on the main points you want to put across.
- Decide what you will do if they don't agree with your proposals.

Photocopy Original © Hodder & Stoughton 2001

ACTIVITY 3 BRIEFING SHEET 2
The Rakyat

It is a year since the big boat sank in the storm and all these foreigners came to settle on the northern shore of Harap. What is worse, it has been the most severe drought anyone can remember. Your crops have failed, trees are dying, game is scarce, and these beasts the foreigners have brought are eating everything. They destroy your crops and shrubs. The food and water situation of the Rakyat is now becoming desperate.

The new settlers call the island 'Esperanza'. It means 'hope' in their language. They have grown plenty of food but they don't seem to know how to harvest it. Your women are very strong and know how to harvest these crops.

You are concerned because there have been several 'incidents' at the Sacred Spring near the settlers' village. It is a holy place, and Rakyat maidens go there to wash their hair and collect water now that all Harap's southern streams have dried up. These new settlers seem to think the spring belongs to them. They got angry when your hunters speared some of their beasts that were eating your last field of corn near the spring.

You think you might be able to do a deal with the settlers. You want to proceed carefully though, because you've heard rumours that they have brought some new kind of killing machine with them that makes a noise like thunder and brings down animals from a great distance. But Rakyat hunters are very cunning, skilled with bamboo spears when they hunt fish and animals and with the leather slings that they use for killing birds. If there is trouble, you will be ready to defend yourselves.

YOUR COMMUNITY NEEDS TO THINK ABOUT THE FOLLOWING AREAS:
- What do they have that you want, and what do you have that they want?
- What are your views about the water supply and the 'incidents'?
- How might you get what you want from them?
- How might they get what they want from you?
- What could you do if the new settlers refuse to do a deal with you?
- Do the new settlers have the same rights as your people?

YOU AGREE TO MEET WITH THE SETTLERS TO DISCUSS THESE THINGS, SO YOU NEED TO DECIDE:
- What conditions will you want to agree about the form of the meeting? E.g. each community will have an equal amount of time to put across their views.
- Decide who will speak for you. Will you all talk or will you choose one or two negotiators?
- Decide on the main points you want to put across to the settlers.
- What you will do if they don't agree with your proposals? How far might you be prepared to compromise?

Photocopy Original © Hodder & Stoughton 2001

ACTIVITY 4 EXERCISE SHEET
Rights and responsibilities

You don't have a right to anything unless you work for it

Famous people forfeit their right to privacy. (What does 'famous' mean?)

Everyone has the right to work (What you mean by 'work'? Paid? Full-time?)

Disabled people have the right to access to all buildings

Everyone has the right to free university education

Everyone has the right to have children

Every parent has the responsibility to ensure that their child behaves properly

Everyone who has the right to vote has a responsibility to vote

Everyone has the right to free health care

We all have a responsibility not to break the law

We all have the right to break unjust laws

Everyone has the right to travel where they like

We all have a responsibility to challenge the denial of other people's rights

Everyone has the right to enjoy their leisure time as they like

Photocopy Original © Hodder & Stoughton 2001

Photocopy Original © Hodder & Stoughton 2001

ACTIVITY 5 BRIEFING SHEET 1
The Long March to Freedom

Human Rights did not just 'arrive on a plate' when the Universal Declaration of Human Rights (UDHR) was adopted by the United Nations in 1948. The movement to demand, establish and to protect human rights has a very long history. Around the world, across the centuries, many ordinary and extraordinary people, men and women, thinkers, teachers, organisers, writers, and social reformers of different cultures and political religious ideas, have stood up against oppression and campaigned for freedom, justice and democracy, for national independence, and equality. They have begun crusades and social movements that have changed the world. Some have given their lives for their cause.

In the half century since the UDHR was agreed many other human rights defenders have campaigned to turn the articles of the Declaration into reality. They have changed the world with the struggles for colonial freedom, the civil rights movement in the United States, the end of apartheid, campaigns for the rights of political prisoners, women and ethnic and sexual minorities. Human rights organisations like Amnesty International and Index on Censorship have been established. Many international human rights treaties have been passed.

Here is a list of some of the human rights defenders who have played a key role in the struggle for justice over the centuries with their dates and their place of birth in present day countries. There may be other human rights defenders in the UK or abroad who are not on this list and whom you may also want to find out about.

Choose one or two of these human rights defenders, and do some research on them. Find their picture (if possible), write down their brief life story, dates, birthplace, their work for human rights, key events taking place during their lives, books they wrote (if any) and a quote from their actual words (if available).

Put your information onto a card. Present it to the class. Then add it to the Long March to Freedom Time Line.

continued

The Long March to Freedom

**'THE LONG MARCH TO FREEDOM' TIME LINE
– SOME OF THE WORLD'S HUMAN RIGHTS DEFENDERS**

NAME	COUNTRY OF ORIGIN	DATE OF BIRTH	NAME	COUNTRY OF ORIGIN	DATE OF BIRTH
Hammurabi	Iraq	2123 BC	Thomas Jefferson	USA	1743
Moses	Egypt	c.1200 BC	Olympe de Gouges	France	1750
Zarathustra	Iran	628 BC	Mary Wollstonecraft	UK	1759
Cyrus the Elder	Iran	600 BC	William Wilberforce	UK	1759
Vardhama Mahavira	India	599 BC	Elizabeth Fry	UK	1780
The Buddha	India	550 BC	Simon Bolivar	Colombia	1783
Lao-Tse	China	6th Century	Sojourner Truth	USA	1797
			Heinrich Heine	Germany	1797
Socrates	Greece	469 BC	Abraham Lincoln	USA	1805
Aristotle	Greece	384 BC	Karl Marx	Germany	1818
Meng-Tse	China	371 BC	Jean Henri Dunant	Switzerland	1828
Zeno of Citium	Greece	334 BC	Emile Zola	France	1840
Spartacus	Greece	110? BC	Emmeline Pankhurst	UK	1858
Marcus Tullius Cicero	Italy	104 BC	Fridtjof Nansen	Norway	1861
Jesus Christ	Palestine	0	Mahatma Gandhi	India	1869
Muhammad ibn Abd Allah	Saudi Arabia	570?	Emiliano Zapata	Mexico	1873
Abdul ibn Rashid	Spain	1126	Eglantyne Jebb	UK	1876
King John I	UK	1167	Eleanor Roosevelt	USA	1884
St Francis of Assisi	Italy	1182	Marcus Gravey	Jamaica	1887
John Ball	UK	1340?	Dr Ambedkar	India	1893
Bartholomé de Las Casas	Spain	1473	Kwame Nkrumah	Ghana	1909
Sir Thomas More	UK	1478	Archbishop Romero	El Salvador	1917
Martin Luther	Germany	1483	Nelson Mandela	South Africa	1918
Hugo Grotius	Netherlands	1583	Prof Andrei D. Sakharov	Russia	1921
John Lilburne	UK	1617	Peter Benenson	UK	1923
Guru Tekh Bahadur	India	1621	Malcolm X	USA	1925
William Penn	UK	1644	Martin Luther King	USA	1929
Voltaire	France	1694	Aung San Suu Kyi	Myanmar	1944
Jean-Jacques Rousseau	Switzerland	1712	The Dalai Lama	Tibet/China	1935
Tom Paine	UK	1737	Vaclav Havel	Czech Republic	1936
Cesare Beccaria	Italy	1738	Lech Walesa	Poland	1943
Toussaint L'Ouverture	Haiti	1743	Rigoberta Menchu	Guatemala	1959

Unit 1: UNDERSTANDING HUMAN RIGHTS

Photocopy Original © Hodder & Stoughton 2001

Photocopy Original © Hodder & Stoughton 2001

The international protection of human rights

In the late 1930s and 1940s the world was shaken by many terrible events: Fascism; World War Two; the atrocities of the concentration camps; the uprooting of millions of people from their homes; the atomic bombs on Hiroshima and Nagasaki. New words and phrases were used to describe the unthinkable: holocaust; genocide; crimes against humanity.

The creation of the United Nations (UN) was intended to ensure that such events never took place again. The UN Charter, signed in San Francisco in June 1945, committed each member state in the new organisation to take action to promote 'universal respect for and observance of human rights and fundamental freedoms for all without distinction as to race, sex, language or religion'.

On 10 December 1948, the UN General Assembly adopted the Universal Declaration of Human Rights (UDHR). This promised 'a world in which human beings shall enjoy freedom of speech and belief and freedom from fear and want' and that the fundamental rights of people would be protected by the rule of law.

Until the end of World War Two, how a government dealt with its citizens was largely seen as its own internal affair, not a matter for anyone outside its borders. With the UDHR, for the first time, such matters became the legitimate concern of all states and their inhabitants.

The UDHR's principles became binding international law in 1966 when the United Nations agreed two important international treaties: The International Covenant on Civil and Political Rights and the International Covenant on Economic, Social and Cultural Rights.

Many other international laws have followed, such as:

1951 Convention on the Status of Refugees
1953 European Convention on Human Rights
1975 Helsinki Declaration
1981 African Charter of Human and People's Rights
1984 Convention against Torture
1989 Convention on the Rights of the Child

The half century that has passed since the UDHR was agreed has been one in which many terrible things have happened in the world to violate the rights and freedoms promised in the UDHR.

It is very clear that the Declaration did not bring about a swift end to abuses of human rights around the world. Since 1948, millions of people have been slaughtered by their governments for their origins, ideas or beliefs. Millions

continued

The international protection of human rights

more have been jailed for their beliefs and ideas and for their struggles for justice and freedom. Tens of millions of refugees have fled from oppression. Poverty, sickness and hunger are everyday experiences for much of the world's population. Each day of the week, every single one of the 30 Articles of the UDHR is being violated somewhere in the world.

Photocopy Original © Hodder & Stoughton 2001

The Universal Declaration of Human Rights (UDHR)

The Universal Declaration of Human Rights has been called 'the world's best kept secret'. The United Nations intended governments to ensure it was displayed everywhere and for everyone to be educated and informed about the UDHR and its importance. This has not happened. Few people know what it says or what it means.

SUMMARY OF THE UDHR

Article 1
'All human beings are born free and equal in dignity and in rights'

Article 2
'Everyone is entitled to all the rights and freedoms set forth in this Declaration, without distinction of any kind.'

Article 3
'Everyone has the right to life, liberty and security of person.'

Article 4
'No one shall be held in slavery or servitude.'

Article 5
'No one shall be subjected to torture or to cruel, inhuman or degrading treatment or punishment.'

Article 6
'Everyone has the right to recognition everywhere as a person before the law.'

Article 7
'All are equal before the law and are entitled without any discrimination to equal protection of the law.'

Photocopy Original © Hodder & Stoughton 2001

continued

The Universal Declaration of Human Rights (UDHR)

Article 8

'Everyone has the right to an effective remedy by the competent national tribunals for acts violating the fundamental rights granted him by the constitution or by law.'

Article 9

'No one shall be subjected to arbitrary arrest, detention or exile.'

Article 10

'Everyone is entitled in full equality to a fair and public hearing by an independent and impartial tribunal.'

Article 11

'Everyone charged with a penal offence has the right to be presumed innocent until proved guilty.'

Article 12

'No one shall be subjected to arbitrary interference with his privacy, family, home or correspondence, nor to attacks upon his honour and reputation.'

Article 13

'Everyone has the right to freedom of movement.'

Article 14

'Everyone has the right to seek and to enjoy in other countries asylum from persecution.'

Article 15

'Everyone has the right to a nationality.'

Article 16

'Men and women ... have the right to marry and to found a family.'

Article 17

'Everyone has the right to own property.'

Article 18

'Everyone has the right to freedom of thought, conscience and religion.'

Article 19

'Everyone has the right to freedom of opinion and expression.'

Article 20

'Everyone has the right to freedom of peaceful assembly and association.'

Article 21

'Everyone has the right to take part in the government of his country.'

Article 22

'Everyone, as a member of society, has the right to social security and is entitled to realisation ... of ... economic, social and cultural rights.'

Photocopy Original © Hodder & Stoughton 2001

continued

Article 23

'Everyone has the right to work ... Everyone has the right to form and join trade unions.'

Article 24

'Everyone has the right to rest and leisure.'

Article 25

'Everyone has the right to a standard of living adequate for ... health and well-being.'

Article 26

'Everyone has the right to education.'

Article 27

'Everyone has the right freely to participate in the cultural life of the community.'

Article 28

'Everyone is entitled to a social and international order in which the rights and freedoms set forth in this Declaration can be fully realised.'

Article 29

'Everyone has duties to the community.'

Article 30

'Nothing in this Declaration may be interpreted as implying ... any right to engage in any activity ... aimed at the destruction of any of the rights and freedoms set forth.'

From The Right Idea *pack, Amnesty International/NUT 1998*

Photocopy Original © Hodder & Stoughton 2001

ACTIVITY 7 EXERCISE SHEET
Human rights in the news

Your group has been given newspapers to find out what kind of coverage it gives to human rights. Cut out anything you can find that deals with a human rights issue. All the cuttings need to be sorted out into one of the following categories:

- A right claimed
- A right respected
- A right denied

Think about which type of right is involved in your cuttings. Can you find the number of any relevant Article in the Universal Declaration of Human Rights? You should write the number on the cutting. Then discuss the following points:

- What can your group find out about this newspaper?
- Who owns it?
- How much does it cost?
- How many people read it?
- What sort of people make up its readership?
- What do you think is the political slant of the paper, if any?
- What is its main headline?
- How much (%) of the paper is given over to: international news; home news; television stories, private lives of famous people and gossip; sport; advertisements?
- Is there anything in the paper that your group feels is itself an abuse of human rights (such as an invasion of privacy, writing that is demeaning to someone because of their race, sex, their disability or sexual orientation)?

You need to agree answers to all these questions amongst your group and write them down on the paper provided. Present your findings to the rest of the class. Which newspaper gives the best and worst coverage to human rights?

ACTIVITY 8 EXERCISE SHEET
Can rights justifiably be curtailed?

Look at the list of measures that governments around the world have used to overrule the rights of the individual. Some of the cases are UK examples. Discuss each example. Decide whether it can be justified.

Can you guess a country in which this restriction has been applied?

A) 'State of Emergency' (natural disaster, war, terrorist threat, political unrest), for example:
- Curfew enforced – nobody allowed out at night
- Imprisonment of suspected terrorists without charge or trial
- Military can shoot suspected looters or troublemakers on sight
- Food, electricity, water rationed by the state
- Use of hose-pipes banned

B) 'Crackdown on crime', for example:
- Police can stop and search anyone without a warrant
- Everyone must carry identity cards
- Parents are fined for their children's truancy
- If you camp without permission, you can be arrested and your home seized

C) 'Religious/moral principles', for example:
- No trading on Sundays
- Monarch must be a Protestant and must marry a Protestant
- Women in public must cover themselves from head to foot
- Women may not work, may not drive a car. Girls may not attend school
- Consumption of alcohol is punishable by flogging
- Euthanasia and suicide are against the law
- Adultery punishable by stoning to death

D) 'The good of the majority overrules individual rights', for example:
- Dance music emitting repetitive beats banned and equipment seized and dancers expelled
- Birth restrictions – one child per family
- Smoking banned in offices and public places
- Seatbelts must be worn
- Speech is a crime if obscene, slanderous, or inciting racial hatred or riot

Photocopy Original © Hodder & Stoughton 2001

ACTIVITY 9 INFORMATION SHEET
Drafting disagreements

Drafting the Universal Declaration, 1948

Even while the Universal Declaration of Human Rights was being drawn up, various conflicts of interest between the countries involved had to be resolved:

The first draft began with Article 1 reading: 'All men are brothers'. The UN's Commission on the Status of Women objected and the phrase was changed to: 'All human beings are created free and equal'. However the second sentence of Article 1 remained '. . . and should act towards one another in a spirit of brotherhood.'

Some delegations, from different religious persuasions, wanted the second sentence of Article 1: '. . . They are endowed with reason and conscience ...' to include an explanation of how reason and conscience got there in the first place. Some delegates wanted the words '. . . endowed by God' to be included. Others preferred 'endowed by nature' instead. This was resolved by not stating how people are endowed with reason and conscience.

South Africa's delegation came from a state which in 1948 was just introducing the machinery of apartheid, and could not accept the wording that 'all human beings are born free and equal' or that 'everyone should be entitled to all the rights and freedoms in the Declaration'. It also opposed Article 7 'all are equal before the law and are entitled without any discrimination to equal protection under the law . . .'. But its objections were defeated by a majority decision.

Delegations from the Communist bloc countries were concerned that the Declaration only dealt with civil and political rights and not with economic and social rights. Finally, Articles 22, 23, 24, 25 and 28 were included.

Saudi Arabia was worried about Article 18 on freedom of thought, conscience and religion, especially about 'to change . . . religion or belief'. In Saudi Arabia, where Islam was the state religion, to renounce the faith was punishable by execution. This objection was defeated.

Some Catholic delegations questioned the references to equal rights of men and women in marriage in Article 16. These references were retained.

Photocopy Original © Hodder & Stoughton 2001

ACTIVITY 10 EXERCISE SHEET
Claiming rights

Your group has been given one of the case studies below to research. You will need to contact relevant organisations to find out about the current law. Think about how you will present your research to the rest of the class, for example:

- devise a short drama in which you role-play the people involved
- create a documentary programme or news item for television/radio

Whilst you are researching your case study, consider the following questions and include some of the answers in your presentation:

- What rights are being claimed?
- How will the person claim these rights?
- Who should they contact?
- What laws exist to support them?
- What skills will the person need to succeed?
- What conflict of rights is involved here?

---

1. I am an 11-year-old girl with a physical disability which means I use a wheelchair which I can operate myself. I live in a small village 25 miles from Newcastle-upon-Tyne. My parents support my wish to go to a mainstream secondary school, not a special school.

---

2. I am a 40-year-old woman. My husband is mentally ill. He has just been discharged from a special hospital which has closed down. I have three school-age children. I have a well-paid, full-time job. My husband needs special care which I do not feel capable of giving.

---

3. I am an 18-year-old woman. I have worked for a year as an apprentice engineer. I was the only woman in my group. The instructor responsible for my group constantly sexually harassed me to the point where I have been forced to leave. I am now depressed and unemployed. I wish to get compensation.

---

4. I am 38 years old, a successful black businessperson with a family. I was recently sent details of a house I was interested in buying. I rang, arranged an appointment and viewed the property. Then the estate agent rang me the next day to say they had made a mistake. The vendors no longer wished to sell the house. A white friend viewed the same property after me and they offered it to him for sale.

Photocopy Original © Hodder & Stoughton 2001

continued

5. I am a devout Muslim. I must say my prayers at certain times whilst I am at work. I need a quiet place where I can do this. My employer has refused me permission to perform my daily prayers.

6. I am 70 years old, a widow on a basic state pension with a very small additional pension. I suffer from severe chest problems for which I need permanent medication. I can no longer afford to heat my home properly, to eat well and to buy my medicines. Now they say I receive £2 a week too much to get any extra financial help from the state.

7. My husband and I are from Pakistan. We recently moved into a council house with our children. It's a mainly white, rural community. Since we moved in, we have had racist slogans daubed on our door. Our phone number is ex-directory but we have started receiving threatening phone-calls in the middle of the night saying they are going to firebomb the house. The local Police and the Council say they can do nothing unless one of us is attacked and the perpetrators are caught.

Photocopy Original © Hodder & Stoughton 2001

ACTIVITY 14 CASE STUDY
Mandela on Democracy

Nelson Mandela as President of South Africa

Nelson Mandela's childhood memories of tribal democracy in Mqhekezweni in the Transkei:

'I watched and learned from the tribal meetings that were held regularly at the Great Place. These were not scheduled, but were called as needed ... All Thembus were free to come – and a great many did, on horseback or by-foot. ... The guests would gather in the courtyard in front of the regent's house and he would open the meeting by thanking everyone for coming and explaining why he had summoned them. From that point on, he would not utter another word until the meeting was nearing its end.

Everyone who wanted to speak did so. It was democracy in its purest form. There may have been a hierarchy of importance among the speakers, but everyone was heard: chief and subject, warrior and medicine man, shopkeeper and farmer, landowner and labourer. People spoke without interruption and the meetings lasted for many hours. The foundation of self-government was that all men were free to voice their opinions and were equal in their value as citizens. (Women, I am afraid, were deemed second-class citizens.)

... I noticed how some speakers rambled and never seemed to get to the point. I grasped how others came to the matter at hand directly, and who made a set of arguments succinctly and cogently. I observed how some speakers used emotion and dramatic language, and tried to move the audience with such techniques, while others were sober and even, and shunned emotion.

continued

... The meetings would continue until some kind of consensus was reached. They ended in unanimity or not at all. Unanimity, however, might be an agreement to disagree, or to wait for a more propitious time to propose a solution. Democracy meant all men were to be heard, and a decision was taken together as a people. Majority rule was a foreign notion. A minority was not to be crushed by a majority.

Only at the end of the meeting, as the sun was setting, would the regent speak. His purpose was to sum up what had been said and form some consensus among the diverse opinions. But no conclusion was forced on people who disagreed. If no agreement could be reached, another meeting would be held.'

In 1957 Mandela was on trial accused of plotting to overthrow the (apartheid) government of South Africa:

'I became testy with Judge Rumpff when he fell into the mistake made by so many white South Africans about the idea of a universal franchise. Their notion was that to exercise this responsibility, voters must be 'educated'. To a narrow thinking person, it is hard to explain that to be 'educated' does not mean only being literate and having a BA, and that an illiterate man can be a far more 'educated' voter than someone with an advanced degree.

JUSTICE RUMPFF: What is the value of participation in the Government of a state of people who know nothing?

NELSON MANDELA: My Lord, what happens when illiterate whites vote ...

JR: Are they not subject as much to the influence of election leaders as children would be?

NM: No, My Lord, this is what happens in practice. A man stands up to contest a seat in a particular area; he draws up a manifesto ... then listening to the policy of this person, you decide whether this man will advance your interests if you return him to Parliament, and on that basis you vote for a candidate. It has nothing to do with education.

JR: He only looks to his own interests?

NM: No, a man looks at a man who will be able to best present his point of view and votes for that man.'

Nelson Mandela, A Long Walk to Freedom, *1994*

Photocopy Original © Hodder & Stoughton 2001

ACTIVITY 14 FACT SHEET
Votes for all

THE RIGHT TO VOTE IN THE UK

1689	The Bill of Rights gave landowners and other powerful people the right to choose Members of Parliament. The system declined until Parliamentary seats could be bought and sold in 'rotten boroughs'. Old Sarum had two Members and no people at all.
1832	The First Reform Act gave the vote to male heads of households with a 'rateable value' of at least £10 (quite a large sum then) and to tenant farmers.
1867	The Second Reform Act widened the franchise to include all rate-paying male householders but still excluded agricultural labourers.
1884	The Third Reform Act included all householders – but not lodgers or women.
1918	Representation of the People Act enfranchised all men over 21 (except those excluded for various reasons) and women over 30.
1928	Equal Franchise Act extended the vote to women over 21.
1983	Representation of the People Act lowered the voting age to 18.

SOUTH AFRICA – THE STRUGGLE FOR DEMOCRACY

In 1910, the new Constitution of the Union of South Africa denied most black people (the vast majority of the population) the right to vote. The African National Congress (ANC) was founded in 1912 with the aim of ending the country's segregationist laws and enabling black people to participate in politics. The struggle to achieve these demands was to take 82 years, thousands of deaths, the torture and imprisonment of thousands more. In the closing years of the apartheid regime South Africa was increasingly isolated from the international community. For millions around the world, the struggle was symbolised by one man: Nelson Mandela, the ANC's most famous leader, who lived through the longest sentence of all – 27 years, in which he never waivered from the struggle for a free multi-racial democracy.

Mandela was freed from jail in February 1990. Four years later, on 26–29 April 1994, the first ever multi-ethnic elections were held in South Africa. Thousands of black people, old and young, queued for hours to vote for the first time. 87% of those registered to vote took part. The ANC obtained 63% of the vote and Nelson Mandela became President of South Africa, an office he held until his retirement in 1999.

Photocopy Original © Hodder & Stoughton 2001

Voting: right or duty?

Voting is compulsory in Australia, Belgium and Luxembourg: it should be compulsory here.
People who don't vote are wasting a right which others have died for – it's our duty to vote.
People who don't vote don't care about society.
Voting is pointless – it doesn't change anything.
If people don't vote, democracy will be in danger.
Forcing people to vote would be an infringement of freedom.
Having the right to do something doesn't mean we have a duty to do it.
Voting is a waste of time – the rich and powerful will always run the country for their own benefit.
Direct action is more useful than voting if you want to change things.

Photocopy Original © Hodder & Stoughton 2001

FREEDOM!

ACTIVITY 15 POETRY
'Tiananmen' by James Fenton

Tinanmen is broad and clean
And you can't tell where the dead have been
And you can't tell what happened then
And you can't speak of Tiananmen.
You must not speak.
You must not think.
You must not dip your pen in ink.
You must not say what happened then,
What happened there
In Tiananmen.

The cruel men are old and deaf
Ready to kill but short of breath
And they will die like other men
And they'll lie in state
In Tiananmen.

They lie in state.
They lie in style.
Another lie's thrown on the pile,
Thrown on the pile by the cruel men
To cleanse the blood
From Tiananmen.

**Man arguing with tank drivers.
Tiananmen Square, 5 June 1989**

Truth is a secret.
Keep it dark.
Keep it dark in your heart of hearts.
Keep it dark till you know when
Truth may return
To Tiananmen.

Tiananmen is broad and clean
And you can't tell where the dead have been
And you can't tell when they'll come again.
They'll come again
To Tiananmen.

Hong Kong, 15 June 1989
From Out of Danger, Penguin Books

Photocopy Original © Hodder & Stoughton 2001

ACTIVITY 15 BRIEFING SHEET
Ten years after Tiananmen

In June 1989 Tiananmen Square in Beijing was the scene of the massacre of hundreds of unarmed civilians – many of them students who had been camping out peacefully in the square, holding a vigil in support of their demands for democracy. On the night of 3 to 4 June heavily armed troops and hundreds of armoured military vehicles stormed into Beijing city to clear the streets of pro-democracy demonstrators, firing at onlookers and protesters in the process. Students and other demonstrators in Tiananmen were crushed and shot. Tens of thousands of demonstrators were arrested in the cities and provinces of China. The authorities were reacting against the wide-ranging support in the country for the pro-democracy movement which had brought millions of people onto the streets in Beijing and other cities. No inquiry has been held into the events and names and numbers of those killed have never been confirmed.

Ten years later, thousands of people in China were still imprisoned for the 'crime' of openly demanding political and economic reform and an end to official corruption. Among them is Liu Baiqiang.

Liu Baiqiang, born in 1968, is serving a prison sentence in Guangdong Province for writing 'counter-revolutionary' messages in support of the 1989 pro-democracy movement. Liu Baiqiang was already serving a ten-year sentence for theft but on 6 June 1989 he was sentenced to an additional eight years' imprisonment for 'counter-revolutionary incitement and propaganda'. According to an official report, Liu Baiqiang secretly wrote several leaflets bearing the words 'Long Live Freedom' and 'Tyranny'. After showing these to his cellmates, he reportedly 'attached these to the legs of locusts and released the insects into the air'. Liu Baiqiang is now serving a combined sentence of 17 years. His sentence will be completed in December 2003.

Ding Zilin is a professor at Beijing University. Her 17-year-old son Jiang Jielian was one of those shot dead on the night of 3 June 1989. She is one of those who formed in 1999 an action group of families of June Fourth Victims. This group appealed to Chinese leaders to use the 10th anniversary at the end of the 20th century to establish a fair and independent inquiry into the events. In 1997 Ding Zilin said:

'If my son were alive ... For 8 years I have been preoccupied with this thought, which cut deeper whenever I saw youths of his age. I would be struck with an empty feeling, a sensation that I was falling into an abyss. If he were alive he would be 25 years old. At that time he was only 17, yet he stood more than six feet. Now he would be taller ...

continued

... Perhaps his was only a momentary passion generated by idealism. However, why don't we adults give something for ideals? A friend once tried to comfort me. She said, "If a person lives just to be alive, his life would be meaningless even if he reached his seventies. Although your son lived for only seventeen years, he achieved a life full of value." ...

... It is often said that children are the continuation of parents' lives, which has been reversed in our family. I am still alive today. Moreover, I have awakened from ignorance and slumber and have regained my dignity, but this rebirth has been achieved at the expense of my son's life. My breath, my voice and my whole being are the continuation of my son's life, forever ...'

Ten Years After Tiananmen, *Amnesty International Report ASA 17 October 1999*

Young people reading near the Monument to the People's Heroes, Tiananmen Square, Beijing, May 1989. Picture by Liu Heung Shing, courtesy Contact Press Images

Photocopy Original © Hodder & Stoughton 2001

Freedom to think, to know, to be, to speak

2

UNIT AIMS

This unit aims to:

- explore the meaning of censorship and its impact on students' lives, with a special focus on music
- enable students to consider some of the issues involved in censorship, freedom of expression and freedom of information
- introduce the recent history of freedom of information in the UK
- consider some of the conflicting rights involved in freedom of expression, especially in the use of words
- introduce the experience of lesbians and gay men as one example of how people have been oppressed for their identity and examine how Amnesty International is challenging lesbian and gay oppression
- explore some of the issues raised by the development of the Internet as a global channel of free expression
- introduce the lives and work of some writers who have been oppressed for their ideas

INTRODUCTION

This unit focuses particularly on Article 19 of the UDHR; issues relevant to Articles 1, 7, 12, 18, 20, 21, 23 and 27 are also raised.

The unit is divided into four sections:

- *Censorship* asks students to consider when censoring might be justifiable and the ways in which it might be dangerous.
- *Freedom of information and expression – what's the limit?* Explores the history of secrecy and freedom of information in the UK; issues around information on the Internet; complex conflicting rights in relation to censorship, in particular the danger of 'hate speech'; and issues around music censorship.

- *The right to be yourself – sexuality and oppression; campaigns for lesbian and gay equality* explores the intolerance and human rights abuses experienced by lesbians, gay men and those whose sexuality is 'different'. Through role play, case studies and a simulation students examine why such prejudice occurs and how such oppression can be challenged in the UK and around the world. Information is presented about campaigns for lesbian and gay equality and the evolution of Amnesty International's policy.
- *Censorship around the world and campaigns for freedom of expression* gives case studies from around the world of

artists, writers, cartoonists, and journalists who have been oppressed or murdered for expressing their views and for exposing human rights abuses. The work of organisations campaigning against censorship is also described.

Teachers and students will be able to update the material via the websites highlighted, and by introducing current campaigns and debates.

SUMMARY OF TOPICS

ACTIVITIES: NOTES FOR TEACHERS

Part 1: Censorship

Activity 1: What is censorship?

Ask small groups to define censorship and think of examples in this country and around the world, from what age young people can view certain films, to censorship as a means of oppression. Students could place any examples they have come up with on a spectrum of extremity. George Bernard Shaw wrote: 'the ultimate form of censorship is torture'. Students could discuss what this means.

Ask students to find dictionary definitions of censorship. How has the meaning of the word changed over the centuries?

Students look at the Universal Declaration of Human Rights (see page 25 and the Amnesty website at **www.amnesty.org.uk/education/index.shtml**) and pick out the articles which directly or indirectly relate to freedom of expression and the right to information.

Activity 2: Taking liberties?

Ask groups to look at the list of situations on the exercise sheet and decide:

• how could censorship be justified?

- what might be 'dangerous' or damaging about it?

Activity 3: Analysing censorship

Ask students to collect information about current issues of censorship and freedom of information, from the newspapers, television, radio and the Internet (e.g. the *Guardian's* 1999 campaign on freedom of information (**www.newsunlimited.co.uk/freedom**)) or use the case studies in this unit.

They can then use the fact sheet 'The many faces of censorship' and the checklist below to analyse censorship and its impact and create a wall display of their findings.

Students can make posters, cartoons or mimes to illustrate examples of censorship.

CENSORSHIP CHECKLIST

1. WHO is doing the censoring?
2. WHAT or WHO is being censored?
3. WHY is the censorship being carried out?
4. HOW is the censorship being carried out?
5. WHEN is the censorship being carried out?

Activity 4: Re-writing history

Ask students to read the two extracts from *1984* by George Orwell and to discuss the following questions:

- What three words best define the society that is being described?
- What are your immediate thoughts and reactions to the slogans?
- How is control maintained?
- Why would it be a struggle to keep 'the few cubic centimetres inside your own skull' your own if you lived in a society like this?
- What does 'palimpsest' mean? Why do you think Orwell used this word?
- Can you think of any societies that have been/are like this?
- Are there any ways in which our own society is like this?
- What are the best ways to prevent a society from becoming like this?

FURTHER ACTIVITIES

- In pairs, find out the meaning of the term 'spin-doctoring'. Choose a current political news story. Discuss how the government and opposition might 'spin-doctor' the story. Write it from these opposing points of view.
- Get some photographs. Photocopy and crop them so that the same photo tells a completely different story. Choose one photograph and write two contradictory headlines and stories.
- Discuss the meaning and purpose of propaganda. When do governments or organisations use propaganda? Can it ever be justified?
- Chose a description of an incident in the history of the 20th century. Rewrite it to completely alter what happened as if you were a historical revisionist working for Big Brother in George Orwell's *1984*.

Part 2: Freedom of information and expression – what's the limit?

Activity 5: Our secret society

Give pairs or small groups of students the exercise sheet and ask them to discuss it.
Give groups the fact sheet 'Towards Freedom of Information in the UK'.

Ask them to make notes on:

- anything which surprised them
- what they think of Andrew Puddephatt's statement
- how the 1999 Freedom of Information Bill was in conflict with Article 19 of the UDHR.

Further activities:

- Visit the websites of Charter 88 (**www.charter88.org.uk**) and the Campaign for Freedom of Information (**www.cfoi.org.uk**) to find out about freedom of information in the United Kingdom.

- Write a short play about a young journalist who stumbles on a 'cover up'.
- Hold a debate or write an essay on 'Ignorance is Bliss' or 'Knowledge is Power'.
- Research the story of Clive Ponting and the sinking of the 'Belgrano'.
- Research the history of Greenham Common and Cruise missiles.
- Investigate freedom of information in your school – what is secret and why?
- Research planning and environmental issues in your area. Try to get information about the quality of the air, funding in the health authority, education or housing.
- Research an inquiry into a recent major accident. Was the information made public?
- Conduct a survey to find out what people know about the ingredients in cosmetics or foods, or the medicines and cleaning materials they regularly use.
- Research the MacPherson Report. What change has come about as a result?
- Imagine you are in your first job after leaving school. You work for the boss of a large charitable organisation. You begin to suspect that senior managers are siphoning off funds for themselves when fictitious invoices are passed to you for filing. Role play a discussion with a friend about the options open to you and the possible consequences.
- Find out more about 'whistleblowing' from The Campaign For Freedom of Information or from Public Concern at Work (0207 404 6609 or **www.pcaw.co.uk**).

Activity 6: Freedom without frontiers?

Ask pairs to draw up lists of the positive and negative features of Internet communication. Compare their lists with the fact sheet 'Some Internet issues'. Complete the statements:
- The best think about the Internet is ...
- The worst thing about the Internet is ...
- If they could censor the Internet, what – if anything – would they censor? Why?
- What limits – if any – do they think there should be on young people's use of the Internet?

FURTHER ACTIVITIES

- Visit the web site of the Global Internet Liberty Coalition (**www.gilc.org**) and Liberty (**www.liberty.org.uk/cacib/**) for an update on Internet censorship issues in the United Kingdom.
- Design a web page for your class or something that you are interested in. What messages do you want to put across? What issues do you need to think about?
- Write an essay or debate: 'The Internet: danger or opportunity?'

Activity 7: Privacy and the right to know

Get pairs to make notes on these questions:
- What parts of your life are private? How/why is privacy important to you?
- How would you feel if your private life became public?
- Would you like to be famous? Why/why not?
- Do you think it is fair that famous people should lose their privacy?

Get groups to read Articles 12 and 19 of the UDHR (see page 21). Where might they be in conflict?

Give out newspapers and magazines. Can groups find examples where they think people's privacy has been invaded? Was this justified in the interests of the public's 'right to know'?

Groups could draft a policy for the press to ensure privacy and the right to know are protected.

Activity 8: Word power

Ask pairs to list some positive and negative ways in which words can be used. Talk about times when others have used words which:
- have made the students feel good about themselves
- have silenced them or made them feel less good about themselves.

Then ask them:
What words have they used that have done this to others?
Have they ever said anything that they wished they could 'unsay'?

Have they ever wished they had said something when it was too late?

On a flipchart write the statement attributed to Voltaire (1694–1778): 'I disapprove of what you say, but I will defend to the death your right to say it'.

Ask groups to come up with three points for the statement and three points against it. Give small groups the extracts from briefing sheet 1 'Hate Speech'. Ask each group to work on one section. They should note the key points and come up with a way of making the rest of the class think about these issues in their own lives.

Groups can then look at the list of statements on briefing sheet 2, discuss them and rank them in order from 'strongly agree' to 'strongly disagree':

FURTHER ACTIVITIES
Find out what cannot be said or written in public in Britain.
Debate on the argument: 'Freedom of speech is an absolute right which should never be limited.'
Visit the web site of Liberty: **www.liberty-human-rights.org.uk** and Index on Censorship: **www.oneworld.org/index_oc** to find out more about freedom of speech.

Activity 9: Banned bands
Ask groups to list any songs/bands they know that have been banned and why.
Have they been offended by any lyrics? Why?
Do they think sexist, racist or homophobic lyrics should be banned? Why?

Give out the fact sheet 'Banned Bands'. Ask groups to list four reasons why songs have been banned. What effect do they think the ban would have had?

FURTHER ACTIVITIES
Hold a debate on the banning of a track with sexist lyrics, with students taking on these different roles:
- Parents opposed to sexually explicit lyrics
- Record company executive
- Record shop keeper
- Fans of the band who think 'slack' lyrics are cool and funny
- A group of girls who are fed up with the terms boys have been using to them since the record came out
- A DJ who refuses to play tracks with sexist lyrics
- Anti-censorship campaigners, who believe, no matter what the lyrics are, the band have the right to be heard

Find out about other bands and songs which have been banned or prosecuted.
Research the origins and history of jazz and rock & roll.
Research the story and music of Paul Robeson, Mikis Theodorakis or Victor Jara.
Research the role that music played in a recent political movement in this country, e.g. CND (1960s), The Miner's Strike (mid 1980s), Gay Liberation, Anti-Apartheid.
Write a song for a campaign which you support.
Visit the website of the journal *Index on Censorship*. Download extracts from their November 1998 issue, 'Smashed Hits': **www.oneworld.org/index_oc**

Activity 10: Whose rights?
Give out the 'Whose rights?' sheet.

Pairs make notes on:
Which rights are infringed in these stories and which are upheld?
Whose right would they defend and why?
What action, if any, should be taken when there is a conflict of rights?
Who should decide?

FURTHER ACTIVITIES:
Ask each group to take one scenario and devise a short play around it.
Identify and investigate recent examples of dilemmas about freedom of speech and censorship: pornography; sex and violence on TV; blasphemy; racist language in private; comedy. Present the arguments for and against restrictions.
Find out about works of art which have been censored in the past.

Part 3: The right to be yourself – sexuality and oppression; campaigns for lesbian and gay equality

Activities from Unit 3 (Women's Rights) and Unit 7 (Genocide) can be used with these activities, to explore identity, exclusion, oppression, and diversity.

Activity 11: The right to be yourself

Ask pairs to discuss an experience of being insulted or taunted:
what happened?
Was the insult based on a real 'difference'?
How did they feel and react at the time?
Why do they think it happened?
What might have motivated the person or people involved?
How would they deal with a similar situation how?

Small groups then pool examples to make a common list which can be grouped into aspects of 'difference', e.g. skin colour, size, physical impairment, sexuality, not conforming to expectations, being unfashionable, etc.

The whole class can then discuss:
What messages do these insults give about what is 'normal' and 'acceptable'?
Which aspect of 'difference' attracts most insults?
How might such insults affect a young person whose identity includes such a 'difference'?
Does their school policy make such insults unacceptable?
How should the school ensure that all young people have a right to be themselves, a right to respect and a right to be included?

Activity 12: Equality for young lesbians and gay men in our schools?

Ask students to find out the meanings and origins of the following terms:
Homosexual, Gay, Lesbian, Bisexual, Transsexual, Transvestite, Heterosexual, Homophobia, Heterosexist.

Give students the information sheet 'Queerbashing surveys'. Ask them to note:
How are the basic human rights of young lesbians and gay men abused?
What factors allow such abuse to happen?
How is it suggested that schools can challenge homophobia?
How are Linda and Stephen treated by their peers, parents, teachers?
What might be the effects of such treatment?

FURTHER ACTIVITIES
Visit Stonewall's website at: **www.stonewall.org.uk**
Design a poster which challenges violence and abuse against young lesbians and gay men.
Role-play a discussion between Linda/Stephen and a friend on the effect of homophobia on young people's lives and what schools should do to combat it.
In pairs, discuss what you might do if someone in your class is subjected to homophobic taunts.
Find out the history of Stonewall.

Activity 13: Breaking the silence

Give students the information sheet and quotes to read.
Ask them to list the different factors which lead to violations of the human rights of lesbians

and gay men. Which articles of the UDHR guarantee the right to be lesbian, gay, bisexual, transsexual or transvestite?

Imagine that you are one of the people quoted. Write a letter to a close friend describing your fears, hopes and dreams.

Activity 14: Is it a crime to be gay?
Ask students to read the briefing sheet on 'Boldovia'.

(Teacher's note: The fictional country of Boldovia has some parallels to the 78 countries around the world where homosexual acts between consenting adults were still crimes in 2000).

Divide the class into small groups. Appoint one group to be the Committee listening to evidence in order to make recommendations about homosexuality to the Boldovian Government. Ask them to prepare questions to put to all the groups offering testimony. Give the other groups the role play cards. Ask them to prepare their testimony.

After hearing all the testimonies the Committee debates and agrees its recommendations. The rest of the class, out of role, take notes: Which testimonies were the Committee most/ least persuaded by?
Did any Committee member's personal views dominate the debate?
What do they think of the Committee's decisions and reasons?

Part 4: Censorship around the world and campaigns for freedom of expression

Activity 15: Amnesty for artists
Distribute information sheets 1 and 2 on Amnesty for Artists and Hong Song-Dam. In groups ask students to:
Draw and tell the story of Hong Song-Dam of Kwangju in a strip cartoon.
Write a report of Hong Song-Dam's arrest and torture for Hangarye newspaper to accompany the smuggled drawing of his torturers.
Design a leaflet for Amnesty's campaign for the release of artist prisoners of conscience.
Use one of Hong Song-Dam's designs to make an appeal card. Visit the Amnesty website (**www.amnesty.org.uk**). Select a recent urgent action case. Write a courteous appeal to the relevant authority on your card and post it.

FURTHER ACTIVITY
Hand out information sheet 3. Write a joke for U Pa Pa Lay.

Activity 16: 'Newspeak'
Ask the students to read the extract on the resource sheet from *1984* by George Orwell, in which Symes tells Winston about his job of writing the dictionary of Newspeak.

Separate the students into pairs and ask them to make notes on:

What impressions do they get of Winston and Symes in this extract?
What do they learn about 'the Party' and the society in which Winston and Symes live?
What words and concepts will 'the Party' abolish?
What do they think 'Newspeak' means?
What ideas or messages do they think the writer is trying to convey?
Orwell was writing *1984* in 1949 – to what extent do they think his nightmare world has come to exist?

FURTHER ACTIVITIES
Write the speech that Winston might make to repudiate Syme's arguments.
Take your favourite poem or an extract from your favourite book, and re-write it in 'Newspeak'.

Activity 17: 'Silence is death'

Give groups one of the case studies to read, asking them to discuss the following questions:

Which articles of the UDHR are being breached?
Does the case study relate to the extract from *1984* that you have looked at?

FURTHER ACTIVITIES AROUND CASE STUDIES
Write a poem or short sketch to illustrate one of the case studies
Find out about human rights in the country in the case study.
Choose one of the articles, and re-write it as if you were the Minister for Propaganda in the country concerned to justify your government's actions.

Activity 18: Spotlight on journalists
When might journalists fact danger? Why might they be perceived as dangerous? Brainstorm why independent media are usually the first targets of oppressive regimes.

Give out the three information sheets. Why do the journalists in Algeria carry on with their jobs despite the danger to themselves and their families?

FURTHER ACTIVITIES
Write the secret diary entry of the journalist in Algeria who has told her family she is a hairdresser for their and her safety.
   Research and write a poem about journalist Veronica Guerin, murdered in Ireland, 1998.
   Visit the Amnesty International website (**www.amnesty.org.uk**). Find out about the life and death of Tahar Djaout, the first journalist murdered in Algeria 1993, and the situation in Algeria in the 1990s. Present the information to the rest of the class.

Activity 19: The Animal and Insect Act
Read the poem by the Malaysian lawyer and human rights campaigner Cecil Rajendra whose passport was once confiscated by the authorities because of his writing. Small groups discuss the following:
What is the key idea in the poem?
What are the writer's feelings about censorship?
Why does he use animals and insects rather than examples of real people from around the world to describe the state techniques of control and censorship?
Which articles of the UDHR are relevant to the poem?
Do you think the poem is effective?

Dramatise the poem using music and sound effects. You could become the animals and insects described in the poem or accompany the reading of the poem with slow motion mime/dance of situations of repression around the world.

Activity 20: Organisations fighting censorship
Give students the information sheet on Article 19 and International P.E.N.

They can find out more about these organisations by visiting the websites at:
www.article19.org and **www.oneworld.org/internatpen/inter.htm**

Design an advert, for television or for a magazine, aimed at a teenage audience, which publicises one of these organisations.
Design a poster campaign to highlight people round the world who are imprisoned or at risk for expressing their opinions, beliefs and creativity. Use information from the websites of International P.E.N., Article 19 and Amnesty International.

ACTIVITY 2 EXERCISE SHEET
Taking liberties?

Look at the following list of situations and decide:

- how could censorship be justified?
- what might be 'dangerous' or damaging about it?

COMPROMISING SITUATIONS?

Your friend asks you if you like her new clothes. You don't, but say that you do.
The media can only report from military briefings in time of war.
Swear words are edited from a television interview.
An employer says trade unions are not welcome; employees can talk to their manager directly if they're unhappy.
A far-right organisation is allowed to march through a racially diverse area.
A civil servant leaks information on contamination in food to the press.
A tabloid newspaper runs an 'exposé' story 'outing' a gay MP.
A government decrees that words of art and literature have to express the values of 'the people'.
Representatives of a 'terrorist' organisation are not allowed to speak directly on TV or radio – instead actors speak their words.
A nuclear leak is covered up 'to prevent mass panic'.
Psychiatric patients are not allowed to see their psychiatric assessments in the interest of their 'stability'.

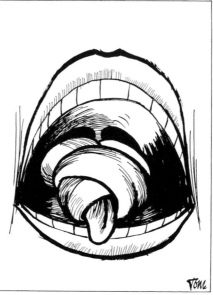

Cartoon by Tom Janssen

Photocopy Original © Hodder & Stoughton 2001

ACTIVITY 3 FACT SHEET
The many faces of censorship

self-censorship: we decide personally not to express an opinion or give out information

social censorship: influenced by society's norms, institutions, pressure groups

legal censorship: imposed through national and local laws on e.g.: obscenity, blasphemy, official secrets, defamation, contempt of court/parliament

extra-legal censorship: government security 'D-notices', police warnings, ministerial warnings, telephone tapping, 'job censorship'

pre-emptive censorship: stopping something from happening

punitive censorship: punishment after the event

physical oppression: arrest, detention, torture, 'disappearance', murder

Cartoon by Jules Feiffer

Photocopy Original © Hodder & Stoughton 2001

WAR IS PEACE

FREEDOM IS SLAVERY

IGNORANCE IS STRENGTH

He took a twenty-five cent piece out of his pocket. There, too, in tiny clear lettering, the same slogans were inscribed, and on the other face of the coin the head of Big Brother. Even from the coin the eyes pursued you. On coins, on stamps, on the covers of books, on banners, on posters and on the wrapping of a cigarette packet – everywhere. Always the eyes watching you and the voice enveloping you. Asleep or awake, working or eating, indoors or out of doors, in the bath or in bed – no escape. Nothing was your own except the few cubic centimetres inside your skull . . .

. . . As soon as all the corrections which happened to be necessary in any particular number of *The Times* had been assembled and collated, that number would be reprinted, the original copy destroyed, and the corrected copy placed on the files in its stead. This process of continual alteration was applied to books, periodicals, pamphlets, posters, leaflets, films, sound-tracks, cartoons, photographs – to every kind of literature or documentation which might conceivably hold any political or ideological significance. Day by day and almost minute by minute the past was brought up to date. In this way every prediction made by the Party could be shown by documentary evidence to have been correct; nor was any item of news, or any expression of opinion, which conflicted with the needs of the moment, ever allowed to remain on record. All history was a palimpsest, scraped clean and re-inscribed exactly as often as was necessary. . . .

From George Orwell, 1984, *1949, Penguin Books*

Cartoon by Len Munnik

Photocopy Original © Hodder & Stoughton 2001

ACTIVITY 5 EXERCISE SHEET
Our secret society

Discuss:

What does the word 'secret' mean to you? Think of situations where it might be important to keep something secret and of examples where it might be dangerous to keep something secret:

in your personal life

in society

What could you do if you found out something 'secret' which you felt that others needed to know? Make two lists:

i) Information that is recorded about you at any time from your birth – tick those things which you think you have a legal right to know about and to see

ii) Information that you want/need about the society in which you live and issues which affect you – tick those where you think you have a legal right to the information

What issues/information do you think should be openly available?
What issues/information do you think should be kept secret?

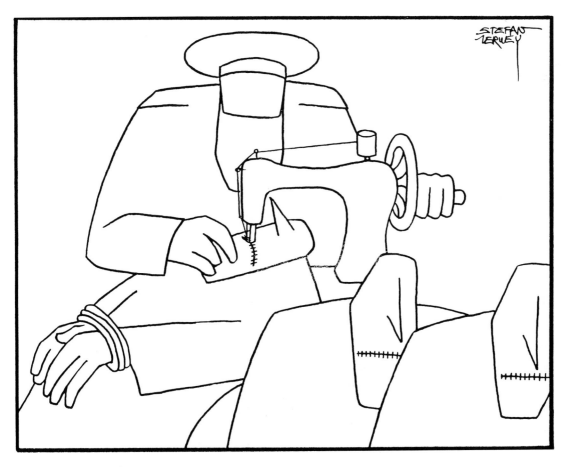

Cartoon by Stefan Verwey

Unit 2: FREEDOM TO THINK, TO KNOW, TO BE, TO SPEAK

Photocopy Original © Hodder & Stoughton 2001

Photocopy Original © Hodder & Stoughton 2001

ACTIVITY 5 FACT SHEET
Towards freedom of information in the UK

1911 Official Secrets Act passed. Section 1 was about espionage. Section 2 made unauthorised disclosure of *any* 'official' information on *any* subject an offence.

1939 During World War Two, information was strictly controlled. The Emergency Powers Act allowed censorship of mail and telephone calls. The Ministry of Information told the papers what they could say. By the 1970s over 100 different laws, in addition to the Official Secrets Act, made the disclosure of information to the public a criminal offence.

1984 The Data Protection Act gave UK citizens the right to see information about themselves held on computer. It did not cover information held on paper. The Local Government (Access to Information) Act gave us wider rights of access to council meetings, reports and papers.

1985   Sarah Tisdall, a young clerk at the Foreign Office, was prosecuted under Section 2 of the Official Secrets Act for 'leaking' information about the arrival in Britain of American Cruise missiles. She was convicted and sentenced to 6 months imprisonment.

Another 'whistle-blower', Clive Ponting, a senior civil servant at the Ministry of Defence, was prosecuted under Section 2. He leaked information to the press showing government ministers had misled Parliament over the sinking of the Argentinian cruiser 'Belgrano' during the Falklands War. His defence was that he was acting in the public interest. The judge said that this defence had no basis in law, but the jury disregarded his ruling and acquitted Ponting.

1987   The Access to Personal Files Act gave us the right to see manually held social work, housing and school records about ourselves.

1988   The Access to Medical Records Act gave us the right to see any report produced by our own doctor for an employer or insurance company.

1990   The Access to Health Records Act gave us the right to see information on our medical records.

1997   A Labour government was elected to bring in freedom of information legislation. A 'white paper' was published promising the new law. It was criticised for excluding the police and the intelligence services.

1998   The MacPherson Report of the Stephen Lawrence inquiry recommended that the police should be subject to the Act and only able to withhold information if its release would cause 'substantial harm'. The Government did not accept this.

The Public Interest Disclosure Act gave protection to people who, 'blow the whistle' on significant wrongdoing.

1999   The Government's Freedom of Information Bill was published for consultation. Many voluntary organisations strongly criticised it for being too weak and said:

continued

Towards freedom of information in the UK

- Public authorities refuse to give information, e.g. on the causes of major accidents; on health risks in foods, medicines and the environment; on police investigations and on the work of the intelligence services.
- People asking for information would have to show why they wanted this information and could be banned from publishing it.
- Andrew Puddephat, Director of the human rights organisation Article 19, said, 'Without amendment, this document will not serve the public interest, and will ensure that the UK remains one of the most secretive democracies in the world.'

"Why, that's a fantastic opinion. Unfortunately I'll have to report it to the FBI." Cartoon by Harley L. Schwadron

Photocopy Original © Hodder & Stoughton 2001

FREEDOM!

ACTIVITY 6 FACT SHEET
Some Internet issues

- Open Access for anyone to publish their opinions and get information

- 'Ordinary people' around the world can contact each other and share ideas and information

- Poorer people and poorer countries are 'left behind'

- Young people may get into 'virtual relationships' with exploitative adults

- News and information can cross borders without censorship or interference from repressive governments

- Lack of accountability/checking for accuracy

- Information overload and confusion

- Young people may get access to pornography

- Racist, Fascist and other 'extremist' groups can publish their views

- People without power, such as street-children's groups, can set up global networks

- Unprecedented public access allowed to information such as the Starr Report on President Clinton and Monica Lewinsky

Photocopy Original © Hodder & Stoughton 2001

ACTIVITY 8 BRIEFING SHEET 1
Hate speech: the speech that kills

'By the time the New York radio station WABC fired its most popular talk show host, Bob Grant, he had spent a good 25 years vilifying Blacks, Hispanics and other minorities with impunity. . . . He was finally sacked because on the day the plane carrying Clinton's Commerce Secretary, Ron Brown, crashed, Grant speculated that Brown (who was black) might be the only survivor, "because I'm a pessimist" . . . The shock jock had no difficulty in finding another job; he was hired by a rival station only two weeks later . . .'

. . . An ABC producer, on being asked whether Bob Grant's remarks were an example of free speech that must be protected . . . or verbal pollution, said: 'If the person has good ratings, a station has to ignore the garbage that he spews out. A radio station always fights for a host's constitutional rights if the show is profitable enough, and Grant had high ratings because he kept beating up on minorities. If his audience had been small, the managers would . . . declare him a bigot. . . . Our advertisers are aware that hate sells their products.'

'Hate speech, as Americans call it, is a troubling matter for people who believe in free speech. It is abusive, insulting, intimidating and harassing. And it might lead to violence, hatred or discrimination; and it kills. The USA, as the least censored society in the world, has held firmly to the first Amendment (of the US Constitution, protecting free speech) and to Article 19 of the UDHR, which has meant that attempts to make provisions against hate speech have almost always been disallowed by the Supreme Court.

International law appears more contradictory. Article 19 of the International Covenant on Civil and Political Rights asserts the right to freedom of opinion and expression . . . but Article 20 states that 'any advocacy of national, racial or religious hatred that constitutes incitement to discrimination, hostility or violence shall be prohibited by law.'

'Catherine MacKinnon and Andrea Dworkin's now famous campaign to outlaw pornography was based on their view that pornography is in effect hate speech: it treats women as sexual objects and subordinates them in a vile way to men. Though they did not succeed in persuading the US courts, the Canadian legislature did introduce a severe censorship law. But the first authors to be prosecuted under the new Canadian statute were not those the feminists had in mind. They were prominent homosexual authors, a radical black feminist accused of stirring up race hatred against white people and, for a time, Andrea Dworkin herself. Liberals who had warned against the dangers of censorship felt vindicated. Censorship backfires; the biter gets bit.'

'In the 1980s, in the United States, the home of free speech, a new form of censorship was born on college campuses. Alarmed at verbal attacks on women

continued

Photocopy Original © Hodder & Stoughton 2001

FREEDOM!

and minority students, some universities introduced so-called speech codes, forbidding remarks that were sexist or derogatory of a particular race or religion. All the great battles for extending liberty in the United States – anti-slavery, anti-segregation, rights of women – had involved parallel battles for the principle of free speech. Yet here were the same kinds of people who had affirmed these civil rights suddenly saying openly they thought free speech was not an absolute right ... that speech must be restricted for the protection of vulnerable groups who were the target of hate speech.'

'The most dangerous threat behind hate speech is surely that it can go beyond its immediate targets and create a *culture* of hate, a culture which makes it acceptable, respectable even, to hate on a far wider scale.... On 4 November 1995, Yitzhak Rabin, Prime Minister of Israel, was assassinated by Yigal Amir, a 25 year-old student. But what part was played by right-wing Israeli radicals chanting, 'Rabin is a traitor! Rabin is a murderer!'? ... Or by placards showing Rabin's features overlaid with the thin black circles of a rifle target? Words can turn into bullets, hate speech can kill and maim, just as censorship can.'

Extracts from 'Hate Speech: the speech that kills', lecture by Ursula Owen for Index on Censorship, 1999. (Full text available on Index website: **www.indexoncensorship.org/back.html)**

Cartoon by Kostas Mitropoulos

Photocopy Original © Hodder & Stoughton 2001

Word power – statements

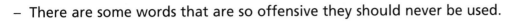

- There are some words that are so offensive they should never be used.

- Everyone should be able to say anything they want to way

- It is all right to say something offensive in private but not in public

- It is better to let hateful opinions be spoken so that they can be known and challenged

- Hate speech is more dangerous than censorship

- Pornography is a form of hate speech

- It is all right for someone to use an offensive word to describe themselves

- It is just as damaging if a woman tells a sexist joke or a black person tells a racist joke

- Politically correct language is a form of censorship

- Principles of equality do not make money

Photocopy Original © Hodder & Stoughton 2001

ACTIVITY 9 FACT SHEET
Banned bands

In 1999 on the Bangladesh state TV 'Band Show', singer Maqsood and his band Dhaka played a 'fusion' version of a favourite song by the revered Bengali poet and songwriter Rabindranath Tagore (1861–1941). 'Cultural activities' – previously supporters of freedom and democracy – were outraged and demanded that the band should be banned from the TV.

Fury against musicians who challenge tradition is nothing new. In the 19th century the waltz was denounced as immoral. In the 20th century jazz – the first big breakthrough by black musicians – was attacked in the US and banned in Nazi Germany for being 'savage' and 'degenerate'. In the 1950s rock & roll – with its roots in black rhythm and blues – was condemned in the US as 'jungle music', threatening American civilisation. In Britain too, rock & roll was considered a threat to British youth. Music journalist Steve Race wrote in the *Melody Maker* in 1956 that 'viewed as a social phenomenon, the current craze for Rock-and-Roll material is one of the most terrifying things to have happened to popular music.'

Music has often been censored for political reasons. The Nazis banned much classical music, especially by Jewish composers and performers. In the Soviet Union, under Stalin, some modern music was banned for being 'decadent' and undermining the spirit of the nation. In the US in the 1950s, singer and actor Paul Robeson was banned from performing because he was a member of the Communist Party. In Greece, the 1967 military coup led to the imprisonment and torture of the internationally famous singer and composer Mikis Theodorakis, whose songs of freedom went on undermining the dictatorship. In Chile, political folksinger Victor Jara went on singing up to the moment of his murder as a prisoner in the Santiago Stadium in 1973. Under Pinochet's regime even to mention Jara's name was an offence.

Musical censorship is still alive and well. References to sex and drugs have led to many songs being banned from the radio, TV or from mainstream shops. Artists whose work has been banned include: Elvis Presley; Billie Holliday; The Rolling Stones; The Beatles; The Sex Pistols; John Lennon; Pink Floyd; Ice T; Biafra Jello. In the US a right-wing group called 'Parents Music Resource Center' pressurised the record industry in 1985 into putting 'Parental Advisory Stickers' on albums with 'explicit lyrics'. Record dealers have been prosecuted for selling 'stickered' albums to minors.

In 1990 the rap group '2 Live Crew' produced an album called 'As Nasty As They Wanna Be', with sexually explicit and sexist lyrics. The band and a record store owner in Miami were prosecuted for obscenity, despite the First Amendment in the US Constitution which protects freedom of speech. This case was a challenge

continued

Photocopy Original © Hodder & Stoughton 2001

Unit 2: FREEDOM TO THINK, TO KNOW, TO BE, TO SPEAK

to people who opposed censorship: although they supported the Crew's right to freedom of expression, it was difficult to defend lyrics which blatantly attacked women.

During the 1991 Gulf War the BBC compiled a list of tracks to be avoided, including 'Boom Bang a Bang' by Lulu, 'A Little Peace' by Nicole and 'Light My Fire' by Jose Feliciano. The band Massive Attack was just referred to as Massive. DJ Giles Peterson was sacked by Jazz FM for playing 90 minutes of 'peace music'.

The music associated with New Age Travellers was even mentioned in law. The 1994 Criminal Justice and Public Order Act: 'defined and proposed to outlaw – when played in certain circumstances – a genre of music: house ... "defined as sounds wholly or predominantly characterised by the emission of a succession of repetitive beats"

Sources: Index on Censorship Issue 6, November 1998 – full text available on **www.indexoncensorship.org/back.html**

The Sex Pistols

The Rolling Stones

The Beatles

Photocopy Original © Hodder & Stoughton 2001

ACTIVITY 10 EXERCISE SHEET
Whose rights?

A newsagent displays pornographic magazines openly. After complaints from customers he puts them under the counter but continues to sell them to those who ask.

A film showing extreme violence is banned from the cinema but is available on video.

The author of a play which criticises the role of Jewish leadership during the Holocaust is told that he will have to change the text before it can be performed.

In an area where there has been a lot of racist violence associated with far-right groups, the local Council bars tenants from putting the Union Jack in their windows.

A painting of a murderer is shown in an art gallery. Objectors damage the picture.

A comedian at a dinner for business people tells racist and sexist jokes. Two waitresses complain. They are told they have no sense of humour. They go to an industrial tribunal and win compensation.

Photocopy Original © Hodder & Stoughton 2001

ACTIVITY 12 INFORMATION SHEET
Queerbashing surveys

Linda: I'm only 16 and to many it won't seem like much, but to me it is. I realised my sexuality when I was 14. I didn't tell my parents because they would chuck me out. I was being beaten up by some girls because I was gay, so in the end I had to tell my form teacher. Her once caring attitude towards me changed. Suddenly she hated me. She told me that I'm going to hell and that I'm concerned with things that shouldn't be thought about let alone by a girl of my age.'

Stephen: 'At school the other kids seemed to know I was gay before I did. Most of the abuse was verbal – they usually refused to touch me because they might become queer too. One kid persistently beat me up right until I was 18. I let him – after all I was gay.'

These quotes come from the 'Queerbashing' survey conducted by Stonewall, the UK campaign for equal rights for gay men and lesbians. Although many lesbians and gays suffer abuse and violence it was clear from the survey that those under 18 had the worst time. In the last five years, 48% of this age group had been attacked, 61% abused and 90% called names. 40% of the attacks took place in schools.

In 1999 the Terrence Higgins Trust and Stonewall commissioned the Institute of Education to carry out a school survey. Its findings confirm the picture painted by Linda and Stephen. 82% of teachers said that they were aware of homophobic bullying, but only 6% of schools had bullying policies that dealt with homophobia. 61% of teachers felt that schools should deal with lesbian and gay issues, but felt unable to do so because of the lack of official guidance, fear of criticism and confusion about Section 28 of the 1988 Local Government Act which forbade local authorities from promoting homosexuality in school and from teaching 'the acceptability of homosexuality as a pretended family relationship'.

Source: Stonewall: Equality 2000 campaign

Photocopy Original © Hodder & Stoughton 2001

Photocopy Original © Hodder & Stoughton 2001

ACTIVITY 13 INFORMATION SHEET
Breaking the silence

LEGAL STATUS OF HOMOSEXUALITY WORLDWIDE (1997)

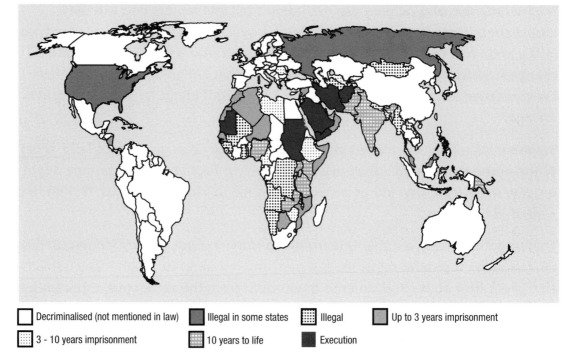

☐ Decriminalised (not mentioned in law) ■ Illegal in some states ▦ Illegal ▨ Up to 3 years imprisonment

▦ 3 - 10 years imprisonment ▨ 10 years to life ■ Execution

In countries all over the world, individuals are being targeted for imprisonment, torture and even murder, simply on the grounds of their sexual orientation. Gay men, lesbians, transvestites, transsexuals, any person who doesn't adhere to the dictates of what passes for 'normal' sexuality may be subject to such persecution at the hands of private individuals or government agents. Abuses may take such subtle forms such as everyday hostility, harassment or neglect. In such cases, antipathetic authorities may refuse to protect the basic rights of gays and lesbians, leaving them vulnerable to exploitation, sexual attack, public or domestic violence and even murder, all without recourse to the law. In other instances, governments are themselves the perpetrators of abuses: unfair trials, imprisonment, ill-treatment (including false 'medical cures'), torture (including rape), and execution are among the violations against sexual minorities recorded by Amnesty International.

Lesbians and gay men were targeted by the Nazis for extermination, but despite the clear indication of their particular vulnerability to human rights abuses, they were not specifically included in the framework for international human rights protection in the UDHR or included in subsequent human rights conventions. The stigmatised position of gay men and lesbians around the world and the lack of recognition of sexuality as a basic human right contributes to their experiences of ill-treatment at the hands of the authorities (in 1995 approximately 78 countries had laws criminalising homosexual acts).

continued

Unit 2: FREEDOM TO THINK, TO KNOW, TO BE, TO SPEAK

'For gays in Colombia, there is no rule of law. The only program the government has for people like me is a program to kill us ... There were a group of 15 of us working the streets that were HIV positive and that the police knew about ... from January to May of this year (1993) 5 of us had been killed.
Luis Alberto, male prostitute

'In 1994 in Lima a very violent raid was carried out in the capital where about 75 lesbian women were beaten up and ill-treated by the police. Prostitutes get a very rough time in jail. But the treatment of lesbians was even worse. Lesbians were beaten up because, however degrading prostitution can be, it is still regarded as normal behaviour, whereas lesbianism is seen as too threatening to the status-quo.'
Peruvian witness

'The laws forbidding homosexual acts often act as a kind of mandate for violations. ... They have killed gays and lesbians in Texas because they believe them to be less than human. I believe it's very important that people understand why murders happen and that such murder is a result of hatred. It is committed by young teenage men. Those men were not born haters. They were taught to hate by a society that continues to pass laws against lesbians and gay men, that continues to demonise lesbians and gays, that preaches hatred from the pulpit.'
Ann, human rights campaigner, Texas, USA

Source: Breaking the Silence: Human Rights Violations Based on Sexual Orientation, *Amnesty International UK, 1997*

FREEDOM!

ACTIVITY 14 BRIEFING SHEET
Is it a crime to be gay in Boldovia?

You live in the newly democratic (imaginary) Eastern European state of Boldovia. After decades of totalitarian government, the country seeks to join the Council of Europe – the organisation of the European democracies which have more tolerant laws towards homosexuality than Boldovia. The Council of Europe will not consider closer political, economic and cultural ties with Boldovia until it decriminalises homosexuality.

The Boldovian government has appointed a Committee to review existing legislation. One of the most controversial laws under review is Section 8 of the Penal Code. This law condemns homosexuality as 'an abomination against nature'. The punishment for promoting homosexuality is two years in jail. The punishment for adults found guilty of involvement in homosexual acts is five years in jail. The uncorroborated testimony of a single person is enough to convict someone under the Act. Section 8 has been used to arrest and discredit many people in Boldovia who were not gay men or lesbians.

A Committee of six members of the Boldovian Parliament has been set up to take testimony from the public, and to recommend if Section 8 should be repealed and, if so, what the consequences might be. The committee will listen to representatives of:
The Boldovian Police, the Boldovian Council for Civil liberties, the Boldovian Council of Faiths, the Boldovian Brigade of Light for Family Values, the Boldovian Institute for Social Research, the Boldovian Medical Association, the Boldovian Committee for Homosexual Equality, Amnesty International.

Role Card 1: The Boldovian police
You represent the police for of Boldovia.
A survey of Boldovian police revealed the following, sometimes conflicting opinions:

Most police do not like homosexuals or homosexuality
Some police are homosexuals. The illegality of homosexual acts gives rise to blackmail of those involved.
Homosexual acts between consenting adults are victimless crimes.
Given the increasing rate of violent crime in Boldovia, resources that are now being used to arrest and jail gays and lesbians could be better used elsewhere.
Decriminalisation of homosexuality may lead to an increase in pornography and prostitution.
The current high rate of violent attacks on lesbians and gay men would decrease if homosexuality were decriminalised.
Police attitudes towards homosexuality would probably remain hostile even if Section 8 was abolished.

Photocopy Original © Hodder & Stoughton 2001

continued

Unit 2: FREEDOM TO THINK, TO KNOW, TO BE, TO SPEAK

Role Card 2: The Boldovian Council for Civil Liberties

You represent the newly established Boldovian Commission for Civil Liberties.

Human rights and civil liberty organisations in Boldovia and abroad believe that:
Sexual minorities should have the right to expect complete equality under Boldovian law as do all other minorities.
Sexual activity between consenting adults is a private matter and is not appropriate for state legislation.
As Boldovia is now a signatory to the European Convention on Human Rights, it must respect the European Court of Human Rights which has ruled that it is illegal for nations to criminalise homosexual relationships between consenting adults.

Role Card 3: The Boldovian Council of Faiths

The Boldovian Council of Faiths speaks for all the main religious faiths in the country – Islamic, Jewish and all the main Christian churches, Orthodox, Catholic and Protestant.
The Council contains a conservative element and a progressive element – both of whom are represented on the delegation. The Council claims to speak for 68% of the Boldovian population.

Some of your Council's conservative members believe:
Homosexuality is evil and unnatural
Holy scriptures condemn homosexual acts as a sin
AIDS is a divine punishment
The state should strengthen traditional morality
Your followers can be mobilised to pressure lawmakers to keep Section 8

Some of your Council's liberal members believe:
Homosexuals should receive support and not punishment
The laws against homosexuality should be abolished
State recognition of lesbian and gay marriages is 'going too far'

Role Card 4: The Boldovian Brigade of Light for Family Values

The Brigade is a conservative group, small in number but very vocal, with some support in the new government and the media. You believe that:

God ordained the natural order of things – men and women – Adam and Eve, not Adam and Adam.

Homosexuality is a perversion and a mental illness.

Homosexuals should be pitied and should receive treatment to try and cure them. This is best done in prison.
No child will be safe from influence and abuse if lesbians and gay men are allowed to become teachers, parents, or youth workers.
The traditional family unit is the only place to bring up children. The Brigade will strongly resist any attempts by the government to broaden the definition of 'family'.

Photocopy Original © Hodder & Stoughton 2001

continued

FREEDOM!

Role Card 5: Boldovian Institute for Social Research

You are a member of the state body that organises social research in Boldovia. From your information you believe that:

Approximately one Boldovian in ten is a lesbian or a gay man – figures that reflect international statistics.

Children suffer no harm from having a lesbian or gay parent.

The current high rate of suicide among lesbian and gays would be prevented if homosexuality were decriminalised.

Role Card 6: Boldovian Medical Association

The Boldovian Medical Association represents the doctors of Boldovia.

Health care and health education should reach as many people as possible. It is impossible effectively to teach safe sex and HIV prevention without acknowledging the reality of homosexuality, and the widespread practice of same sex relationships in Boldovia.

More people would be tested for HIV infection if lesbian and gay relationships were not illegal

Role Card 7: Boldovian Campaign for Homosexual Equality

You are members of the recently formed Boldovian Campaign for Homosexual Equality.

Some of your members are prominent Boldovian lesbians and gay men. You have gathered international support for your campaign for equal status and rights for lesbians and gays. The main points of your campaign are:

Gay men and lesbians should be full citizens with equal protection under the law. All laws against homosexual acts amongst consenting adults and against the promotion of homosexuality should be abolished.

Evidence does not support the argument that children suffer negatively from having lesbian or gay parents; on the contrary, most child sex abusers are heterosexual men. You therefore demand full parental rights for lesbians and gay men.

Decriminalisation of homosexuality is not linked to an increase in prostitution and pornography, especially since the overwhelming majority of both pornography and prostitution is heterosexual.

Role Card 8: Amnesty International (AI)

You represent an international human rights organisation. AI maintains that it is a violation of human rights to imprison people on the grounds of their homosexuality. You are therefore demanding that:

Section 8 be repealed and homosexuality be decriminalised in Boldovia.

All persons imprisoned because of consensual relations with a partner of the same sex be released immediately.

Source: Adapted from AIUSA Human Rights Education Resource Notebooks, Gay and Lesbian Rights, 1995

Photocopy Original © Hodder & Stoughton 2001

ACTIVITY 15 BRIEFING SHEET 1
Amnesty for Artists

'In the jails of the world, artists are imprisoned. Their words, their songs, their pictures and their ideas have disturbed those in power. Some suffer torture. Some pay for exercising their right to freedom of expression with their lives.'

From the Amnesty for Artists campaign, Glasgow, 1990 calling for the release of three artist prisoners of conscience: Jack Mapanje, jailed poet from Malawi; Nguyen Chi Thien, jailed poet from Vietnam; and Hong Song-Dam, jailed Korean painter.

Amnesty International Campaigning For Human Rights

Amnesty for Artists Leaflet from woodblock print by Hong Song-Dam

Photocopy Original © Hodder & Stoughton 2001

Photocopy Original © Hodder & Stoughton 2001

ACTIVITY 15 INFORMATION SHEET 2
Hong Song-Dam

Hong Song-Dam is a well-known graphic artist from Kwangju, a city in the South East of the Republic of Korea. He made many woodcuts, prints and paintings for the labour movement in his country, often on human rights themes. In May 1980, the military took power in Korea and martial law was declared. Hong was involved in the massive protest demonstrations for democracy and against martial law that took place in Kwangju at that time. The protests were brutally suppressed during 'The Kwangju Incident', when many hundreds of Kwangju citizens were killed by paratroopers of the Korean army, thousands more were injured and thousands were jailed. (Those imprisoned included the opposition leader Kim Dae-Jung, who was initially sentenced to death. He was elected President of Korea in 1998.)

Under martial law all political activity was banned, strikes were forbidden, the spreading of 'baseless rumours' became a crime, and criticism of previous Presidents was made illegal. Under the strictest censorship all reports of the Kwangju protests and their repression were suppressed. The city was sealed off by the military. All photographs and film were seized and confiscated. In the early 1980s Hong Song-Dam made and printed a series of woodcuts of the massacre he had witnessed, the first published records of the events that had taken place.

Some of Hong Song Dam's woodcuts in the 1980s depicted the brutal torture of political prisoners – ill treatment that he himself was to undergo when he was arrested in 1989, tortured, and jailed as a prisoner of conscience.

During his interrogation Hong was tortured, deprived of sleep, stripped naked, and beaten on the hands and feet. He was hung up by his feet and thrown

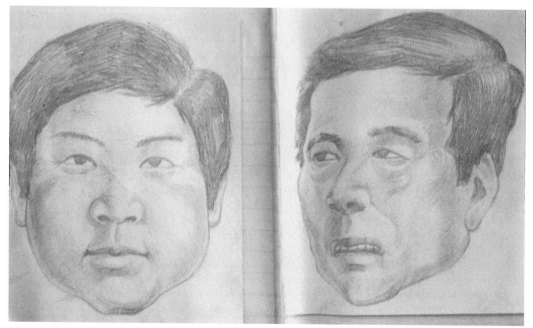

Hong Song-Dam's drawings of his torturers, 1989

continued

against the walls of his cell. Worst of all was the water torture, a series of mock executions by drowning. Despite his damaged hand, Hong was later able to draw portraits of two of his torturers on a smuggled scrap of paper that he managed to pass out to his mother. The picture was published the next day in Hangarye Daily, a progressive newspaper.

Hong's 'crime' had been to post a set of colour slides of a series of 17 large mural paintings he and his friends had made to North Korea. The wall hangings – each 17 feet long and 10 feet high – depicted the history of Korea's struggles for national independence. The artists wanted them to be displayed in the World Youth Festival that was taking place in Pyonyang, North Korea that summer. Most of the paintings were subsequently destroyed by the authorities.

Hong was eventually sentenced to seven years imprisonment under Article 7 of Korea's notorious National Security Law which prohibited any form of expression, or the production of any document or drawing that 'praises, benefits or encourages' North Korea.

After his arrest Hong was adopted as a prisoner of conscience by Amnesty International. Many thousands of people, particularly in Scotland, signed appeals to the Korean authorities calling for his release. He was freed after three years in jail. He has become one of the most celebrated artists in Korea, and has since made many paintings of his torture and imprisonment.

Source: Free Expressions, *Amnesty International Art Education Pack, Sara Selwood, 1991*

Unit 2: FREEDOM TO THINK, TO KNOW, TO BE, TO SPEAK

Photocopy Original © Hodder & Stoughton 2001

FREEDOM!

Jailed for a joke

No laughing matter ... Portrait of Burmese comedian, U Pa Pa Lay who was jailed for seven years in 1997 for telling jokes against the military government of Myanmar.

The portrait, by Lancaster artist, Chris Robinson, made from 1.6 million of the 17 million thumbprints and signatures collected by Amnesty International and the Body Shop in support of the Universal Declaration of Human Rights. It was displayed at the National Portrait Gallery in London and in Paris in 1998.

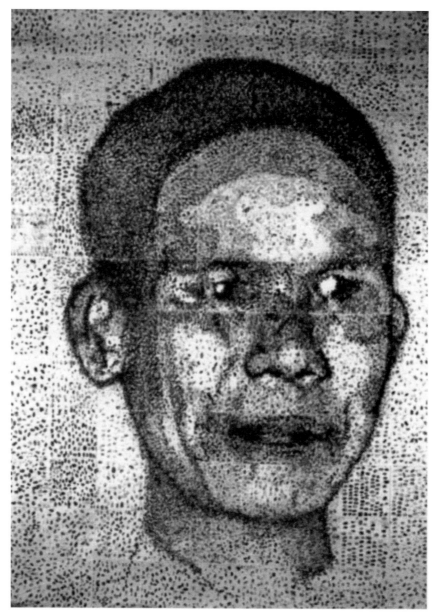

Thumbprint portrait of U Pa Pa Lay by Chris Robinson 1998

Photocopy Original © Hodder & Stoughton 2001

ACTIVITY 16 RESOURCE SHEET
'Newspeak'

'... what justification is there for a word which is simply the opposite of some other word? A word contains its opposite in itself. Take "good" for instance. If you have a word like "good", what need is there for a word like "bad"? "Ungood" will do just as well – better, because it is an exact opposite, which the other is not. Or again, if you want a stronger version of "good", what sense is there in having a whole string of vague useless words like "excellent" and "splendid" and all the rest of them? "Plusgood" covers the meaning; or "doubleplusgood" if you want something stronger still ...'

Syme immediately detected a certain lack of enthusiasm.

'You haven't a real appreciation of Newspeak, Winston ... you don't grasp the beauty of the destruction of words ... Don't you see that the whole aim of Newspeak is to narrow the range of thought? In the end we shall make thoughtcrime literally impossible, because there will be no words in which to express it. Every concept that can ever be needed will be expressed by exactly *one* word, with its meaning rigidly defined and all its subsidiary meanings rubbed out and forgotten ... By 2050 – earlier, probably – all real knowledge of Oldspeak will have disappeared. The whole literature of the past will have been destroyed. Chaucer, Shakespeare, Milton, Byron – they'll exist only in Newspeak versions, not merely changed into something different, but actually changed into something contradictory of what they used to be. Even the literature of the Party will change. Even the slogans will change. How could you have a concept like "freedom is slavery" when the concept of freedom has been abolished? The whole climate of thought will be different. In fact, there will *be* no thought, as we understand it now. Orthodoxy means not thinking – not needing to think. Orthodoxy is unconsciousness.'

One of these days, thought Winston with sudden deep conviction, Syme will be vaporized. He is too intelligent. He sees too clearly and speaks too plainly. The Party does not like such people. One day he will disappear. It is written in his face.

From: 1984 by George Orwell, 1949, Penguin Books

Cartoon by Ivan Steiger

ACTIVITY 17 CASE STUDY 1
Turkey rewrites the journalists' dictionary

In May 1999 the Turkish government issued a directive to journalists working for the official press, TV and radio, warning them to mind their language during the trial of Kurdish leader of the PKK, Abdullah Ocalan, who was sentenced to death. Here are some of the terms that were ruled unacceptable, and the alternative words and phrases that the reporters were to use instead:

Instead of 'Guerrilla' use *'Terrorist'*
Instead of 'Rural guerilla' use *'Bandit'*
Instead of 'Separatist' use *'Terrorist'*
Instead of 'Kurdish uprising/Kurdish national independence war/Kurds' independence struggle' use *'Terrorist actions'*
Instead of 'PKK' use *'Terrorist organisation PKK/Bloody terrorist organisation/Murder gang'*
Instead of 'Kurdish/of Kurdish background' use *'Turkish citizen/Our citizens who are identified as Kurds'*
Instead of 'Refugee' use *'Shelter seeker'*
Instead of 'Kurdish people' use *'People from separatist environments'*
Instead of 'Kurdish Parliament in exile' use *'Meeting under the PKK terrorist organisation's control'*
Instead of 'Kurdish flag' use *'Symbol of the terror organisation'*
Instead of 'Low-intensity warfare' use *'Fight against terrorism'*
Instead of 'Kurdish nation' use *'Formation in northern Iraq'*

Source: New York Times, *6 June 1999*

Photocopy Original © Hodder & Stoughton 2001

Unit 2: FREEDOM TO THINK, TO KNOW, TO BE, TO SPEAK

ACTIVITY 17 CASE STUDY 2
'Turkey – freedom of thought?'

'In Turkey I am involved in a campaign which challenges the continued imprisonment of people in Turkey for the peaceful exercise of their right to freedom of expression.

Although the Turkish Constitution (Article 28) guarantees a free press which "shall not be censored", Article 8 of the Turkish Legal Code makes it a crime to write anything which falls within the widely drawn offence of "separatist propaganda". It is also an offence for anybody to publish a criminal article even if the publisher makes it clear he disagrees with what he published. Many people have found themselves in front of the judges and then in prison under these laws.'

What a beautiful article! If Abdullah Ocalan (the leader of the PKK) makes a statement, nobody can publish it, and nobody can read it. We can only hear what are supposed to be his words coming from the mouth of the Turkish authorities.

In January 1995 one of our most famous writers, Yasar Kemal, had to appear before the State Security Court in Istanbul to face charges arising from an article on Turkey that he wrote in the German magazine *Der Spiegel*. When people heard about his arrest our phone started to ring. 90 intellectuals turned up at the courthouse to support him. We began a signature campaign there and then. We took Voltaire's words from, 250 years ago as our slogan: "I may disagree with your ideas but I am ready to die for your right to express them". Within a month hundreds of Turkish intellectuals, writers, publishers, and artists jointly published: *Freedom of Thought*, a book consisting of 10 banned articles including Yasar's.

A mass trial started against 185 of the co-publishers under Anti Terror Law 3713 – one of over 500 articles of the Turkish legal code that currently define "thought crime". We were liable to up to a minimum of 20 months imprisonment each. We all turned up in a long queue at the Constitutional Court. What would happen in Turkey if we were locked up? Five of the most popular TV programmes would have to be suspended. Five soap operas would need their story lines rewritten as their writers or directors were in jail. The media would lose 30 of the most popular newspaper columns. Eight professional chairs will be left vacant and whole universities would need new teaching staff. Film studios and theatres would close. But on the positive side at least 20 new books will be added to the Turkish bibliography on prison conditions.

On 12 March we invited authors from other countries to co-publish another book with us called *Mini Freedom of Thought*. It contained just one paragraph from each banned article. The co-publishers include James Kellman, Arthur

Photocopy Original © Hodder & Stoughton 2001

continued

FREEDOM!

Miller, Harold Pinter and 144 other writers from all over the world. The State Prosecutor was embarrassed and refused to prosecute. So we took a case against him for violating the State Constitution by not taking any action against us. If nothing happens in 60 days, we take the case to the European Court in Strasbourg for our right to be prosecuted!

One of the accused is the actor and theatre director Mahir Gunsherai. The only words he would use in court were quotations from Franz Kafka's play *The Trial*. It was the first time that the judge had heard these famous words. He kept asking: "What's he saying? This man is insulting the court!" A new case has now opened against the 'Gunsherai/Kafka' tendency.

Sanar Yurdatapan, Turkish musician, writer, composer and human rights activist addressing the Amnesty International UK's AGM in 1997.

Yasar Kemal

Yurdatapan has been imprisoned in Turkey for investigating village massacres by the security forces, and for 'promoting the PKK' (when a piece of music he had composed was used as background to a programme on MEDTV – Satellite Turkish television on the Kurdish question).

AIUK Group Newsletter, April 1997

Sanar Yurdatapan: cartoon by Dan Jones

Photocopy Original © Hodder & Stoughton 2001

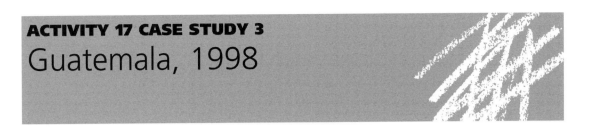

ACTIVITY 17 CASE STUDY 3
Guatemala, 1998

Human rights defender Bishop Juan Jose Gerardi, aged 75, was bludgeoned to death at his home two days after handing in his findings on atrocities committed during Guatemala's 36-year-old civil war which ended in 1996. The Bishop's dossier, entitled 'Never Again', blamed the army for most of the violations which led to 150,000 deaths and 50,000 'disappearances'. A man, previously convicted of assault, was arrested for the Bishop's murder, but human rights activists said the authorities were trying to claim the murder was criminal, not political.

Sources: The Guardian, *Amnesty International*

Cartoon by Stefan Verwey

Photocopy Original © Hodder & Stoughton 2001

ACTIVITY 17 CASE STUDY 4
China 1999

A Chinese Internet user who distributed 30,000 e-mail addresses to a democracy magazine in the United States has been jailed for crimes against the state.

Lin Hai, the 30-year-old owner of a software company in Shanghai, was found guilty of subversion. His wife Xu Hong said yesterday that he had been jailed for two years.

Beijing is trying to draw a clear line between approved use of the Internet, which is seen as an essential part of the technological revolution, and its use for 'improper purposes'. These include gambling, pornography, selling goods and the spreading of 'subversive' political ideas. . . . Beijing has confirmed plans for monitoring units to supervise Internet use.

Mr Lin was detained in March and held for eight months before being charged.

Source: John Gittings, The Guardian, *21 January 1999*

The world's journalists under siege

Fifty journalists were killed around the world in 1998, nearly twice the number of the year before. 22 of them were killed in Latin America – ten in Colombia and six in Mexico. In Peru, the National Association of Journalists registered 121 attacks on journalists or media outlets.

During the 1990s, Algeria was the most dangerous country in the world for journalists, with 60 deaths between 1988 and 1997.

Source: International Federation of Journalists, 1999

Photocopy Original © Hodder & Stoughton 2001

FREEDOM!

ACTIVITY 18 INFORMATION SHEET 2
Four more journalists murdered

Mexico, 1998: Pedro Valle Hernandez, correspondent for the Guerrero state television network, was shot in his car in the city of Zihuatanejo on 29 October. His last report, broadcast after his death, exposed a child prostitution ring.

Colombia, 1998: Nelson Carvajal, a teacher and local radio producer, was assassinated on 16 April as he left the school where he taught. His radio programmes were frequently critical of local government corruption.

Bangladesh, 1998: Saiful Alam Mukul, editor of the Dainik Runner, was killed by unknown gunmen while returning to his home in the town of Jessore on 30 August. The paper was well known for its outspoken criticism of political corruption.

Canada, 1998: Tara Singh Hayer, publisher of the Indo-Canadian Times, was shot dead on 18 November at his Vancouver home. Hayer, who was partially paralysed after an assassination attempt in 1988, is thought to have been killed by Sikh fundamentalists, of whom his paper was fiercely critical.

Source: The Guardian, *media section, 26 April 1999*

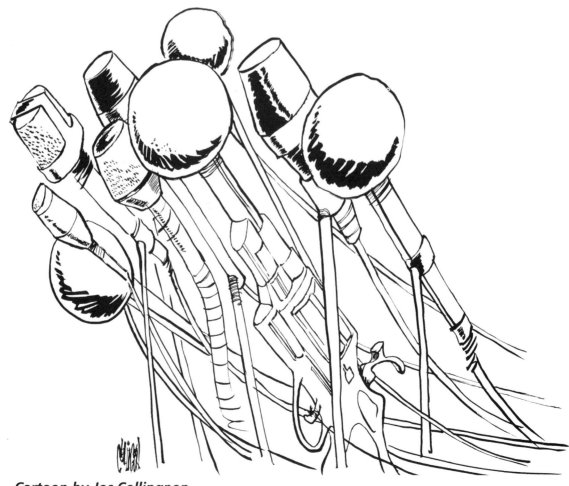

Cartoon by Jos Collingnon

Photocopy Original © Hodder & Stoughton 2001

ACTIVITY 18 INFORMATION SHEET 3
Truth under attack in Algeria

Silence is death: Algerian women demonstrate in Algiers, March 1994

'Silence is death
If you are silent you are dead
And if you speak you are dead
So speak and die . . .'

Tahar Djaout, journalist, Algeria, assassinated May 1993

'The most difficult times are when I take pictures after the massacres. . . . I have to stay in control, I can't be touched emotionally, but it's very hard what we see, very hard'. . . . Photographers such as Khared (not his real name) are in the front line of a civil war which has torn apart this former French colony. It is a conflict which claimed 80,000 lives in just six years.

'It is an extremely vicious war', one journalist put it, 'fought without mercy'. Whole villages have been massacred by extremists and 'death squads'. Checkpoints can turn into ambushes, and thousands have 'disappeared'. This is a war in which children and babies have frequently had their throats cut, and pregnant women disembowelled.

Yet there is another, unnoticed, battle here; one fought by a fledgling independent press and the journalist and proprietors who run it. Caught

continued

76

FREEDOM!

between a repressive regime keen to silence criticism, and Islamic fundamentalists who regard them as traitors, journalists have often been critical of both sides – with deadly results. Seventy journalists and photographers have lost their lives here since May 1993, killed by the fundamentalists...

... Many journalists use pseudonyms, dare not publish pictures of their faces, and often lie about their profession. One woman I met at El Khabar, the largest selling Arabic newspaper, even told her family she works as a hairdresser. ...

Deep in El Watan's archives, Hakim, the paper's economics correspondent, shows me a simple brown folder, gathering dust on a back shelf. The harsh, artificial light reveals little at first of what lies within; the yellowing photographs staring out, beneath such headlines as shot, dead, assassinated, mutilated.

'Some of these were my friends,' he says. 'This one is Tahar Djaout', he murmurs pointing to an earnest, bespectacled man. 'He was the first of us to die.'

I ask him what effect these deaths have had on him. 'We've lost our friends, our colleagues. It's very hard to live with this.' Yet he is still insistent. 'We will never stop. In fact, we are more motivated. It's a kind of resistance'. ... 'This is the journalists' fight, and society's fight, to build a democracy and a free press.'

Source: edited from The Guardian, *media section, 20 July 1998, and International P.E.N.*

Photocopy Original © Hodder & Stoughton 2001

ACTIVITY 19 POETRY

'The Animal and Insect Act'
by Cecil Rajendra

Finally, in order to ensure
absolute national security
they passed the Animal and Insect
Emergency Control and Discipline Act.

Under this new Act, buffaloes
cows and goats were prohibited
from grazing in herds of more
than three. Neither could birds
flock, nor bees swarm . . .
This constituted unlawful assembly.

As they had not obtained prior
planning permission, mud-wasps
and swallows were issued with
summary Notices to Quit. Their
homes were declared subversive
extensions to private property.

Monkeys and mynahs were warned
to stop relaying their noisy
morning orisons until an official
Broadcasting Licence was issued
by the appropriate Ministry.
Unmonitored publications and broad-
casts posed the gravest threats
in times of a National Emergency.

Similarly, woodpeckers had
to stop tapping their morse-
code messages from coconut
tree-top to chempaka tree.
All messages were subject
to a thorough pre-scrutiny
by the relevant authorities.

Java sparrows were arrested in
droves for rumour-mongering.

continued

Photocopy Original © Hodder & Stoughton 2001

'The Animal and Insect Act' by Cecil Rajendra

Cats (suspected of conspiracy)
had to be indoors by 9 o'clock.
Cicadas and crickets received
notification to turn their amp-
lifiers down. Ducks could not
quack nor turkeys gobble during
restricted hours. Need I say,
all dogs – alsatians, dachshunds,
terriers, pointers and even
little chihuahuas – were muzzled.

In the interests of security
penguins and zebras were
ordered to discard their
non-regulation uniforms.
The deer had to surrender
their dangerous antlers.
Tigers and all carnivores
with retracted claws were
sent directly to prison
for concealing lethal weapons.

And by virtue of Article
Four, paragraph 2(b)
sub-section sixteen
under no circumstances
were elephants allowed
to break wind between
the hours of six and six.
Their farts could easily
be interpreted as gunshots.
Might spark off a riot . . .

A month after the Act
was properly gazetted
the birds and insects
started migrating south
the animals went north
and an eerie silence
handcuffed our forests.

There was now Total Security.

Photocopy Original © Hodder & Stoughton 2001

Unit 2: FREEDOM TO THINK, TO KNOW, TO BE, TO SPEAK

ACTIVITY 20 INFORMATION SHEET
Organisations fighting censorship

ARTICLE 19

Article 19, founded in 1986, is an international human rights organisation which promotes freedom of expression and fights censorship all over the world. It takes its name from Article 19 of the UDHR.

The right to freedom of expression and information is a fundamental human right without which all other rights, including the right to life, cannot be protected. The full enjoyment of this right is the most potent force to preempt repression, war and genocide and safeguard other fundamental human rights.

From the banning of books to the torture and murder of dissenters, from undisclosed nuclear disasters to war propaganda, from the denial of the existence of a famine to forbidding adults to watch a film about Jesus Christ, from the smallest slash of the censor's pen to the blanket muzzling of the media, censorship pervades every culture. It can be blatant or subtle, including hidden threats and harassment that result in self-censorship.

The torture and murder of dissenters takes place in many countries. In the absence of a free press international pressure is vital. Censorship can cause mass starvation as despotic regimes hide the facts. Failure to provide information on health issues such as reproductive health or AIDS causes unnecessary deaths around the world. The dumping of toxic waste, exploitation of agricultural land by multi-national companies and the long-term effects of chemicals and nuclear accidents are often shrouded in secrecy.

Article 19 monitors, researches, publishes, lobbies, campaigns and litigates on behalf of freedom of expression wherever it is threatened. With partners in 30 countries, it works to monitor and protest censorship.

INTERNATIONAL P.E.N.

'If a single writer in a country is in chains, then there are some links of that chain that binds us all'

Vaclav Havel

International P.E.N. is an international organisation founded in 1921. It has branches in almost 100 countries. It is a strictly non-political organisation. It promotes the universality of literature and works of art, international cultural co-operation in literature and the need to dispel class, race and national hatreds; and to oppose any suppression of free expression or censorship. International P.E.N. speaks for writers who are harassed, imprisoned, 'disappeared', tortured and murdered for the expression of their views. It currently lobbies on behalf of 900 such writers each year

Photocopy Original © Hodder & Stoughton 2001

Women's rights

UNIT AIMS:

- highlight the principle that 'human rights are women's rights'
- investigate the gendered language of rights
- survey some aspects of gender inequality around the world
- look at religious fundamentalism and the oppression of women
- introduce the topic of violence against women globally and in the UK
- explore how gender roles are played out in students' own lives
- outline progress towards women's rights around the world and in the UK
- offer some examples of women who are working for change and invite students to find more for themselves

INTRODUCTION

The topic of women's rights is huge – this unit can only offer a taster and there are many other excellent resources which can be used for more in-depth work. Of course, all human rights issues affect women and this is reflected throughout the whole of **Freedom!** However, we include a unit of women because of the oppression and denial of rights that women experience specifically because of their gender.

The activities in this unit are divided under seven headings, which can again be used selectively or in full. *Gendered language of rights* explores the way in which language can be a vehicle to oppress or limit women. *Global gender inequality* presents information about women's economic, social and political inequality for students to consider and analyse. *No human rights without women's rights* explores the work of the United Nations, Amnesty International and the Beijing Women's Conference and Platform for Action in defining and promoting the rights of women.

Violence against women looks at the facts

and asks students to reflect on the links between power and oppression. *Religious fundamentalism and the oppression of women*, aimed at older students, presents information and research for students to analyse, with a focus on the USA and Afghanistan. *Claiming women's rights* looks at the struggle for equality over the past two centuries in Europe and America. Activities in *Committed to creating a better world: women working for change* highlight and celebrate some of the individuals and organisations challenging inequality and improving the lives of women.

In using activities from this unit you will need to bear in mind that some of your students may have witnessed or experienced violence against women or other violations of women's rights.

Mixed classes may find it useful to work on some activities in single-sex groups to enable freer discussion – reporting back and sharing perspectives will be useful.

One important issue which is not explored here is that of Female Genital Mutilation

(FGM). You can find information on this on the Amnesty International website (**www.amnesty.org.uk/action/camp**). Other organisations with information on this issue are FORWARD, 40 Eastbourne Terrace, London W2 3QR (020 7725 2606) and Anti-Slavery International, The Stableyard, Broomsgrove Rd, London SW9 9TL (020 7501 8920).

SUMMARY OF TOPICS

ACTIVITIES: NOTES FOR TEACHERS

Part 1: Gendered language of rights

Activity 1: Language, expectations and limitations

Give individuals/pairs the exercise sheet to work through. When they have completed this, the whole group can discuss the expectations and messages that language promotes about men and women in both subtle and more obvious ways. They can then compare their results and discuss:

- the number of negative or patronising words used to describe men/women
- what is stereotyped as masculine and feminine
- ways in which men as well as women are limited by the stereotypes
- how they think language is linked to discrimination

Small groups could then make a list of other ways in which gender stereotypes are promoted, e.g. through children's toys, advertising. They can then come up with five suggestions, in priority order, about how such stereotyping could be avoided.

Activity 2: Powerful language

Some students will find this activity too difficult to handle; there may be embarrassed laughter; you will need to decide whether it is appropriate to leave it out or adapt it.

Introduce this topic with the following statement: 'Sticks and stones may break my bones but words can never hurt me' – asking students to go to different corners of the room according to whether they agree/disagree, then to discuss their views/experiences with someone in the opposite corner.

Ask the class:

- Can language be violent?
- Can language be used to 'keep people in their place', to discriminate or oppress people, to create high or low expectations levels of opportunity on people?

Ask small groups to list all the words they can think of that are commonly used as terms of insult or abuse. They can then sort these expressions into categories – for example, words that refer to: women (and women's sexuality); men (noticing words which are used to insult boys/men by comparing them to girls, gay men, etc.); black people; disabled people; other groups. They can then discuss:

- Which groupings of insults are the largest?
- Are there many insults which specifically refer to white, middle-class, heterosexual, non-disabled men? If not, what does this suggest?
- What do words of insult about gender, race, sexual orientation and disability (and any other groups that have come up) tell us about individual power and institutionalised power?
- What messages do the insults send out to girls and boys, women and men about the way they are supposed to be and act?
- Can the group think of ways in which people who have been, or are, oppressed by language, have created their own positive language about themselves or have campaigned to have themselves described by their own definitions rather than the labels of others?

Groups could improvise responding to a real situation where language is used to oppress with examples from their own experience. They can experiment with different ways of challenging the abuse.

FURTHER ACTIVITIES
Write an essay on Simone de Beauvoir's statement; 'Language is inherited from a masculine society. It contains many male prejudices.'

Part 2: Global gender inequality

Activity 3: Women hold up half the sky
This section introduces some aspects of global gender inequality at the start of the 21st century. There are many possibilities for further work on this topic, using regularly updated resources like the UN Human Development Report; the Progress of Nations Report (UNICEF); The State of the World Population Report (UNPFA). *The State of Women in the World Atlas*, ed. Joni Seager, Penguin, 1997.

Give out fact sheets on 'Gender inequality' and 'Changing times'.

Give each group a different aspect to focus on, e.g.: decision making; health; education; economic power, and ask them to pick out the information from both sheets relevant to their area. How does each inequality affect women's quality of life? How might each inequality be eradicated?

Each group then presents their area to the rest of the class.

- Are these issues interrelated?
- Do these issues differ according to where you are born?

Groups design posters about inequality from a baby girl's birth through her life (using their own ideas and actual initiatives). The posters should be based on research on the global and local situation.

What are the facts and figures about women in their local area? What proportion of local councillors are women? Senior managers and professionals? Unemployed people? Workers in part-time/low-paid jobs?

FURTHER ACTIVITIES
- Make a banner on the theme 'women of the world'.
- 'In no society do women enjoy the same opportunities as men.' Write an article for a magazine which explores this statement.
- In the year 2000 17% of British MPs were women, a huge increase from previous years. Look at the parliaments of two other countries from the Inter Parliamentary Union web page: www.ipu.org/iss-e/women.htm. Present your findings to the rest of the class.

Activity 4: Gender and work
- Give out the fact sheet 'Does she work?' Ask groups to come up with some suggestions about why 'women's' and 'men's' work are seen in different ways.
- Organise a Housework Survey. Get students to make a list of the main household chores

which need doing. Devise a questionnaire to find out who undertakes these tasks in the home, and how long each takes per week. Students can either conduct their own research at home, or can interview other school students. (Be sensitive here about different types of situation in which students may be living.) Students can make graphs or charts of their findings, showing the gender breakdown of the various chores and the time they take to do.

FURTHER ACTIVITIES

- Role play the conversation from 'Does she work?', but set in Britain. Explore the similarities and differences.
- Get students to bring in a piece of equipment used for a household chore: iron, hoover, scrubbing brush, frying pan, dog's lead, sponge and hosepipe. Make careful drawings of these instruments and turn them into giant posters or large sculptures in wire and tin foil to illustrate 'invisible work' and survey.

Part 3: No human rights without women's rights

Activity 5: Beijing 1995 and the Platform for Action

Give students the information sheet, 'Beijing 1995'.

Find more about the Beijing Platform For Action on the Womenwatch website

www.un.org/womenwatch/daw/beijing/platform

FURTHER ACTIVITIES

- In small groups, research the Beijing Platform For Action. What does it mean? What are the issues it raises for women? Share your findings as a class. Get the whole class to make an illustrated exhibition explaining the key points of the PFA in simple language that people will understand.

Activity 6: International Women's Day

After reading the information sheet, students could:

- Write a news report on the 1909 New York march.
- Find out about International Women's Day events in your area (from the library, local paper, or the Council). Who organises them? Who goes? Would the programme be attractive to young people? What would they like to add? Have they ever been to such an event – what did they think of it?
- Plan an International Women's Day celebration for your school.
- Write a song for International Women's Day.

Part 4: Violence against women

Activity 7: Women and male violence

Ask the class to come up with different forms of violence which targets or affects women.
Give out the fact sheet, 'Violence against women'. Ask:

- What did they find surprising in the fact sheet? How do they feel after reading it?
- Can they think of other examples of violence against women
- Research campaigns and organisations which challenge violence against women, e.g. the 1999 ZERO TOLERANCE 'Respect' campaign (email address: **zerotolerance@dial.pipex.com**).
- Research and create your own guide or make a short video for young women on: dealing effectively with harassment/feeling safe on the streets/self-defence techniques/relationships – respect is a right.
- Write a poem, song or short play challenging violence against women.

Activity 8: Rape

6th form activity

In small groups:

- Look at the newspaper article about rape in information sheet 1. What does the writer believe to be the main reasons for such low conviction rates for rapists? What additional reasons can you think of?

- What do you think of the notion that the way a woman dresses affects her rights?
- Recent UK legislation puts limitations on the questioning judges can allow about a woman rape victim's past sexual history. Will this make a difference to conviction rates?
- Look at the information sheet 2 and the extract from the Amnesty Report. Discuss the links between individual acts of rape during peacetime and rape as an act of war. What contributes to such acts of violence? How could such factors be eradicated? What kinds of support and action do women survivors of such violence need?
- During the First World War false propaganda claimed German soldiers were raping their way across Belgium. What was the purpose of such propaganda?
- Research recent cases of prosecution of war criminals who are being tried for using or condoning rape as a weapon of war and 'ethnic cleansing'.

Part 5: Religious fundamentalism and the oppression of women

Activity 9: Women oppressed

6th form activity

Ask small groups to define 'fundamentalism'. How have they seen this word used? Look it up in different dictionaries. Download the briefing *What is fundamentalism?* from the Amnesty website **www.amnesty.org.uk**

Divide the students into small groups and ask them:

- Why do the writers claim religious fundamentalists try to limit the role of women?
- Did anything surprise you in these passages?
- The writers explain that some women embrace religious fundamentalism as a way of transcending racism and classism. Why else might some women welcome prescribed gender roles?

Look at information on the website on *Women in Islam* and *Christianity and the Oppression of Women*. Small groups can discuss:

- What surprises or interests you in each piece of writing?
- Pick out five main points from each article. Which do you most agree with?

Look at information sheet 3 on the website on Afghanistan in the late 1990s. Ask the students:

- Which articles of the UDHR are being breached?
- If the practice of Taliban denies the teachings of Mohammed.
- How the Taliban came to power.

Students read information sheet 4 on the website and:

- Note what the author considers dangerous about this form of religious fundamentalism.
- Discuss why Satan and Sex might be 'twin obsessions'.
- Discuss what the underlying attitudes towards women's sexuality are.
- Find out links between politics and neo-evangelical Christianity in the USA and the UK.

FURTHER ACTIVITIES

- Research fundamentalist movements amongst different religious groups in Britain. Find out what they have to say about women's roles and responsibilities.
- Explore the portrayal of Eve in the Creation story. St Augustine (early 5th century) said 'What is the difference whether it is in a wife or in a mother, it is still Eve the temptress that we must beware of in any woman.' St Thomas Aquinas, in the 13th century, described women as 'defective and misbegotten'. Read 'The Hidden Face of Eve' by Nawal el Saadawi. Write Eve's story, challenging the way she has been portrayed and interpreted by male writers and theologians.
- Collect papers over a period of time (including religious papers). Cut out all articles which use the word 'fundamentalism'. Analyse how it is used in relation to specific religions. Write an essay exploring media coverage of 'fundamentalism'.
- Create a chart: on one side, show ways in which religion may empower women, and on the other ways in which religion may oppress women.

- Find out more about the movement for the ordination of women priests in the Church of England.
- Investigate and prepare a short report on the women in Afghanistan. With the help of these websites (**www.womenaid.org**, **www.rawa.org** and **www.amnesty.org.uk** design an advertising campaign for Amnesty to highlight the situation of women in Afghanistan.

Part 6: Claiming women's rights

Activity 10: Claims for women's rights in Europe and America

Give students the fact sheet 'Claims for women's rights'. Ask different pairs to 'update; and simplify the words of Olympe de Gouges and Mary Wollstonecraft. Some of the words may need looking up in a dictionary.

- Research Olympe de Gouges, Mary Wollstonecraft and Sojourner Truth. Write a short play in which the three women meet. Discuss their different life experiences and shared vision.

Activity 11: Women's fight for the vote in the UK

Ask students when women achieved the vote in the UK. Give them the fact sheet 'Votes for women in the UK' to read.

- Get students to imagine one of the leading Suffragettes visits the UK today. Write her diary. What would she be most surprised at? Proud of? Disappointed about?
- Get groups to role-play the debate in the National Union of Women's Suffrage Societies on whether to continue with peaceful tactics to gain the vote, or whether to use more militant measures to get publicity and support.

FURTHER ACTIVITIES

- Can you find anything about campaigns for the vote for women in your area?

Activity 12: The fight towards equality in the UK

Separate the dates and the landmarks on the exercise sheet, cut them up and get the students to try and arrange them in the correct order. Which of these achievements have had the most significance. What other achievements should be added?

For further information visit: **www.lgu.ac.uk/fawcett/main.htm**, **www.eoc.org.uk**, **www.womens-unit.gov.uk**

Part 7: Committed to creating a better world – women working for change

Activity 13: Women's organisations working for change

From the Amnesty International website download the fact sheets on six different women's organisations. Ask groups to:

- List the women's rights which the organisation is working for.
- Discuss whether these are relevant to women where you live.
- Note two points about the way the organisation works, and two ways in which the organisation is changing women's lives.

Groups share information about 'their' organisation and identify what they have in common.

FURTHER ACTIVITIES

- Find out about women's groups in your area. What do they do? Who runs them?
- Find out more about The British Council's equality project: 'Working to Promote gender equality'. Visit their website at **www.britishcouncil.org/governance.gendev/index.htm**
- Read more about SEWA on their website **www.sewa.org**
- Research micro finance on the website of the Micro-Credit Summit (**www.microcreditsummit.org**). Visit the Grameen Bank website (**www.grameen-info.org**) to learn about their work in Bangladesh.
- Find out more about Demus and BEWDA from Oxfam.
- Role play a meeting of WUAR, where the group has the chance to provide a speaker at a big anti-racist rally. At first nobody is prepared to do it ...
- Design a poster to encourage women to register to vote.
- Investigate Engender's website: **www.engender.org.uk**

- What percentage of Members of the Scottish Parliament are women?
- Research the rules for asylum in the UK and how they affect women. Get information from the Refugee Council website (**www.refugeecouncil.org.uk**)
- Create a set of posters on Womankind's 'Four Literacies'
- Find out more about teenage pregnancy in the UK and about government initiatives to reduce the numbers of teenage pregnancies. How does teenage pregnancy relate to women's rights?

Activity 14: Women of courage

Ask pairs to read the fact sheet 'They can't kill everyone'. Then discuss:

- What do these three women have in common?
- What adjectives would you use to describe them?
- What difficult decisions have they had to make?
- What do you think inspires them?
- What sets them apart from, and what unites them, with other women?

Groups make a list of women, past and present, whom they admire. Do they like the term 'heroine'? (Why does Maya Angelou use the term 'sheroes' to describe women she admires?)

Pairs can use the Internet to find out more about women, known and less well known, who have worked for change:

'Distinguished Women of Past and Present' **www.distinguishedwomen.com**

'Women of Accomplishment' **www.education-world.com/**

FURTHER ACTIVITIES

- Create a 'Heroines' Gallery', with picture and stories about the women you have researched.
- Think of a woman you admire in your own life. What are the qualities you admire about her? Interview her and write a profile of her.

ACTIVITY 1 EXERCISE SHEET

What do words convey?

1. Look at each word and quickly write down 'M' or 'F' next to the word according to whether you think it is a more masculine or feminine word. Add other words you can think of that strike you as being masculine or feminine.

Fire   Steel
Water   Sun
Glass   Moon
Stone   Ship
Machine   Silk
Bullet
Willow
Oak

2. Think of some words which are used to describe men and women under the following headings. Put a plus or minus sign next to them to indicate whether they are positive or negative (or patronising):

Men talking: e.g. Debate   Women talking: e.g. Natter

Men as food: Women as food:

Men as animals: Women as animals:

Men who are sexually active: Women who are sexually active:

3. Write down the images/words which are associated with the following words:

Masculine   Feminine

Bachelor   Spinster

Master   Mistress

4. List as many words and phrases as you can think of in which the word 'man' is used. Find an equivalent word or phrase to it which includes women, e.g. manning/staffing.

(Exercise adapted from: Crown Woods School English Department)

Photocopy Original © Hodder & Stoughton 2001

ACTIVITY 3 FACT SHEET 1
Gender inequality

Women are half the world's population, yet they do two-thirds of the world's work, earn one-tenth of the world's income and own less than 1% of the world's property.

In 1999 only Finland and Sweden made an unqualified commitment to equal political rights for women and legal protection against sex discrimination.

In 1994 eight countries did not allow women to own land.

In 1999 out of 1.3 billion people in the world living in absolute poverty, over 70% were women.

At the present rate of progress, it will take 450 years before women reach equality with men as senior managers.

Women hold less than 5% of the top positions in international organisations like the UN and the European Community.

Of the 960 million illiterate people in the world, two-thirds are women.

In 1997 140 million young people in the world were not in school. Two-thirds were female.

World-wide in 1999, women's wages were 30 to 40% lower than those for men for comparable work.

Only 6.2% of government ministers world-wide were women in 1995.

In 1995 there were 34,306 MPs in the world. 3,737 were women.

In Switzerland, Japan and Belgium, for every 100 men enrolled in higher education in 1995, there were respectively 53, 63, and 78 women.

At the end of the 20th Century, 500,000 women die each year from causes related to pregnancy and childbirth.

An estimated 300 million women world-wide had no access to contraception.

43% of all women suffered from anaemia.

Sources: Focus on Women, UN 1995; Human Development Report, UNDP 1995; Women: Challenges for the Year 2000, UN 1991; Progress of Nations 1997; State of the World Population, UNFPA 1995; World Health Report, WHO 1995; New Internationalist, August 1995; The World Guide 1999–2000.

Photocopy Original © Hodder & Stoughton 2001

ACTIVITY 3 FACT SHEET 2
Changing times

Women and girls are better educated than ever before.

Primary school enrolment for girls now equals that of boys in Africa and Asia.

Literacy rates for adult women rose from 33% in 1970 to 50% in 1995.

Women now make up more than half of the formal labour force.

In the 1997 UK election, 137 of the 630 MPs elected to Westminster were women – 17% – double the previous record.

Women are increasingly entering areas of activity previously reserved for men and the number of women in professions is growing.

Gender inequality has been recognised as a crucial issue and is high on the UN agenda for action, and the UN has developed a new system – the Gender-related Development Index (GDI) – to measure health, education and living standards for women and men in each country.

Sources: UNDP 1995; The World Guide 1999–2000; Beijing 1995 Platform for Action

***Women in Sri Lanka's capital, Colombo, demanding
equal rights on International Women's Day***

Photocopy Original © Hodder & Stoughton 2001

ACTIVITY 4 FACT SHEET
Does she work?

'Have you many children?' the doctor asked.

'God had not been good to me. Of sixteen born, only nine live,' he answered.

'Does your wife work?'

'No, she stays at home.'

'I see. How does she spend her day?'

'Well, she gets up at four in the morning, fetches water and wood, makes the fire and cooks breakfast. Then she goes down to the river and washes clothes. After that she goes to the town to get corn ground and buys what we need in the market. Then she cooks the midday meal.'

'You come home at midday?'

'No, no. She brings the meal to me in the fields – about three kilometres from home.'

'And after that?'

'Well, she takes care of the hens and pigs. And of course she looks after the children all day. Then she prepares supper so that it is ready when I come home.'

'Does she go to bed after supper?'

'No I do. She has things to do around the house till nine o'clock.'

'But you say your wife doesn't work?'

'No, I told you. She stays at home.'

Source: International Labour Organisation

On average women around the world work more than 16 hours a day. Data produced by the Danish Development Agency in four villages in Tanzania show that out of women's 14-hour working day: 25% of time was spent on farm work; 28% on food preparation; 8% on washing and cleaning; 8% on collecting water and firewood; 2% on child care; 15% on other activities; 14% on resting.

Source: J.L.P. Lugalla, in Review of African Economy, 6 March 1995

A survey of young people aged 14 to 25 in England and Wales showed: 21% of males and 7% of females never did the washing up; 52% of males and 26% of females never washed their own clothes; 3% of males and 22% of females always made meals for others in the family.

Source: Youth Lifestyle Survey, Home Office, 1993

A UK survey of weekly hours spent on household tasks by parents showed: preparing food took 2.50 hrs/week for fathers, 13.30 hrs for mothers; cleaning, fathers 2 hrs; mothers 13.15 hrs; washing & ironing, fathers 0.55 hrs, mothers 9.05 hrs. All household tasks: fathers 23 hrs, mothers 62 hrs.

Source: Research Services Ltd for Legal and General, 1996

Photocopy Original © Hodder & Stoughton 2001

ACTIVITY 5 INFORMATION SHEET
Beijing 1995

In September 1995 the Fourth World Conference on Women was held in Beijing, the Chinese capital. 15,000 official delegates, journalists and NGO representatives attended the official Conference. About 35,000 women (and a few men) from all around the world were at the NGO (Non-Governmental Organisations) Forum. The Forum was a 'rainbow' of diversity and difference, solidarity and sisterhood. It reflected the huge diversity of organisations working for women's rights. The Conference debated the Platform For Action (PFA) and with governments pledging to take action on its agenda.

The PFA deals with:
- women and human rights
- women in poverty
- women's education and literacy
- women's health care
- the girl-child
- violence against women
- the effects of war and armed conflict on women
- women's role in politics and decision making
- women and the environment
- ways of enabling women to advance
- the mass media and women

There were many results from the Conference:
- commitments to protect women involved in human rights activities
- recognition that systematic rape in armed conflict is a war crime
- agreement that children have rights to privacy, respect and access to counselling

In the end, the success of the Conference can only be measured by how effectively the Platform For Action is achieved.

Amnesty International vigil in Beijing against violence against women, 1995

ACTIVITY 6 INFORMATION SHEET
International Women's Day

International Women's Day, 8 March, was recognised by the United Nations in 1977, but the event has a much longer tradition. The date is linked to one of the first organised protests by working women anywhere in the world. On 8 March 1857, after a fire in a New York clothing factory in which women workers were killed, hundreds of women workers in garment and textile factories went on strike against low wages, long working hours and terrible working conditions. In 1909, women workers in those same factories rose up in a longer strike which eventually led to shorter working hours, better pay and the right to unionise. The 1909 strike was launched with a women's march through New York, on 8 March, the anniversary of the earlier events.

In 1910 Clara Zetkin, German Social Democrat MP and delegate to the Women's Socialist International meeting in Copenhagen, called for 8 March to be celebrated as International Women's Day all over the world. In 1913 a Women's Day rally was held in St Petersburg. Later, 8 March became part of the Soviet calendar (perhaps as a way of 'repackaging' the Easter festival) and an official event in many countries.

The first celebration of International Women's Day in Britain was in 1926, the year of the General Strike. The event has grown even since. In many parts of the country women get together to share ideas, plans, music and food, and to try out new activities.

Photocopy Original © Hodder & Stoughton 2001

ACTIVITY 7 FACT SHEET
Violence against women

Violence against women, in the home and outside, is a global phenomenon. It can take many forms:

Worldwide, 60 million women are 'missing' – killed by infanticide, sex-selective abortion, deliberate under-nutrition or lack of access to health care.
World Bank Discussion Paper, 1995

Worldwide, more than 20 per cent of women experience some degree of domestic violence during marriage.
New Internationalist, Jan/Feb 1998

Worldwide gender violence causes more deaths and disability among women aged 15 to 44 than cancer, malaria, traffic accidents or war.
The Global Burden of Disease, Harvard University, 1996

In a survey of 796 Japanese women, 77% said they had experienced some form of domestic battery. 58.7% reported physical abuse. 59.4% reported sexual abuse.
New Internationalist, Jan/Feb 1998

In the USA a woman is beaten every 15 seconds.
New Internationalist, Jan/Feb 1998

Hospitals in Pakistan treat four new cases of young wives doused in kerosene and set alight by husbands and parents-in-law every day.
Progressive Women's Assn of Pakistan report on domestic violence and murder, 1999

In the UK, more than 25% of violent crimes reported to the police are acts of domestic violence by men against women, the second most common violent crime.
New Internationalist, Jan/Feb 1998

Domestic violence kills two women every week in England and Wales.
Home Office, 1997

In the UK one woman in ten is severely beaten by a partner every year. The cost to health and social services is estimated at over £1 billion per annum
'Counting the Costs', Crime Concern, London 1998

Each year an estimated two million girls suffer female genital mutilation.
New Internationalist, Jan/Feb 1998

BUT ... 44 countries have passed laws against domestic violence. 17 countries have made marital rape a criminal offence. 27 countries have passed laws against sexual harassment.
New Internationalist, Jan/Feb 1998

Source: WOMANKIND Worldwide Fact sheet: Violence against women, ZERO TOLERANCE fact sheet.

ACTIVITY 8 INFORMATION SHEET 1
Rape

'When in Rome . . . don't wear jeans. In London, stay away from stilettos . . .'

The failure of the law to address the problem of rape was highlighted by the Italian Court of Appeal last week. It overturned the conviction of a 45-year-old driving instructor found guilty of raping an 18-year-old pupil on the grounds that she could not have been raped because she was wearing jeans . . .

. . . Criminal justice systems all over the world have failed adequately to address the problem of rape. It is estimated that in Switzerland only 1 per cent of rapes result in a conviction. In the UK, where under 10 per cent of reported rapes result in a conviction and where surveys indicate under one in 10 cases are reported, the percentage must be roughly the same. The problem is that the burden of proof rests on the credibility of the witness. The criteria used to test this is pernicious: In England, it can include not only questions regarding past sexual history but also details of her lifestyle – her lingerie, her make-up, even her menstrual flow.

In one case at the Old Bailey in 1993, a 24-year-old student reported how she had been raped twice on her way home from a nightclub by a mini-cab driver. She managed to run away after the rape, leaving her coat behind. No contraception was used and the complainant had contracted a sexually transmitted disease. In the trial, she was cross-examined at length about whether her dress and shoes could be described as 'dressy' and her jacket as 'flimsy'. She was then asked to describe the material of her jacket and whether or not it was transparent. . . . The defence counsel insinuated that she had not been wearing knickers or tights which she strongly denied. In his summing up, the judge, without explaining why, said the jury had to decide whether she was wearing a G-string or a pair of flimsy panties. The defendant was acquitted.

In another case in which the defendant was acquitted in spite of injuries inflicted, the complainant was asked about red shoes she was wearing. The defence asked: "You would admit these shoes are not leather. They are of the cheaper end of the market?" If her shoes were cheap, the implication was that she must be too . . .'

Sue Lees, The Guardian, 16 February 1999

ACTIVITY 8 INFORMATION SHEET 2
Rape

Up to one in five women will be victims of rape in their lifetime. *The Progress of the Nations, UNICEF, 1997*

Rape as a weapon of war has become more evident in recent conflicts. In Rwanda from April 1994 to April 1995 250,000 women and girls were raped. *New Internationalist, Jan/Feb 1998*

Estimates suggest 40,000 women were victims of war-rape in Bosnia. *Human Rights Watch, New York, 1995*

RAPE: A WEAPON OF WAR

Rape by soldiers of vanquished women has a long history. The Crusaders in the 12th century raped women in the name of religion. In the 16th century the 'conquest of the Americas' saw the mass rape of indigenous women by the invading forces. English soldiers in the 18th century systematically raped Scottish women during the subjugation of Scotland.

Half a century ago, rape in war was outlawed by international humanitarian law. The Geneva Convention (1951), states: 'Women shall be especially protected ... against rape, enforced prostitution, or any form of indecent assault.'

However, women are being raped, terrorised, degraded and violated in every modern conflict on the planet. Women are raped because their bodies are seen as the legitimate spoils of war. Rape by combatants is an act of torture ... yet few governments or armed opposition groups have taken action to prevent rape during conflict.

Rape by the armed forces in the conflicts in Bosnia-Herzegovina received unprecedented publicity. The extent of sexual abuse there caused shock and dismay. Women were raped in their homes by soldiers from their own town or strangers passing through. Women prisoners were raped by soldiers and guards in detention centres. Women were raped in an organised and systematic way: they were imprisoned in hotels and other buildings specifically so that they could be raped by soldiers.

The UN Special Rapporteur on the Conflict in the Former Yugoslavia reported:

'... rape was being used as an instrument of ethnic cleansing ... There are reliable reports of public rapes, for example, in front of a whole village, designed to terrorise the population and force ethnic groups to flee.'

Adapted from: 'Human Rights Are Women's Right' Amnesty International 8 March 1995: ACT 77/01/95

Claims for women's rights in Europe and America

Olympe de Gouges

In 1791 a Frenchwoman, Olympe de Gouges, a butcher's daughter, playwright and a political pamphleteer, wrote 'The Declaration of the Rights of Woman'. She argued that the Declaration of the Rights of Man, which had arisen from the French Revolution, excluded women, and called for equal rights in law, government and education. In 1793 she was executed by the Jacobins as a troublemaker.

Her declaration claimed women's rights and stressed the need for education:

'Women, wake up; the tocsin of reason is being heard throughout the whole universe; discover your rights. The powerful empire of nature is no longer surrounded by prejudice, fanaticism, superstition, and lies. The flame of truth has dispersed all the clouds of folly and usurpation. Enslaved man has multiplied his strength and needs recourse to yours to break his chains. Having become free, he has become unjust to his companion. Oh, women, women! When will you cease to be blind? What advantage have you received from the Revolution? A more pronounced scorn, a more marked disdain.'

Mary Wollstonecraft

continued

Claims for women's rights in Europe and America

Inspired by the French Revolution, Mary Wollstonecraft wrote 'Vindication of the Rights of Women' in 1792. Known as the 'Mother of Feminism', she argued that femininity was a construct; women are born equal but taught to be subordinate to men. She called for universal co-education, women's right to work in trades, professions and civil and political life. She died without recognition.

'. . . when men contend for their freedom, and to be allowed to judge for themselves respecting their own happiness, it be not inconsistent and unjust to subjugate women, even though you firmly believe that you are acting in the manner best calculated to promote their happiness?

In this style argue tyrants of every denomination, from the weak king to the weak father of a family; they are all eager to crush reason, yet always assert that they usurp its throne only to be useful. Do you not act a similar part when you force all women by denying them civil and political rights, to remain immured in their families groping in the dark? For surely, sir, you will not assert that a duty can be binding which is not founded on reason?'

Sojourner Truth

Sojourner Truth, a black American activist, born a slave in New York State in 1777. She became free in 1827 and travelled the country preaching against slavery and for women's rights. She made a passionate plea for women's rights in one of her speeches at the Broadway Tabernacle in September 1853.

'I come forth to speak about Women's Rights . . . We have all been thrown down so low that nobody thought we'd ever get up again; but we have been long enough trodden now; we will come up again . . . Now, women do not ask for half a kingdom, but their rights, and they don't get them.'

Photocopy Original © Hodder & Stoughton 2001

FREEDOM!

Votes for women in the UK

In Britain, in 1865 Emily Davies and Elizabeth Garrett gave the first women's petition demanding votes for women to John Stuart Mill to present in the House of Commons. Women wanted the vote to give them the power to push for all the other reforms that women needed to gain equality in education, employment, marriage and family life.

For most of the 19th century, married women did not have legal control over their own children, could not obtain a divorce, had no control over their earnings, which belonged to their husband and did not legally own any possessions, whether clothes or belongings.

Meanwhile, women:
- could not attend university or enter any of the professions. Those working in factories and in 'sweated labour' could not earn enough for a living wage.

THE SUFFRAGISTS

In the 1860s the women's suffrage movement started with groups in London, Manchester, Birmingham, Bristol and Edinburgh. Until the early years of the 20th century these groups tried to gain the vote through 'constitutional' means. The National Union of Women's Suffrage Societies, led by Mrs Fawcett, held meetings, collected petitions, lobbied Members of Parliament, published pamphlets, wrote letters to the press and enlisted the support of prominent public figures. All with no success.

THE SUFFRAGETTES

From 1903, with the foundation of the Women's Social and Political Union many

WSPU ex-prisoners in suffragette demonstration

continued

Photocopy Original © Hodder & Stoughton 2001

women activists gradually became more militant, believing that the 'polite' strategies were not working. From 1905 to 1914, the tactics of resisting arrest, public demonstrations, window smashing arson and the destruction of property were used, which resulted in the arrest and imprisonment of hundreds of women. In 1909 the suffragette Marion Wallace Dunlop went on hunger-strike in Birmingham jail. She was the first of many women to endure the violence of forcible feeding. Despite a huge public outcry the Liberal government of the day continued to imprison and ill-treat the women.

Suffragette protester

VICTORY

In February 1918 women over 30 who were married or owned property achieved the vote. Only in 1928 did women over 21 achieve the vote – after 63 years of campaigning to achieve voting equality.

Photocopy Original © Hodder & Stoughton 2001

Photocopy Original © Hodder & Stoughton 2001

ACTIVITY 12 EXERCISE SHEET

Feminist achievements of 20th-century Britain

Women achieving the vote was just a beginning. Throughout the 20th century women have had to continue campaigning to gain equal access to education, jobs and pay, for control over their own fertility, for safety and justice, for equal political and civil rights, for free childcare provision, for freedom from sexual exploitation. Some of these rights have been won, some are still to be won.

1918	Married or property owning women over 30 won the vote; Countess Constance Markievicz was the first woman elected as an MP (but as a representative of Sinn Fein in Dublin, she would not take her seat in Parliament as a protest against British rule in Ireland).
1919	First woman MP who took her seat: Lady Nancy Astor. The Sex Disqualification (Removal) Act allowed women to do jury service and become magistrates.
1921	Marie Stopes opened the first English birth-control clinic.
1928	All women over 21 won the right to vote.
1929	First woman Cabinet Minister: Margaret Bondfield (Labour).
1930	Amy Johnson flew a plane from Britain to Australia.
1943	First female President of the Trades Union Congress: Anne Loughlin.
1945	Family Allowance (child benefits) introduced and paid directly to mothers.
1958	Women admitted into the House of Lords. First Peeress: Baroness Wooton First female British Nobel Prize-winner: Dorothy Hodgkin (chemistry).
1964	First female High Court Judge: Elizabeth Lane.
1965	Abortion Act made abortion legal for the first time.
1969	Family Law Reform Act: wives can enter into financial and legal contracts.

continued

Feminist achievements of 20th-century Britain

1971	First refuges set up to help women escaping from domestic violence.
1979	First female Prime Minister in Britain: Margaret Thatcher.
1980	Social Security Act: married women entitled to claim Supplementary Benefit if main breadwinners.
1984	Equal Pay (Equal Value Amendment) Act: women entitled to the same pay as men for jobs of equal value.
1985	Sexual Offences Act: kerb-crawlers liable for prosecution.
1986	Sex Discrimination (Amendment) Act: allows women to retire at the same age as men.
1987	London-born Diane Abbott becomes the first black woman MP.
1988	Finance Act: independent taxation for husband and wife.
1991	Rape inside marriage recognised as a crime.
1992	Sexual harassment in the workplace recognised as a crime.
1993	Church of England votes to allow women to become priests.
1994	'Zero Tolerance': first national campaign against violence against women.
1999	Rape and domestic violence recognised as grounds for asylum.

Photocopy Original © Hodder & Stoughton 2001

ACTIVITY 14 FACT SHEET
'They can't kill everyone'

Salima Ghezali

'Salima Ghezali is 40. Editor of *La Nation* in Algeria, she was the only female editor of a national newspaper throughout the Middle East – until, that is, the Algerian authorities closed it down just over a year ago. Over 70 journalists have been murdered in Algeria, but although she can now only publish abroad and on the Internet, Salima goes on writing, arguing for human rights and a negotiated end of the conflict. When I met her in April, her casual bravery was daunting. "I hear from a friend that someone has told someone they know that I talk too much and will be found in a ditch with my throat cut. They may kill me, but they can't kill everyone."'

Mark Lattimer, Amnesty International, The Independent, *23 June 1998*

Dr Nawal el Saadawi

Dr Nawal el Saadawi was born in Egypt in 1931. Her first rebellion was her refusal to get married at 10 years old. 'This was the first challenge and when I succeeded it gave me a lot of strength.' The strength led her to overcome many obstacles and qualify as a doctor and later to become Egypt's Director of Public Health. Realising that 'writing was a stronger weapon than medicine in the fight against poverty and ignorance', she began to write poems, stories, novels and plays. Gradually her writing, in books like *The Hidden Face of Eve*, focused more on women's oppression and rights essential to freedom. 'Women are the first target because we are politically weak and because our status in religions is inferior.' Her books were banned for many years in Egypt.

Although she has worked mainly for women's rights, Nawal el Saadawi believes that human rights cannot be divided: 'We need a movement ... which seeks unity in diversity by breaking down barriers built on discrimination (by gender, class, race, religion) and by discovering what we have in common as human beings.' Through her controversial writing she lost her job, was prevented from practising medicine, imprisoned and exiled. Now back in Egypt, her work is mainly on projects which inform rural women of their rights in order to liberate them economically from male domination. 'I am in danger ... but it has become

continued

Photocopy Original © Hodder & Stoughton 2001

Unit 3: WOMEN'S RIGHTS

part of me. I no longer feel it. It is like sitting on a train; after a time you no longer feel the movement; you become part of it.'

Sources: Katrina Payne Paying the Price of Freedom, interview with Nawal el Saadawi, *New Internationalist 298 Jan/Feb 1998*; Nawal el Saadawi Reader, *Zed Books 1997;* Encyclopaedia of the Orient; *Nawal el Saadawi,* The Hidden Face of Eve, *Beacon Books 1980*

Aung San Suu Kyi

Aung San Suu Kyi was born in Burma in 1945. Her father, Aung San, was the national hero of Burma who led struggles against British colonialism and the Japanese invasion. Aung San was assassinated just before Burma gained its independence in 1948. While studying at Oxford Suu Kyi (pronounced Soo Chee) married a British academic and had two sons.

In 1988 Suu Kyi returned to Burma/Myanmar to care for her dying mother. Her return coincided with the Burmese people's uprising against the repressive military regime which had ruled for 26 years. Suu Kyi became the leader of the movement and the party which she founded, the National League for Democracy, won a massive victory in the general election held in 1990. But the military regime refused to hand over power and kept Suu Kyi under house arrest for six years. For nearly two and a half years she was not allowed any contact with her husband and children. She has said that she did not feel afraid or really lonely because 'I didn't feel hostile to the guards or soldiers surrounding me and I think fear comes from hostility. So I felt quite relaxed . . . I had the radio . . . and my books. And I think loneliness comes from inside.'

In 1991 Aung San Suu Kyi was awarded the Nobel Peace Prize. Since her release from house arrest Suu Kyi continued to campaign for the restoration of democracy as the first step towards rights for all. 'People keep asking me about women's rights and I find it a little difficult to answer because the men in Burma have no rights either. I feel that first we have to get basic rights for everyone and then we have to attack this area. Women are particularly discriminated against.' Her husband became ill with cancer but the regime denied him a visa to make a last visit to her. She decided not to leave the country to visit him, believing she would be prevented from returning. He died in 1999.

Sources: John Pilger Burma: a cry for freedom, *New Internationalist 28 June 1996; Arlene Gregorius, BBC Online News, 29 July 1998*

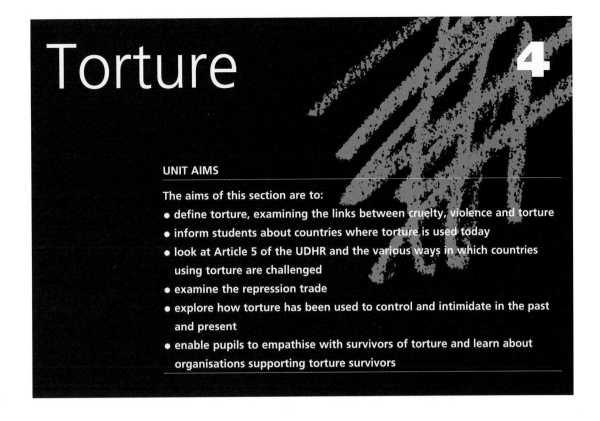

Torture

4

UNIT AIMS

The aims of this section are to:
- define torture, examining the links between cruelty, violence and torture
- inform students about countries where torture is used today
- look at Article 5 of the UDHR and the various ways in which countries using torture are challenged
- examine the repression trade
- explore how torture has been used to control and intimidate in the past and present
- enable pupils to empathise with survivors of torture and learn about organisations supporting torture survivors

INTRODUCTION

This unit covers the difficult subject of torture, a subject some might consider marginal; a phenomenon that happens 'somewhere else'. However, the prevalence of torture in the world today means that the subject cannot be ignored. At the time of publication, over 120 countries, including countries in Europe, have been reported to Amnesty International for torturing their own citizens. Many countries, including the UK, profit from selling the equipment of torture.

Activities start from students' own understanding of what constitutes torture, which they can then compare with international definitions under Article 5 of the UDHR and the 1984 Convention Against Torture. Real case studies are used to explore whether certain groups are more vulnerable to forms of oppression such as torture and to examine the links between discrimination, inequality and repression.

Students are asked to consider and re-evaluate their preconceptions about which countries have practised torture in the last few years of the 1990s by being given the facts in a variety of formats. This includes examining the moral and practical responsibility of industrialised nations not just for instances where they have used torture in direct contravention of their laws, but for perpetuating torture around the world through the vastly lucrative trade in instruments of repression and military training.

Students are asked to reflect on the capacity for cruelty demonstrated by some people, to understand how and why human beings can reach a point where they are able to inflict severe physical or psychological pain, and often death, on another human being. The question of impunity and the case of ex-General Pinochet is explored in detail. To dismiss torturers as 'inhuman monsters' means that the forces in society that shape and influence human behaviour are also dismissed. In order to fight against the practice of torture it is necessary to understand what brings people to the point where they can become involved in such a practice. This is an uncomfortable process, because it necessitates our confronting ourselves and our weaknesses. It is not enough to brand others as 'evil' without asking some searching questions of ourselves.

Clearly the selection of activities needs to be appropriate to the ages, emotional maturity and life-experiences in the class. There may be students whose families have witnessed or experienced torture, for example, where students are from refugee communities, or where students live or have lived in an environment of domestic violence. Even where this is not the case, students may find it a difficult and painful subject to engage with.

To balance the grim reality of such human rights violations, the positive aspects of human nature are also highlighted, in particular the courage and resistance of individuals who have experienced torture and the organisations and international treaties that challenge and fight against torture. Students are also asked to explore the work of the Medical Foundation for the Treatment of Victims of Torture and the material it works with. Students are encouraged to consider how their awareness of, and personal reactions to, the practice of torture can be translated into positive activity to prevent the circumstances in which torture can happen.

SUMMARY OF TOPICS

TITLE	CURRICULUM LINKS	PAGE
1. What is torture?	14+: PSHE/Pastoral/Citizenship/General Studies/English/ Geography: *e.g. KS4 Infringement of Rights*/Law/ Government & Politics/History/Sociology/BTEC National in Public Services/Media Studies	*109/113*
Citizenship	***Knowledge and Understanding:*** *legal human rights and responsibilities underpinning society* **Key Skills:** *communication*	
2. The experience of torture	14+: PSHE/Pastoral/Citizenship/English/Humanities/Drama/ Theatre Studies/Media Studies/Law/Government and Politics/ RE/Sociology/General Studies/BTEC National in Public Services: *e.g. Examine Human Rights and their violation*	*110/114*
3. World map of torture	14+: PSHE/Pastoral/Citizenship/General Studies/Geography/ Media Studies/Law/Art and Design: *e.g. drawing, painting, graphics, textiles, three dimensional studies, photography*/ Sociology/Government and Politics/Economics/BTEC National in Public Services	*110/119*
4. Torture and Amnesty's concerns in the UK	14+: PSHE/Pastoral/Citizenship/General Studies/Humanities/ Media Studies: *e.g. KS4 –analyse and interpret media representations of individuals, groups, events and issues*/Drama/Theatre Studies/English/Sociology/Law/BTEC National in Public Services/Religious Education/Economic and Business Studies	*110/121*
Citizenship	***Knowledge and Understanding:*** *legal and human rights and responsibilities* **Key Skills:** *communication*	
5. Profit from torture	14+: PSHE/Pastoral/Citizenship/General Studies/Humanities/ Government and Politics/Sociology/English/Law/Business Studies and Economics/Geography: *e.g. KS4 trade and economic status*/BTEC National in Public Services/Media Studies/Theatre Studies	*111/123*
Citizenship	**Knowledge and Understanding:** *how the economy functions, the role of business* **Key Skills:** *communication*	
6. Is torture ever justified?	16+: PSHE/Pastoral/Citizenship/ Sociology/Humanities/ General Studies/Law: KS4/16+/Media/Theatre Arts/Drama/ Government and Politics/BTEC National in Public Services/RE	*111/—*

TITLE	CURRICULUM LINKS	PAGE
7. People who torture	16+: PSHE/Pastoral/Citizenship/General Studies/English/ Drama/Theatre Studies/Media Studies/Law/Sociology/RE/ BTEC National in Public Services	*111/125*
8. Pinochet – a question of impunity	16+: PSHE/Pastoral/Citizenship/English/Humanities/Drama/ Theatre Studies/Media Studies/Law/Government & Politics/ RE/Sociology/General Studies/BTEC National in Public Services	*112/127*
9. Survivors	14+: English/Drama/Theatre Studies/Sociology/RE/Art	*112/130*
Citizenship	**Knowledge and Understanding:** *voluntary groups and social change* **Participation Skills:** *empathy*	
10. The strength of the human spirit – poetry	14+: English	*112/133*
11. Working against torture	14+: PSHE/Pastoral/Citizenship/General Studies/Economics and Business Studies/Government and Politics/Law/ Sociology: e.g. KS4 – the individual in society/English/ Geography/RE/BTEC National in Public Service Media/ Theatre Studies	*112/136*
Citizenship	**Knowledge and Understanding:** *Legal and human rights* **Participation Skills:** *considering others' experiences*	

ACTIVITIES: NOTES FOR TEACHERS

Activity 1: What is torture?

Ask groups to try and define 'torture' in 20 words.

Compare and discuss results.

Divide the room into three areas; 'agree', 'disagree', 'undecided'.

Read out statements from the list below. Ask students to move to a designated area of the room: 'agree', 'disagree', 'not sure'. Those who agree or disagree have to persuade those undecided to join them. Where numbers on one side are few, the teacher can play devil's advocate.

Is it torture:
- to deny a detainee medical treatment?
- to deprive detainees of sleep?
- to put a bag over a prisoner's head?
- to forcibly sterilise a prisoner?
- to keep a prisoner in extended solitary confinement?
- to threaten a child of the prisoner?
- to execute a prisoner?
- to deport prisoners to a country where they will be ill-treated?
- to use drugs on a prisoner to extract information?
- to place a child of 12 in jail?
- to separate a new-born baby from its imprisoned mother?

Give out the briefing sheet 'What is torture?' for pairs to discuss.
- Do any of the court decisions on what constitutes torture surprise you?
- Write down reasons why a state might use torture.

The whole class can then share their list of reasons why countries use torture.

Activity 2: The experience of torture

Give out the briefing sheet 'Interrogation'. In groups, define interrogation.

Groups research three famous trials in the UK that depended on false confessions extracted from suspects under pressure, and led to miscarriages of justice:

The Guildford Four, The Birmingham Six, Timothy Evans.

Then write up their findings as a radio programme and report back to the rest of the class.

Ask students if they consider some people might be at more risk of being tortured than others. Give out the exercise sheet 'Who is tortured?'. Ask them to rank people on the list in order of their risk of torture. (In fact every category listed was found amongst Amnesty International's recent records of torture victims.)

Cut up and hand out one of the case studies of torture to pairs or small groups. Ask them to make notes on these questions:

● Is this a case of torture as defined under the UN Convention Against Torture (see Activity 1 briefing sheet, page 113)?

● Why do you think this happened?

● Was the aim of the torturer to: Punish the prisoner? Extract a confession? Gather information? Intimidate the detainee? Who was the person responsible? When and where did the torture take place?

Share thoughts and findings about these cases, and make an exhibition about torture based on these cases.

Activity 3: World map of torture

Ask the students to name countries in the world where they think Amnesty International is likely to have recorded reports of torture in recent years.

Give out the information sheet 'The world map of torture'.

Ask students to tick ✔ countries that they are NOT surprised to see on the list. Ask them to underline any countries which they are surprised to see.

Pairs can then discuss whether they can find any pattern in the countries in which torture has been reported – does torture tend to take place in a particular continent, under a particular political system, economic situation, system of religious belief? Discuss.

Give groups a blank map of the world. Ask them to colour in countries where Amnesty International did NOT record any reports of torture between 1993 and 1998. Get them to design a poster for Amnesty International's campaign for the abolition of torture including this map and its information.

FURTHER ACTIVITIES:

Ask groups to pick out three countries from the list on 'The world map of torture' sheet. Visit the Amnesty International website at **www.amnesty.org.uk** to look up reports on these chosen countries.

For each country: make a report on the circumstances in which torture, or other cruel, inhuman or degrading treatment of detainees takes place.

– Who are the victims? Who are the torturers? What methods of torture are used? Has any action been taken against those responsible?

Activity 4: Torture and Amnesty's concerns in the UK

Ask students what human rights issues Amnesty International might have been concerned about in the United Kingdom in recent years.

Hand out briefing sheet 1 'United Kingdom cases' and briefing sheet 2 'Emergency legislation and practice in Northern Ireland'. Groups of students search Amnesty International's recent reports on the UK on the Amnesty International website. Summarise the main categories of concern. Link these to Articles in the UDHR.

Groups write up the cases in briefing sheet 1 as short newspaper articles including an interview with a family member, or write a newspaper article about the report of the UN special rapporteur in briefing sheet 2.

Activity 5: Profit from torture

Give students the briefing sheet 'Profit from Torture'.

Organise a radio debate on the UK's involvement in the repression trade. Allocate different roles to groups of students:

- The manufacturer of equipment that may be used for torture
- A worker from the factory
- A government official promoting the sale of UK products in the defence industry
- A speaker from Amnesty International
- A witness who has been the victim of the trade, like Sipho Pityana, who was held in UK-made shackles in South Africa, or Sevgi Erdovan, a woman who was tortured by the Turkish authorities with electric shock equipment similar to that sold by ICL Technical Plastics.

Give groups time to collect information and prepare their case. Visit Amnesty International's website **www.amnesty.org.uk** for information on the repression trade. People involved in the trade may argue:

'If we did not sell clients this equipment they would go somewhere else and there would be thousands of job losses in the UK.'

'I do not ask questions. I need a job, and I need the money.'

Activity 6: Is torture ever justified?

Give groups the following scenarios to discuss.

1. A member of your family has been kidnapped. They are in very great danger and may be suffering very much. You manage to apprehend one of the kidnappers, who knows where the person you are looking for is, but will not tell you.
   - How would you try to get the information you need?
   - How far would you go to get this information?

2. You are the chief of police. A terrorist has been detained. You have reliable information that s/he has planted a bomb in a main-line railway station. It is due to go off in rush hour when thousands of people will be at risk. You don't know which station.
   - How would you try to get the information you need?
   - How far would you go to get this information?

In pairs discuss and makes notes on:
- a time when you have witnessed an act of deliberate cruelty
- a time when you have felt like inflicting mental or physical pain on somebody
- a time when you have been on the receiving end of deliberately inflicted mental or physical pain
- a time when you have been swept along/stood by/been involved in treating someone badly and why.

Activity 7: People who torture

Hand out briefing sheet 1 'The Milgram experiment'. Ask groups to discuss:
- What does the experiment show us about obedience to authority and inflicting of suffering.
- Is the capacity to inflict pain and suffering part of our nature – are people born to torment or kill?
- Explain the three different responses of the volunteers.

Hand out resource sheet 'Re-writing history' from *1984* on page 46 and briefing sheet 2 on Michalis Petrou. If possible show the Amnesty International film *Your Neighbour's Son* on the training of torturers in Greece.
- Groups make a list of reasons how/why people might become torturers.
- How should torturers be punished?

Individuals write an article entitled 'In each of us there is the potential for torture.'

Activity 8: Pinochet – a question of impunity

Get students to look up and define the word 'impunity'.

Hand out the briefing sheet on the Pinochet case.

Make several copies of the UN Convention Against Torture 1984 on the Amnesty International website **www.amnesty.org.uk/education/index.shtml**

– Get the class to replay the Pinochet hearing in the House of Lords

– Select seven students to act as Law Lords, hear the arguments and make up their minds on the issue.

– Divide the rest of the class up into two halves, to prepare the arguments either for or against Pinochet being deported to Spain to face trial for crimes against humanity. Encourage each side to get further information to strengthen their arguments using the Amnesty website and other sources, and quoting international human rights law. Each side should select some of the group to act as witnesses such as Pinochet himself, the families of victims, Sheila Cassidy, Chilean and Spanish government representatives, Amnesty International researchers, or prominent political figures.

– At the end of the trial the Law Lords decide what will happen to the ex-general.

Activity 9: Survivors

Hand out the briefing sheet 'The Medical Foundation for the Treatment of Victims of Torture'. Groups are invited to:

● List the physical and mental after-effects of torture.

● Write and perform M's story as a radio play.

● Write an illustrate M's story as a strip cartoon.

● Design a fund-raising leaflet for the Medical Foundation, describing and illustrating its work.

● Write a five-minute Sunday morning radio commercial for the Medical Foundation.

Activity 10: The strength of the human spirit – poetry

Hand out the two poems 'Touch' and 'I will live and survive'. These two poems can be used separately or together.

Ask students:

– What the poets convey about the experience of torture and imprisonment?

– How do they do this?

– What do the poets say about how they were able to survive?

– Which poem do you find most powerful and why?

● Research the human rights situation in South Africa and the Soviet Union when these poems were written

● Write a poem to one of the people in these poems or to someone who is currently suffering torture in prison

Activity 11: Working against torture

Torture was described as 'a cancer of society' by the writer and philosopher Albert Camus, writing about its occurrence in colonial Algeria during the struggle for national independence in the early 1960s.

Give out briefing sheet 1 'Torture – an epidemic' and briefing sheet 2 'Torture – the cure'. Ask groups to try and analyse the phenomenon of torture in the manner of doctors meeting together to try to combat a plague or epidemic. Their task is to formulate a plan of action for governments to combat torture at its most vulnerable points.

Ask them to compare their proposals with Amnesty International's programme for eliminating torture in briefing sheet 3 'Eliminating torture'.

The class pools its proposals and makes an exhibition of sets of posters entitled 'Torture – an epidemic' and 'Torture – the cure'.

ACTIVITY 1 BRIEFING SHEET
What is torture?

Universal Declaration of Human Rights, Article 5:
'No one shall be subjected to torture or to cruel, inhuman or degrading treatment or punishment.'

The article distinguishes between mental and physical cruelty which is considered torture and 'cruel, inhuman and degrading treatment or punishment' – treatment or conditions that have the effect of intimidating, humiliating, hurting and de-humanising a detainee. It forbids all such abuse of prisoners.

Torture is defined under international law (The UN Convention Against Torture [CAT] 1984) as the deliberate inflicting of severe physical or mental pain or suffering by public officials in order to intimidate, punish or obtain a confession or information from the victim.

Physical torture mostly consists of the brutal methods of the Middle Ages, but it may be inflicted using the sophisticated equipment of modern technology.

Psychological torture may include:
- denial of sleep and sensory deprivation
- the threat of violence, mock execution
- the use of drugs which induce fear or lack of physical control

Courts have also decided that all the following also constitute torture, or cruel, inhuman or degrading treatment or punishment of prisoners:
- sterilisation without consent
- the denial of adequate or correct medical treatment
- flogging, beating of the soles of the feet, confinement in painful positions
- sensory isolation – denial of light, sound, all human contact – if harmful to the physical or mental health of the prisoner
- rape
- sensory bombardment: bright light, noise
- subjecting detainees to electric shocks
- the forcible administration of drugs
- deportation to countries where the prisoner can expect ill-treatment
- keeping a detainee on death row for years awaiting execution
- denial of food

ACTIVITY 2 BRIEFING SHEET
Interrogation

Interrogation means the interviewing of 'suspects' of a crime. A confession during an interrogation helps to secure the prosecution and conviction of the suspect in court.

Public 'confessions' for political purposes were a feature of show trials in the Soviet Union in the 1930s and the McCarthy witch hunts in the United States in the 1950s.

Suspects may not tell the police what they want to know. The police try and persuade them to own up or to change their story during interrogation. There are great differences in the methods used by police forces to obtain confessions in different countries and what is admissible in court. In the USA, police may use psychological pressure and deception to obtain a confession (deliberate lies are not generally allowed in British courts). The techniques of questioning have changed over the years. Before the 1930s confessions were routinely obtained through 'third degree methods' of inhumane treatment; brute physical force, pain, discomfort and torture including the use of a rubber hose (which left no marks) to be a confession from suspects; physical duress – such as the denial of sleep and food; and psychological coercion including threats of violence and isolation from outsiders through incommunicado detention. Other methods to pressurise suspects that are akin to torture include confinement in painful body positions, hooding, and blindfolding.

Sometimes the psychological methods used are more subtle than brute force. Suspects are promised easier treatment by the court if they confess. Police exaggerate the weight of the evidence they possess. The suspect is told they have incontrovertible evidence – an open and shut case.

In 1986 the Police and Criminal Evidence Act (PACE) was passed covering England and Wales, and Judges' Rules which said that statements had to be made voluntarily, not forced out by fear, inducement or oppression. Confessions are discounted by the court if they are obtained by methods or in conditions which are likely to make them unreliable.

Interrogations can go wrong when justice miscarries on flawed evidence:
- When the statement obtained by the police is incomplete, false, misleading or unreliable
- When the way the interview is conducted will make any statement obtained inadmissible in court
- When those interrogated react with anger, believing they have been manipulated, tricked or pressured into giving a statement
- Suspects may not tell the truth for fear of incriminating themselves

continued

- Police may believe suspects are lying and pressurise them to tell the truth, confronting the suspect with alleged lies and urging them to agree an account that is false or misleading.

A number of factors may make some vulnerable people's confessions in an interrogation unreliable:

- Suspects of low intelligence
- Those who are suffering from mental illness during the interrogation
- Suspects in an abnormal mental state during custody and interrogation – including severe anxiety, the survivors of torture who suffer post-traumatic stress disorder (PTSD), fear of confinement, drug withdrawal – which can affect their ability to cope with the interrogation
- Suspects with personality disorders such as heightened suggestibility or compliance that will tend to make them give unreliable information when asked leading questions, placed under pressure or psychologically manipulated
- Some vulnerable suspects may be traumatised by the humiliation of being arrested, detained and interrogated.

Many suspects who make confessions subsequently deny their guilt and say they were forced or induced to confess by abuse, threats or promises. However, a number of cases of grave miscarriages of justice in the UK have arisen out of false or forced confessions. In recent years these have included the long-term imprisonment of the Birmingham Six, the Guildford Four and the execution of Timothy Evans.

Birmingham Six, with campaigner, Chris Mullin, MP, on their release, March 1991.

Unit 4: TORTURE

Photocopy Original © Hodder & Stoughton 2001

FREEDOM!

ACTIVITY 2 EXERCISE SHEET
Who is tortured?

Are some groups of people at greater risk of being tortured than others?

How would you place the following people in order of being tortured if they are detained? Give 20 points to the most likely to be tortured, all the way down to 1 point for the least likely to be tortured.

A student		A suspected terrorist	
A human rights activist		A trade union shop steward	
A member of an ethnic minority		A judge	
A soldier		A car mechanic	
A street child		A university professor	
A princess		A homeless person	
A business man		A rag picker	
A government minister		A transvestite entertainer	
A nun		A general	
A suspected thief			
A member of an opposition party			

Photocopy Original © Hodder & Stoughton 2001

ACTIVITY 2 CASE STUDIES
Torture

Albertino Soares, a student at East Timor University, Dili, was arrested by the Indonesian security forces. His forehead bears a deep scar from rifle butts; his legs have cigarette burns. He was subjected to electric shocks which at one point made his heart stop beating. The last time he was released he was told: 'Albertino, you be careful of us.' He is careful, but he is not prepared to abandon his struggle. He said: 'If Indonesia always stays here it will be difficult but we will not give up.'
(*adapted from Stephen Vines,* The Independent, *30 July 1998*)

Doru Marian Beldie, a man of 19, was arrested in Bucharest. He was charged with having sex with an under-age youth. He was reportedly beaten with truncheons on the palms of his hands and the soles of his feet for several hours by police officers in the 17th District Police Station in Bucharest in order to force him to sign a confession admitting to the offence. He was sentenced to four and a half years' imprisonment. In prison he was allegedly raped repeatedly by other prisoners.
(*Source: Amnesty International,* Breaking the Silence, *1996*)

In Turkey, children as young as 12, some detained on suspicion of very minor offences, have been very cruelly treated in police custody. They have been subjected to beatings, electric shocks, hosing with cold water, and sexual abuse. In 1995 12 year-old Halil Ibrahim Okkali was kicked and beaten with a truncheon during his interrogation in a police station in Izmir. He ended up with a broken arm and in intensive care. Two police officers were put on trial for the assault. They were found guilty of ill-treatment and fined the equivalent of £5 each.
(*Source: Amnesty International: Eur 44/176/96*)

Rexhep Bislimi, aged 32, an ethnic Albanian human rights activist from Urosevac in Kosovo was arrested by Serbian security forces on 6 July 1998. He died in custody. Photographs of his body show that his left arm had been burnt by something like an electric iron. His legs are black and blue, his right arm is broken and two fingers have been turned back.
(*Source:* The Guardian, *26 August 1998*)

continued

Photocopy Original © Hodder & Stoughton 2001

FREEDOM!

Asam Halman, 27, a car mechanic from Bethlehem, was arrested on 25 July 1997. During his interrogation by the Israeli authorities, Asam was made to squat in an agonising position for hours at a time. Hooded, and bombarded with deafening music, he was forced into a chair with his knees pressed against his chin, his arms pulled backwards and his hands tied to the back of the chair. When Amnesty International received information about his case an Urgent Action was set in motion. Within days, the torture had stopped. Within weeks Asam was free. No charge was ever brought against him. On his release, suffering from swellings and infected wounds on his hands, Asam stated: 'Amnesty International . . . helped to stop the terrible torture I was suffering.'
(*Source: Amnesty International, September 1998*)

Richard Post, a paraplegic prisoner confined to a wheelchair, was admitted to Madison Street Jail, Phoenix, Arizona, United States of America. Detention officers removed him from his wheelchair, and strapped him to a four-point restraint chair, with his arms pulled down towards his ankles and padlocked, and his legs secured in metal shackles. He developed severe ulcers. The tightness of his restraints reportedly damaged his spinal cord, resulting in significant loss of upper body mobility.
(*Source: Amnesty International, USA – Rights for All, 1998*)

When Firoz from Bangladesh was 9 he helped his father to move a family to a new home. He was accused of stealing their mobile phone. They beat him. The next day Firoz was arrested, tied up, beaten and taken to the Police Station. He was hung from a bar for many hours. Police squeezed his thumb with pliers until he lost consciousness. After two days he was released.
(*Source: Amnesty International: AI Index: ACT 7 6/07/00*)

Ravi and Ramesh live in Ahmedabad in India. Ravi's parents died when he was six. He earned his living picking up garbage for recycling. Ramesh's mother had died and he was working in a market, earning money to send home to his family. In 1995 Ravi, 11, and Ramesh, 12, were picked up by the police on suspicion of stealing copper wire. They were beaten. When they arrived at the police station, Ravi was given electric shocks several times on his hands. The boys were kept at the police station for two and a half days, tied to the bars of the cell. On the third day they were brought in front of a magistrate. They had been threatened by police if they revealed what had happened to them in custody. They were sent to a Remand Home, without being formally charged with any offence.
(*Source: Amnesty International: AI Index: ASA 04/03/98; ASA 04/12/97*)

Photocopy Original © Hodder & Stoughton 2001

ACTIVITY 3 INFORMATION SHEET
The world map of torture

Countries where reports of the torture of detainees appeared in Amnesty International Annual Reports for 1993–1998

Afghanistan	Denmark	Latvia
Albania	Djibouti	Lebanon
Algeria	Dominican Rep	Lesotho
Angola	Ecuador	Liberia
Argentina	Egypt	Libya
Armenia	El Salvador	Macedonia
Australia	Equatorial Guinea	Malawi
Austria	Eritrea	Malaysia
Azerbaijan	Ethiopia	Maldives
Bahrain	France	Mali
Bangladesh	Gambia	Mauritania
Belarus	Georgia	Mexico
Belgium	Germany	Moldova
Benin	Ghana	Morocco
Bhutan	Greece	Mozambique
Bolivia	Grenada	Myanmar
Bosnia	Guatemala	Nepal
Botswana	Guinea – Bissau	Netherlands
Brazil	Guinea	New Zealand
Bulgaria	Guyana	Nicaragua
Burkina Faso	Haiti	Niger
Burundi	Honduras	Nigeria
Cambodia	Hong Kong	Oman
Cameroon	Hungary	Pakistan
Canada	India	Palestine
Central African Rep	Indonesia/East Timor	Panama
Chad	Iran	Papua
Chile	Iraq	Paraguay
China	Israel	Peru
Colombia	Italy	Philippines
Comoros	Jamaica	Portugal
Congo	Japan	Qatar
Costa Rica	Jordan	Romania
Côte d'Ivoire	Kazakstan	Russia
Croatia	Kenya	Rwanda
Cuba	Korea (Rep)	Saudi Arabia
Cyprus	Kyrgyzstan	Senegal
Czech Republic	Laos	Sierra Leone

continued

Photocopy Original © Hodder & Stoughton 2001

The world map of torture

Singapore
Slovakia
Somalia
South Africa
Spain
Sri Lanka
Sudan
Swaziland
Sweden
Switzerland
Syria
Taiwan

Tajikistan
Tanzania
Thailand
Togo
Trinidad
Tunisia
Turkey
Turkmenistan
Uganda
Ukraine
UAE
United Kingdom

USA
Uruguay
Uzbekistan
Vanuatu
Venezuela
Yemen
Yugoslavia F R
Zaire/D R Congo
Zambia
Zimbabwe

Photocopy Original © Hodder & Stoughton 2001

ACTIVITY 4 BRIEFING SHEET 1
United Kingdom cases

Joy Gardner, a Jamaican immigrant woman, died in Metropolitan Police custody in July 1993. Unauthorised equipment was used to gag and restrain her in such a manner as to lead to her death.

Three police officers went to her home to deport her and her five-year old son to Jamaica. When she physically resisted arrest, they placed her in a body-belt with handcuffs, bound her thighs and ankles with leather straps and gagged her with 13 feet of adhesive tape wound at least seven times around her head. She died from brain damage due to asphyxiation caused by the mouth gag. The three police officers were charged with manslaughter; they stood trial and were acquitted in June 1995.

In 1997 an inquest jury ruled that asylum seeker Ibrahima Sey had been unlawfully killed while in police custody in East London in March 1996. Ibrahima Sey had been handcuffed, sprayed in the face with CS gas, and then held face down for about 15 minutes by several police officers.

Roisin McAliskey, four months pregnant, was arrested in November 1996 and held, without charge, in custody pending extradition to Germany for questioning about an IRA attack on an army base. Despite her fragile physical and mental health, as a Category A prisoner she was subjected to frequent strip-searches, 'closed visits' and severe restrictions on her right to meet with other prisoners and to exercise. Restrictions were eased towards the end of her pregnancy, but Amnesty International remains very concerned about the treatment to which she was subjected, which further damaged her physical and mental health and endangered her pregnancy.

ACTIVITY 4 BRIEFING SHEET 2
Emergency legislation and practice in Northern Ireland

A United Nations investigation of emergency law practices in Northern Ireland in 1998 criticised:

- The special interrogation centres – the subject of many allegations of police ill-treatment of detainees since the 1970s. Detainees could be held incommunicado for up to seven days without charge, and denied access to lawyers. Interviews were not taped.
- The lack of provision for investigating abuses – there was no impartial process for investigating complaints about interrogation methods, disputed killings by police officers, allegations of collusion between the Royal Ulster Constabulary and Loyalist paramilitary groups, and methods of crowd control including the firing of plastic bullets.
- The intimidation and harassment of lawyers, particularly lawyers representing suspects arrested under emergency legislation – from mild harassment and interference to physical abuse and death threats.
- The 1989 murder of Patrick Finucane – a prominent criminal defence and civil rights lawyer, by a Loyalist armed group. Strong evidence emerged suggesting collusion between military intelligence and Loyalist paramilitaries in his killing.
- Diplock Courts – special courts with a single judge and no jury – were established under emergency legislation in 1973 to try serious offences linked to alleged terrorist activities. Some of those convicted by such courts claimed unfair trial and miscarriages of justice.

(References: AI Index: Eur45/06/98, Report on the mission to the United Kingdom by the UN Special Rapporteur on Torture)

Patrick Finucane

Photocopy Original © Hodder & Stoughton 2001

ACTIVITY 5 BRIEFING SHEET
Profit from torture

While a great deal of the torture of prisoners involves the crude brutality of the boot, the club, and the fist, the technology of equipment for torture and repression has also become a highly sophisticated process using modern technological and scientific advances. The equipment for torture which is used in prisons, 'safe houses' and interrogation centres has been invented, designed, manufactured and sold for profit by companies world-wide.

The United Kingdom has been extensively involved in the manufacture and export of equipment used for torture, and in the training of the military and police in countries where security forces are involved in torture and repression.

ELECTROSHOCK WEAPONS
Electronic stun weapons – batons that deliver electric shocks of up to 40,000 volts – were banned in the United Kingdom in 1985. They may not be bought, manufactured or sold in the UK. But in 1995 an undercover investigation team working for the ITV Channel 4 programme *Dispatches* and pretending to be foreign buyers for clients in Lebanon were offered £4 million of orders of electroshock batons from Royal Ordnance, part of British Aerospace (BAe) one of the leading UK engineering firms, as well as thousands more batons by ICL Technical Plastics in Glasgow. Export licences had been issued by the UK government for these banned weapons.

Frank Stott, the ICL boss, said his firm had sold the batons to the apartheid regime in South Africa and to Abu Dhabi and to China via Hong Kong. Another UK company manufacturing such equipment was Tactical Arms International UK.

In 1992 the *Guardian* newspaper reported that this equipment has been reproduced on a massive scale in China, with the Tianjin Bohai Radio Works manufacturing 80,000 of the batons each year. The use of electric shock weapons is endemic in China, particularly within the penal system.

LEG IRONS
In 1983 Hiatts and Co, a company in the West Midlands, was discovered to be manufacturing leg-irons. The company had originally been engaged in the manufacture of leg-irons 200 years ago for the slave trade. Now its equipment was being sold to restrain prisoners. The use of leg-irons as a form of restraint for detainees is prohibited under international law (the UN Standard Minimum Rules for the Treatment of Prisoners Rule 33). Amnesty International led a successful campaign against this trade, and called on the UK government to refuse subsequent licences for the export of this particular equipment. In 1984 the UK government banned the export of leg-irons, shackles, belly chains and gang chains.

continued

Photocopy Original © Hodder & Stoughton 2001

FREEDOM!

Hiatts 'leg-cuffs' on display

Ten years later in an exhibition in Miami for the Caribbean and Latin American markets Hiatts leg-irons were still being promoted through the UK company's American associate based in Chicago. This equipment was described as 'leg-cuffs' and defended by its manufacturers as a legitimate means of controlling prisoners, widely used in the United States and other countries.

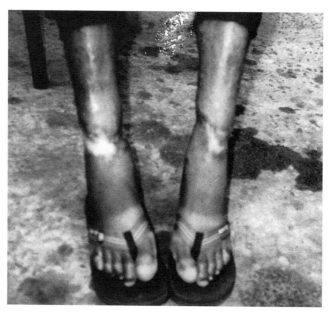

The effects of leg-irons, Zaire

Photocopy Original © Hodder & Stoughton 2001

The Milgram experiment

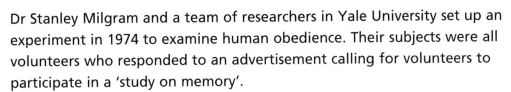

Dr Stanley Milgram and a team of researchers in Yale University set up an experiment in 1974 to examine human obedience. Their subjects were all volunteers who responded to an advertisement calling for volunteers to participate in a 'study on memory'.

They were given an introductory talk by the Experimenter on theories of learning. They were told 'people learn things when they get punished for making a mistake such as when parents smack a child . . .'

The volunteers did not know that the 'Learner', strapped into an electric chair in another room, and the Experimenter were acting. Nor did they know that no electric shock was really being administered. The volunteers were seated in front of an instrument panel with a row of four electric switches labelled from 15 to 450 Volts. The last switch was also marked 'Danger: severe shock'.

The volunteers were told to move one level higher on the shock generator each time their Learner in the electric chair gave the wrong answer. The Learner started to scream as the shocks appeared to become more painful. Though many of the 40 volunteers protested verbally at having to continue, 26 of them still carried on, giving greater and greater shocks, until the maximum voltage was reached. They were aware they were causing more and more pain and potentially killing their Learner, but most persisted even when the Learner had gone quiet and volunteers feared he might have died. Volunteers checked with the Experimenter to get him to accept responsibility for what happened, but then continued to obey their instructions.

One volunteer turned to the Experimenter at this point and said, politely: 'What if he is dead in there . . . I don't mean to be rude, but I think you should look in on him . . .'

Another volunteer had his Learner placed in an electric chair, not in another room but actually sitting next to him. When the Learner refused to put his hand on the 150 Volt plate this volunteer, disgusted at his pupil's refusal to co-operate, physically forced the man's hand down on the plate, ignoring his pleas for mercy.

A minority of the volunteers objected forcefully to the experiment. They refused to continue with the exercise. When told by the Experimenter that they had no choice and had to continue, one said: 'I do have a choice. I am a volunteer. I thought I would help in a research project. I cam here on my own free will. But if I have to hurt somebody to do that I just can't continue. I have probably gone too far already.'

Photocopy Original © Hodder & Stoughton 2001

continued

ACTIVITY 7 BRIEFING SHEET 2
Michalis Petrou

YOUR NEIGHBOUR'S SON – THE TRAINING OF A TORTURER

Between 1967 and 1974 Greece was ruled by a military dictatorship. One method the Greek colonels used to sustain their control was through the military police, ESA, which trained National Service conscripts on a specially designed course to become the regime's torturers. Some of the torturers were later put on trial.

Selected trainees were usually 18-year-old conscripts from the countryside, with little formal education and from conservative or right-wing families. During three months of intensive training the recruits were subjected to intense discipline, beatings, humiliation and punishment. One recruit, Michalis Petrou, testified how recruits were woken in the middle of the night, had heavy sacks placed round their necks, were given full back packs, metal helmets on their heads from which the padding had been removed and a rifle to hold at arm's length while they were forced to 'bunny hop' for two or three hours at a time.

Petrou said the treatment made them feel 'totally lost', isolated from the normal world. He felt unable to go to a superior officer to complain – 'your fear was greater than your will-power'. The brutalising treatment 'left you with no chance of thinking like a human being'. They had to obey every order, 'to kill their own mothers', if that was the command.

Those exhibiting the right attitude were recruited into the Prison Service, and expected to beat and humiliate prisoners who were suspected of being enemies of the state. As newly qualified ESA officers, they were treated as equals by their instructors and told how important they had become. They were 'the Eye of the Revolution'. They must protect the state against its Communist foes who were everywhere. They were now important people. One recruit described how the possession of such power can intoxicate and flatter you. He said they were able to do this work as their suppression had to find some release.

Michalis Petrou became a prison officer, and was made a Chief Police Warden. He was one of the most infamous of the regime's torturers from 1972 to 1973. Petrou recalled that he did everything asked of him. Every time he 'succeeded' in making a prisoner talk, he was rewarded with leave. His conditioning made him believe that hundreds of detainees in the ESA HQ were, indeed, his nation's enemies.

In 1973 when democracy had been restored to Greece, Petrou gave himself up to the authorities. He spent six years in prison after giving evidence against military officers. He said his training had been intended to 'produce tools, people with no will of their own – who would submit', transforming him from a human being into an animal.

Photocopy Original © Hodder & Stoughton 2001

127

ACTIVITY 8 BRIEFING SHEET
Ex-General Pinochet and the question of impunity

Ex-General Pinochet

In October 1998 Balthazar Garzon, a Spanish judge, issued a warrant for the arrest and deportation of Augusto Pinochet Ugarte, ex-dictator of Chile, who was on a visit to Britain. On 16 October 1998, members of Scotland Yard's anti-terrorist squad duly arrested the ex-general in his bed in a private hospital ward in West London.

He was to be extradited to Spain to face charges of gross human rights violations including torture, crimes against humanity and other grave crimes committed in Chile in the 'dirty war' during his military dictatorship (1973 to 1989). Requests for his extradition followed from France, Switzerland and Belgium.

In 1945, the Nuremberg trials established the principle that crimes against humanity were subject to universal jurisdiction. The UN Convention Against Torture (1984) required the United Kingdom to extradite anyone charged with such offences. General Pinochet had seized power from the democratic government of his country in 1973 in a bloody military coup. During his 17 years in power, a pattern of systematic torture had taken place, with tens of thousands of victims. More than 3,000 Chilean citizens and numbers of foreigners were assassinated by the security forces, died under torture or 'disappeared' after interrogation in secret 'safe houses'. General Pinochet created and controlled the Chilean intelligence services, the DINA and the CNI, who were responsible for most of these abuses.

In 1980 General Pinochet also passed a self-amnesty law in Chile which absolved him and his armed forces from responsibility for any crimes the military had committed from 1973 to 1978. On retiring as Head of the Army in 1999 he became a Senator-for-life, guaranteeing him total Parliamentary impunity from any charges brought against him.

Following his arrest in London, General Pinochet's lawyers appealed against the extradition order. The High Court decided Pinochet should not be deported because as ruler of his country at the time of the alleged offences, he had automatic immunity from prosecution for any acts carried out (the doctrine of 'sovereign immunity').

The Director of Public Prosecutions and lawyers for Pinochet's victims appealed to the House of Lords against the High Court decision. Two protracted appeals were heard. Witnesses from Amnesty International, Human Rights Watch, the Medical Foundation for the Victims of Torture, and the Association of the Families of the 'Disappeared' of Chile gave evidence of human rights abuses that had taken place under Pinochet's rule.

continued

Photocopy Original © Hodder & Stoughton 2001

FREEDOM!

Ex-General Pinochet and the question of impunity

Dr Sheila Cassidy

One witness was Dr Sheila Cassidy, who was working in Chile at that time as a medical missionary. A priest had asked her to give medical help to a wounded man with a bullet in his leg. She was arrested, interrogated about terrorism, tortured and sexually abused.

'They tied me to the bottom half of the bunk, tying my wrists and ankles and upper arms and placing a wide band around my chest and abdomen. Then it began. I felt an electric shock pass through me, and then another and another. I made to scream but there was a gag in my mouth. Then the questions began. The hope of release was a very important factor in my initial ability to withstand the pain. For it did not occur to me that this could go on for long, and it seemed a matter of hanging on till help came. I was taught in medical school that pain had three components: the actual pain experienced, the memory of that pain and the fear of future pain. Thus at the very beginning, with no knowledge of how severe the pain could become and believing it would be of short duration, I was able to act more bravely than I did later. I believed that the lives of two of my friends depended on my silence. This is also very important. Resistance to torture is closely related to motivation for not talking.'

William Beausire

Another witness was Adriana Borquez, a Chilean woman who had been detained in a converted nightclub known as 'El Disco', a DINA interrogation centre in Santiago. Amongst her fellow detainees was a young English businessman called William Beausire. Borquez had managed to smuggle out secret letters containing information about Beausire and about her own torture. She had sewn these into the lining of clothes she had made and had sent to her daughter with the help of a sympathetic guard. Despite his own suffering, water torture and psychotropic drugs, Beausire had continuously tried to protect her from rape by the guards. Beausire had also been tortured in the DINA's notorious Villa Grimaldi where blindfold victims were tied on to 'the grill' where electric current surged through every orifice. He became anaemic, sick and pale, suffering from pain in the kidneys and testicles. He had refused to bow to his captors, and anyway did not know the whereabouts of his sister whom the intelligence services were hunting. He was last heard of in June 1975, one more statistic amongst Chile's 1,000 'disappeared'.

Ex-General Pinochet faced charges in Spain of being responsible for deliberately causing the suffering of Spanish citizens, 'in purported performance of official duties'.

– Maria Lidia Urgarte Roman – by suspending her from a pole in a pit, pulling out her finger nails and toe nails, and burning her

Photocopy Original © Hodder & Stoughton 2001

continued

Ex-General Pinochet and the question of impunity

- Meduardo Paredes Barrientos – by systematically breaking his wrists, pelvis, ribs and skull; and burning with a blowtorch or flame thrower
- Adriana Luz Pino Vidal – a pregnant women, by applying electric shocks to her ears, hands, feet, mouth and genitals and stubbing out cigarettes on her stomach
- Father Antonio Llido Menual – a priest from Valencia, by applying electric current to his genitals and repeatedly burning his whole body.

The Chilean authorities and a number of leading British politicians campaigned for Pinochet's immediate release and return to Chile. They argued he was too old and infirm to face trial at 83; that he should be immune from prosecution because of his diplomatic and Parliamentary status; that his alleged crimes should be investigated and tried in Chile, not abroad; that he had helped the UK during the Falklands conflict with Argentina; and that fragile democracy in Chile would be in danger if the trial went ahead. The former British Prime Minister, Mrs Thatcher, an old friend of the ex-general, described the moves to extradite Pinochet as 'international lynch law' and described the former dictator as 'Britain's only political prisoner', seized from his 'bed of pain' and 'not even allowed to set foot in his garden', held under house arrest in his Surrey mansion and facing 'a lingering death in a foreign land'.

The Law Lords finally ruled by six to one in March 1999 that: former rulers were not protected by 'sovereign immunity', that widespread torture was no part of the job of any head of state, and that Pinochet should be extradited to Spain, under the terms of the UN Torture Convention (1984) which the UK, Spain and Chile had ratified, to face the charges against him.

In 1999 ex-general Pinochet; reportedly in deteriorating health, was considered unfit to stand trial by the Home Secretary and was allowed to fly back to Chile.

Photocopy Original © Hodder & Stoughton 2001

The Medical Foundation for the Treatment of Victims of Torture

The Medical Foundation for the Treatment of Victims of Torture was founded in London in 1985 by Helen Bamber and doctors in the Medical Group of Amnesty International. In 1945 Helen Bamber, as a young social worker, had gone to Belsen concentration camp to help rehabilitate concentration camp survivors. What she saw has never left her. She has since dedicated her life to helping the victims of state-sponsored cruelty. The Medical Foundation has a staff of over 40 part-time and full-time staff and many volunteers, working with 2000 torture survivors, from nearly 70 countries, mostly refugees. Other centres have been established in many countries including Denmark, Uganda, the Philippines, France, Canada, and Chile.

Helen Bamber at work

The Foundation's clients come initially for help with what seem to be practical reasons – inexplicable back pains, acute insomnia and nightmares, or they urgently need medical evidence for asylum.

Darker matters often erupt only when the Foundation starts to address these immediate problems. The effects of torture on its survivors are often severe and intractable. Aftereffects can take many forms, physical, psychological, social or cultural. They may last a short or a long time. They may be obvious or hidden. 'You have to place torture in a proper context – otherwise you are merely looking at a body that has been assaulted or mutilated' says Helen Bamber. When a doctor investigates a disease she wants to look at its causes. 'In the case of torture, it's not a pretty picture. It's about power, about privilege, about poverty. I get very tired of people looking at torture only as some horrible phenomenon, without actually saying this is a preventable thing.'

continued

The Medical Foundation for the Treatment of Victims of Torture

The Medical Foundation uses a combination of medicine, social work, physical therapy, psychotherapy and self-help programmes to help torture survivors. Central to its work is a place where a person's work can be remade, where time slows down, and where anger and pain can be acknowledged as staff, volunteers and survivors work to try to reverse what torture does.

'Everything begins with the body, and a careful, sympathetic clinical examination of the client.' The Foundation explains how, in torture, the body has been abused to gain access to the mind. Torture is associated with extreme pain and mental disturbance. Profound mental damage, deliberately inflicted, is a form of bondage through which the torturer ensures his intervention will last. Many survivors have developed defence mechanisms to protect themselves during torture – over-breathing to develop a trance-like state, or numbing through to take the mind off the pain. In the Foundation the physical after-effects of torture on the body are dealt with medically, while damage to the mind is treated through sustained emotional support.

Helen Bamber and her colleagues have become expert in identifying the hidden effects of torture: soft tissue damage to muscles and ligaments from beating with sticks and rifle butts on the trunk, damage to soles of the feet, injury to the lumbar region which hurts not only the back but also the legs; painful shoulder joints from 'Palestinian hanging' in which the victim is suspended from a rope by his arms tied behind his back; eye injuries like the degeneration of the optic nerve, so vision blurs, and epilepsies caused by blows to the head. Other forms of torture are directed primarily at vicitms' mind like mock executions or being forced to witness violence to friends or relatives.

M was a young man who had been held in prison for more than three years, and tortured. Before his detention at the age of 20 he had been physically strong – a sportsman – and reasonably happy. Now he was anorexic, far below his optimal weight, had a poorly healed fracture of one wrist, and damaged, painful soles of the feet. He had recurrent headaches, disordered sleep, and morbid thoughts. Any discussion of his treatment produced dramatic convulsions and spasms with no apparent medical cause.

He told of having been blindfolded and thrown into a cell with a former friend whose toes had been severed. Later he was taken to a small room. The walls were bloodstained and the floor strewn with broken glass. Three men stripped him naked, bound his hands and feet, and hung him upside down from a bar on the ceiling. He was beaten with wire cables and his feet were cut. They burnt him with lighted cigarettes between his fingers and on the back of his hands. A bloodstained blanket was stuffed in his mouth to muffle his cries. Urine was passed into his mouth. They punched him there, broke six teeth and pulled out the stumps with pliers. A day later he was tied to a pole along with five other prisoners. When the shots rang out he alone was left alive. Then he was locked in the back of a van with the corpses.

The initial examination of each torture survivor at the Foundation is carried out with a caseworker, a doctor and often an interpreter. M needed an interpreter

continued

Photocopy Original © Hodder & Stoughton 2001

FREEDOM!

The Medical Foundation for the Treatment of Victims of Torture

until his English improved, a family friend, who stayed with him during the first months of treatment. Foundation neurologist John Rundle described the interview process as 'an identification, an entering in.' He says 'You have to come into the torture chamber with them. Each question makes the situation clearer. Were you wearing a blindfold? Was there a light? Were you seated? What did they use to hit you? How were your hands tied?'

Trust is gradually developed before any medical tests take place. Early history is explored. M's actual torture was not mentioned for six months. The Foundation uses many complementary techniques to help its work including massage, osteopathy, relaxation, dietary advice, grief counselling, the interpretation of dreams and nightmares, aromatherapy, exercise, physiotherapy and Alexander technique. Help, as in M's case, may take practical form – special soft slippers to help walking, a bicycle to ride. Work often takes place in group sessions, including gardening, cooking, and storytelling.

Over time M was helped physically, and enabled gradually to come to terms with what had happened to him and his friends, his personal loss and to find the courage to take up life again.

Sources: A Glimpse of Hell, *Duncan Forest, Amnesty International/Cassell, 1996*
The Good Listener, *Neil Burton, Weidenfeld and Nicholson, 1999*

Photocopy Original © Hodder & Stoughton 2001

ACTIVITY 10 POETRY 1
'Touch' by Hugh Lewin

When I get out
I'm going to ask someone
to touch me
very gently please
and slowly,
touch me
I want
to learn again
how life feels.

I've not been touched for seven years
for seven years
I've been untouched
out of touch
and I've learnt
to know now
the meaning of
untouchable.

Untouched – not quite
I can count the things
that have touched me
One: fists
At the beginning
fierce mad fists
beating, beating
till I remember
screaming
Don't touch me
please don't touch me.

Two: paws
The first four years of paws
every day
patting paws, searching
– arms up, shoes off
legs apart –
prodding paws, systematic
heavy, indifferent
probing away
all privacy.

Cartoon courtesy Amnesty International USA

Photocopy Original © Hodder & Stoughton 2001

continued

'Touch' by Hugh Lewin

I don't want fists and paws
I want
to want to be touched again
I want to say
when I get out
Here I am
please touch me.

Hugh Lewin, a poet from South Africa, was held for seven years in Pretoria Central Prison in the 1970s under the Suppression of Communism Act. He has written poems and books about his prison experiences.

Photocopy Original © Hodder & Stoughton 2001

ACTIVITY 10 POETRY 2
'I will live and survive' by Irina Ratushinskaya

I will live and survive and be asked:
How they slammed my head against a trestle,
How I had to freeze at nights,
How my hair started to turn grey . . .
But I'll smile. And will crack some joke
And brush away the encroaching shadow.
And I will render homage to the dry September
That became my second birth.
And I'll be asked: 'Doesn't it hurt you to remember?'
Not being deceived by my outward flippancy.
But the former names will detonate my memory –
Magnificent as old cannon.
And I will tell of the best people in all the earth,
The most tender, but also the most invincible,
How they said farewell, how they went to be tortured,
How they waited for letters from their loved ones.
And I'll be asked: what helped us to live
When there was neither letters nor any news – only walls,
And the cold of the cell, and the blather of official lies,
And the sickening promises made in exchange for betrayal.
And I will tell of the first beauty
I saw in captivity.
A frost-covered window! No spyholes, nor walls,
Nor cell-bars, nor the long-endured pain –
Only a blue radiance on a tiny pane of glass,
A cast pattern – none more beautiful could be dreamt!
The more clearly you looked, the more powerfully blossomed
Those brigand forests, campfires and birds!
And how many times there was bitter cold weather
And how many windows sparkled after that one –
but never was it repeated,
That heavy upheaval of rainbow ice!
And anyway, what good would it be to me now,
and what would be the pretext for that festival?
Such a gift can only be received once,
And perhaps, it is only needed once.

The poet Irina Ratushinskaya was sentenced to seven years' hard labour for 'anti-Soviet agitation' – and held in the 'Small Zone', a special unit for women political prisoners.

Photocopy Original © Hodder & Stoughton 2001

ACTIVITY 11 BRIEFING SHEET 1
Torture – an epidemic

In 1960, the writer Albert Camus described the phenomenon of torture as a plague. At the beginning of the new millennium torture of detainees was taking place in over 100 countries in the world.

Think about and list all the conditions that are necessary for the plague/epidemic of torture to begin and to flourish.

- When does the epidemic occur?
- What is the scale of it?
- What does it need to survive?
- Whereabouts exactly does it lurk?
- How does it grow and flourish?
- What are the various forms that this illness takes?
- Who are the vicitms?
- What are the effects of this disease on the victims?
- What are the effects of this disease on the perpetrators?
- Can it be detected? How?
- What do we know about its cause?

Hand shackles

ACTIVITY 11 BRIEFING SHEET 2
Torture – the cure

(Make sure that your programme of cure and eradication includes all the points you raised in your answers to the questions on sheet 1.)

Think of steps that will end the epidemic of torture.

- What should be done about the places where torture takes place?
- What should governments do?
- What should judges do and not do?
- What should soldiers and policemen do, and what should they not do?
- What can be done to help the victims of this epidemic, physically and mentally and in other ways?
- What can be done to protect those who report this disease?
- What action should be taken against the perpetrators of this epidemic?

Photocopy Original © Hodder & Stoughton 2001

Photocopy Original © Hodder & Stoughton 2001

ACTIVITY 11 BRIEFING SHEET 3
Eliminating torture

Amnesty International has worked against the torture of prisoners for many years. Through its long experience of one of the ugliest areas of human rights abuse, Amnesty International has learned a great deal about the torture – the torturers, the victims, the places where torture is carried out and the circumstances in which it is allowed to flourish.

Here is a summary of Amnesty International's 12-point programme for governments to use to stamp out torture.

1. OFFICIAL CONDEMNATION OF TORTURE
Governments should show they are completely against torture. All law-enforcement staff should be told that torture is not allowed under any circumstances.

2. LIMITS ON INCOMMUNICADO DETENTION
Torture often takes place when the victims are held *incommunicado* – locked up in a place where they cannot contact anybody outside who could help them or find out what is happening to them. Governments must make sure that any incommunicado detention does not allow torture to take place. All prisoners must be brought before a judge as soon as possible after they are put in custody. Relatives, lawyers and doctors should be able to see them early on and meet with them regularly.

3. NO SECRET DETENTION
In some countries torture often takes place in secret centres, where prisoners are taken who have been made to 'disappear'. Governments should make sure prisoners are only held in proper and recognised places of detention. Relatives and lawyers should be told where they are.

4. SAFEGUARDS DURING INTERROGATION AND CUSTODY
Governments should regularly inspect prisons, and any place of detention and interrogation where prisoners are held in custody. Prisoners should be told their rights early on, including their right to complain about their treatment. There should be regular independent inspections of places of detention. Different people should be responsible for detention and interrogation.

5. INDEPENDENT INVESTIGATION OF REPORTS OF TORTURE
Governments must make sure that any complaint or report of torture is properly investigated by independent people. The public should be told how it was investigated and what the findings were. People complaining about torture and witnesses should be protected from any threats.

continued

Unit 4: TORTURE

6. NO USE OF STATEMENTS EXTRACTED UNDER TORTURE
Governments should make sure that confessions or other evidence obtained through torture are never used in court.

7. PROHIBITION OF TORTURE IN LAW
Governments should make sure their laws punish torture as a crime. International law never allows the ban on torture to be lifted under any circumstances, including war or other emergency.

8. PROSECUTION OF ALLEGED TORTURERS
People responsible for torture should be brought to justice, whoever or wherever they are, wherever the crime was committed and whatever the nationality of the torturer or the person tortured. There should be no 'safe haven' for torturers anywhere in the world.

9. TRAINING PROCEDURES
Anybody involved in the custody, interrogation or treatment of prisoners must be trained to know that torture is a crime. They should be instructed that they must refuse to obey any order to torture.

10. COMPENSATION AND REHABILITATION
Victims of torture and their dependants are entitled to financial compensation and be provided with appropriate medical care or rehabilitation.

11. INTERNATIONAL RESPONSE
Governments should take action when other states are accused of torture. Intergovernmental mechanisms should be set up to investigate reports of torture and to take action against it.

Governments should make sure that they are not supplying equipment, personnel or training for military, security or police abroad which could help the practice of torture.

12. RATIFICATION OF INTERNATIONAL INSTRUMENTS
All governments should ratify international treaties against torture, including the International Covenant on Civil and Political Rights (ICCPR) and the UN Convention Against Torture.

The death penalty

5

UNIT AIMS

This unit aims to:

- give current information on the death penalty around the world
- provide a history of the death penalty in the UK
- examine how factors such as politics, poverty and racism influence the use of the death penalty
- explore arguments for and against the death penalty
- give examples of miscarriages of justice and explore their implications
- give students opportunities to develop their own views on the basis of evidence
- explore some underlying issues: 'justice', appropriate punishment, morality, compassion, reconciliation

INTRODUCTION

The death penalty is a controversial human rights issue. Many people have very strong opinions on it, frequently unsupported by facts. Public debate about the issue often draws on emotions rather than information.

This unit contains material which students may find frightening or disturbing. Fuller and more realistic information is given about the process of execution in order to help students to investigate what capital punishment involves and to consider the legal, moral and humanitarian issues of the process.

Please read the material carefully and assess its suitability for your students. Remember too that young people may deal with their fear by joking about frightening topics. It is important to try to make them recognise that these situations are real – not just horror stories.

You need to be prepared for the possibility that students may have very

strong feelings, for example, about those who kill children. You may wish to explore why this is, but such discussions will need to be very sensitively handled and could lead to disclosure and/or to students needing particular support.

Get the class to research and explain some terminology before beginning these activities, e.g., capital punishment homicide, manslaughter, abolition, retribution.

Activities start with students' own experience of punishment. Students can explore their ideas about crime and the purpose and appropriateness of forms of punishment. They can compare this with information about the arbitrary use of the death penalty in the past in the UK, and other countries today. Cases are examined where innocent people have been executed and other miscarriages of justice.

The use of the death penalty in the USA is highlighted in some detail so that students can explore the influences of racism, inequality and political expediency in state executions. Arguments for and against the death penalty are presented for analysis, because (whilst Amnesty International campaigns for the abolition of the death penalty) it is important that students are able to consider all sides of the argument.

SUMMARY OF TOPICS

TITLE	CURRICULUM LINKS	PAGE
1. Your experience of punishment	14+: English/PSHE/RE	*143/—*
Citizenship	**Knowledge and Understanding**: *human rights and the operation of the criminal justice system* **Key Skills**: *communication*	
2. What is a crime?	14+: English/PSHE/RE	*143/148*
3. 'Criminal' activities	14+: English/PSHE/RE/General Studies	*143/149*
4. The death penalty around the world	14+: English/PSHE/RE/Geography/General Studies/Law	*144/150*
Citizenship	**Knowledge and Understanding**: *legal rights and the operation of the criminal justice system* **Key Skills**: *communication*	
5. Execution methods	16+: English/PSHE/RE/History	*144/151*
6. Poetry	14+: English//PSHE/RE	*144/152*
7. Fair trials	14+: English/PSHE/RE/Geography/General Studies/Law	*144/155*
Citizenship	**Knowledge and Understanding**: *human rights and the operation of the justice system* **Key Skills**: *communication*	
8. Execution of the innocent and miscarriages of justice	14+: English/PSHE/RE/Geography/Sociology/General Studies/Media Studies/Law	*145/156*
9. Case studies on state killings	14+: Geography/English/PSHE/RE/Geography/General Studies/Law	*145/158*
Citizenship	**Knowledge and Understanding**: *legal rights and the operation of the criminal justice system* **Key Skills**: *communication*	
10. The history of the death penalty in the UK	14+: English/PSHE/RE/Geography/History	*145/160*
11. The death penalty in the USA	14+: English/PSHE/RE/Geography/History/Law/General Studies	*145/163*
12. Racism and the death penalty in the USA – a case study	16+: English/PSHE/RE	*145/165*
Citizenship	**Knowledge and Understanding**: *legal rights and the operation of the criminal justice system, need for mutual respect* **Key Skills**: *communication* **Participation Skills**: *considering others' experiences*	
13. Death Row	16+: English/PSHE/RE	*145/166*

TITLE	CURRICULUM LINKS	PAGE
14. Bill Clinton's choice	16+: Drama/Theatre Studies/English/PSHE/RE/General Studies/History/Law/Sociology	*146/167*
Citizenship	**Enquiry Skills:** *analysing topical moral and political events*	
15. The deterrence argument	14+: English/PSHE/RE/General Studies/History/Sociology	*146/168*
16. Terrorism – a special case?	14+: PSHE/English/Media Studies: *e.g. KS4/16+ – developmentand use of stereotypes in generating 'moral panics.'Significance of differences in the reporting of foreign news between newspapers*/RE/General Studies/ History/Sociology	—
17. The case against capital punishment	14+: General Studies/PSHE/English/RE	*147/—*
Citizenship	**Knowledge and Understanding:** *legal and human rights and responsibilities* **Enquiry Skills:** *researching topical political and moral events*	
18. The humanitarian and moral arguments	16+: General Studies/PSHE/English/RE/Sociology	*147/170*
Citizenship	**Enquiry Skills:** *researching topical political/moral events by analysing information from different sources*	

ACTIVITIES: NOTES FOR TEACHERS

Activity 1: Your experience of punishment

Ask the whole group to brainstorm all the words they associate with punishment.

Ask pairs to think of an occasion when each of them has been punished and felt the punishment was just, and an occasion when they felt the punishment was unjust. Give them the following questions to talk through:

What had you done? Why were you punished and by whom? How did you feel? What do you think punishment should achieve? Did your punishment achieve this? Why/why not? What is 'fair' punishment?

The whole group can make two lists: what caused them to feel that they had been justly treated, and what caused them to feel they had been unjustly treated.

Activity 2: What is a crime?

Ask small groups to make a list of all the crimes they can think of. Put a star by any that are considered very serious.

Pool all the suggestions into a single list. Discuss with the students:
- What do we mean by 'crime'?
- Who decides what is a crime and how serious it is?

Give small groups the exercise sheet 'Crime and punishment' and three pieces of paper, one for each crime chosen from the class list. Groups answer the questions on the exercise sheet on this crime and discuss the purpose and effectiveness of different 'punishments', and whether the desire to 'punish' and seek revenge should be carried out.

Activity 3: 'Criminal' activities

DEFINITIONS

Get groups to research and define these words: trial, punishment, deterrence, capital punishment, execution, homicide, offence, manslaughter, abolitionist, crime, retribution. (You might like to point out that some of the terminology implies that victims are male.)

Ask small groups to come up with arguments for and against the restoration of the death penalty in the UK. Compile two separate lists from the points that the groups make.

Ask the class whether they think any of the Articles of the Universal Declaration of Human Rights are infringed by the death penalty.

Give pairs the exercise sheet ''Criminal' activities?' Ask them to discuss whether these are all crimes.

Explain that each of these activities were capital crimes, punishable by execution somewhere in the world in 1999.

Ask small groups to suggest why a state might retain the death penalty for any activity they did not consider a crime. Share these as a whole class.

Activity 4: The death penalty around the world

In pairs, students look at the briefing sheet, and discuss these questions:
- why do you think the trend is towards abolition?
- why do you think particular countries retain the death penalty?
- why does international law ban the use of the death penalty for young offenders?
- why might a state carry out executions in public?

FURTHER RESEARCH ACTIVITIES

- Look on the Amnesty International website **www.amnesty.org.uk**. List all the countries that have carried out judicial executions in the last five years and the countries that have not.
- Choose one executing country. List the reasons given for executions.
- Choose one abolitionist country. Find out how the death penalty was abolished.

Activity 5: Execution methods

Ask students to read the briefing sheet 'Execution methods'.

Discussion questions:
- What does the word 'execution' suggest/mean?
- Is any method of execution quick and painless?

Activity 6: Poetry

Hand out the two poems 'Hang' and 'The Ballad of Reading Gaol'.

The two poems in the sheets can be used separately as a stimulus for discussion and writing, or together, to compare and contrast. Small groups could read a poem to the rest of the class.

Discussion questions:
- What is each writer's experience and view of capital punishment?
- Which words, images or poetic devices are the most powerful in each poem. Why?
- Who are 'they' in the poems by Oscar Wilde and Hugh Lewin?
- Which poem do you find most effective?
- These poems about hanging were written a century apart, in different countries. What are the similarities and differences?
- Explain how Hugh Lewin uses irony to convey his views in the poem 'Hang'. What other devices does he use to portray the inhumanity of hanging?

FURTHER ACTIVITIES

- Write a poem from the point of view of one of the other people involved in the execution.
- Find out more about executions in 19th-century England and 20th-century South Africa. Write a story about the events leading up to a hanging.

Activity 7: Fair trials

What is a fair trial? Ask small groups to brainstorm and draw up two lists:
1. all the factors they can think of ensure due process of law
2. all the factors they can think of which would make a trial unfair

Pool ideas in a class list. Hand out the briefing sheets for Activity 8. Ask groups to compare their list with Article 14 of the International Covenant on Civil and Political Rights (Activity 7 briefing sheet).

Can students think of trials in the UK when people have been wrongly convicted? What made these trials unfair?

Activity 8: Execution of the innocent and miscarriages of justice

Ask students to read the breifing sheets, then consider and discuss the following:

- Have you ever been blamed for something someone else did? How did that feel?
- If you had been wrongly imprisoned for a number of years, how might this affect your life? Could anything compensate you?
- Imagine the atmosphere after a terrorist bomb attack – why might police officers use improper methods to find evidence or get confessions?

FURTHER ACTIVITIES

- In 1998 the Criminal Cases Review Commission was established. Within a few months over 1,800 cases of possible miscarriages of justice had been submitted to the Commission. Information: Telephone 0121 633 1800, email: **info@ccrc.gov.uk**
- Find out about miscarriages of justice in the UK, wrongful executions such as Timothy Evans, Derek Bentley, Mahmood Hussein Mattan; wrongful conviction and imprisonment such as the Bridgewater Three.

Activity 9: Case studies on state killings

Give pairs or small groups the case studies 'State killings' and Article 14 of the ICCPR from Activity 7 briefing sheet (page 155).

Ask them to decide:

- were the defendants' rights infringed? If so, how?

Feedback findings and thoughts to the whole group.

Activity 10: The history of the death penalty in the UK

Give pairs the quiz sheet on the death penalty in the UK, and the fact sheet.

- What was the purpose of the death penalty in the UK?
- Which groups of people were most likely to be executed?
- Which groups of people were least likely to be executed?
- Why were children executed?
- Do they think that the judicial system today is affected by such inequalities and prejudices?

Activity 11: The death penalty in the USA

Give small groups the information sheet on the death penalty in the USA. Ask them to list ways in which human rights are violated in the use of the death penalty.

Activity 12: Racism and the death penalty in the USA – a case study

Give groups the case study of Wilburn Dobbs and a copy of the UDHR (see pages 20–22) and ICCPR (from **www.amnesty.org.uk**).

Ask groups to list the ways in which Wilburn Dobbs' human rights were infringed at his trial.

- Imagine you are a defence lawyer whom Wilburn Dobbs asks to help him re-present his case. Write to the State Governor setting out your arguments for re-trial.
- Visit the website of Lifelines, an organisation that writes to prisoners on death row: **www.lifelines.org** Select a prisoner to write to and send them a letter.

Activity 13: Death Row

Give out the information sheet on Death Row. Ask them to discuss the following questions:

- What is life like for Tim Davis?
- How old was he when he was sentenced to death?
- How many prisoners are under sentence of death in the USA (see information sheet for Activity 11, page 163)?

FURTHER ACTIVITIES

- Imagine you are a relative of someone on Death Row. Write a letter to them to try to encourage them. Write to the State Governor appealing for clemency.
- Role play a meeting between Pierre Sané and a prisoner on Death Row.

Activity 14: Bill Clinton's choice

Ask pairs to look at the case study of Ricky Ray Rector and draw up arguments to put to Bill Clinton

- for clemency
- for carrying out the death penalty.

The whole class could devise a role play in which various characters meet and discuss the case. Start from the point at which the appeal for clemency is being made, and finish when a year after the execution, Bill Clinton is elected as President.

The characters could include:

Bill Clinton's advisors, both pro and anti-clemency, Ricky Ray Rector's attorney, members of Ricky Ray Rector's family, members of the family of the two men Rector shot (with different ideas on revenge and forgiveness), Rev. Jesse Jackson, Bill Clinton, Jerry Jewell, the four people on death row that Jerry Jewell saved from execution, a social worker who works on death row, psychologists and doctors, the executioner who administered the lethal injection, campaigners against the death penalty, campaigners for the death penalty.

Activity 15: The deterrence argument

Hand out information sheet 1 'The deterrence argument: evidence from around the world' and information sheet 2 'The deterrence argument: crime and capital punishment in the UK'. Two main arguments for the death penalty:

- deterrence – preventing crime
- retribution – taking revenge on behalf of the victims of crime

Pairs could look back to their original list from Activity 3 and see which of the cases for the death penalty fit into these two arguments. They can then read the information sheets on deterrence.

Discussion questions:

- What points suggest the death penalty is not a deterrent, in the past or now?
- What other reasons suggest that the death penalty is no deterrent to crime?
- What suggests the death penalty is a deterrent?

Activity 16: Terrorism – a special case?

Get groups to define 'terrorism'.

Some people believe that terrorism is a special case for which the death penalty should be restored.

Terrorism consists of politically motivated acts of violence, aimed at government targets or at the general public that aims to draw attention to a particular cause; to disrupt society; and to achieve some of the group's aims through fear.

Students could research recent terrorist events exploring:

- the common factors involved, the targets, the objectives of the terrorists, the effects on local people, the national/international response

The argument that capital punishment should be restored for terrorists has three main weaknesses:

- It would be unlikely to deter terrorists who already risk their lives carrying explosives and undertaking other dangerous tasks – even 'suicide missions'.
- It would create martyrs and publicity and recruit others to their cause.
- There could be reprisals, with more people being killed.

FURTHER ACTIVITIES

- Write an essay debating the pros and cons of restoring the death penalty for terrorists.

Activity 17: The case against capital punishment

Ask small groups to look back at their original points against restoring the death penalty in Activity 3 and see which of the arguments they covered are made by abolitionists:

- religious and humanitarian principles of respect for life
- belief that no-one is 'evil' and anyone can learn and change
- the myth of the deterrence argument
- unfairness in the judicial process of administering the death penalty
- the cruel process of awaiting execution
- the inevitability of mistaken convictions
- execution as the ultimate cruel punishment

Activity 18: The humanitarian and moral arguments

Ask students to read the resource sheet and list the reasons why these two witnesses oppose the death penalty.

Discussion question:

- How were George Orwell and Jimmy Boyle changed by the experiences they describe?

FREEDOM!

ACTIVITY 2 EXERCISE SHEET
Crime and punishment

Choose three crimes from the list that the class has come up with. Write down each crime at the top of a large sheet of paper.

Make notes on your responses to the following questions:

1. What are the reasons someone might commit this crime?
* Are some of these reasons more understandable than others?
* Are there any situations where it would be justifiable to commit this crime?

2. List the different ways in which you think the person committing the crime could be dealt with.
* Should everyone who commits a particular crime be dealt with in the same way?
* Does it make a difference if the person committing the crime is a child/young person, is mentally ill or in a desperate situation?
* Should the victim of the crime or their family be involved in deciding what happens to the criminal?

3. Write down the purpose of each of the ideas you have mentioned in 2. Are they designed:
* to get revenge and make the person suffer for what they have done?
* to get the person to understand the effect of their crime and make amends?
* to put other people off committing the same crime?
* to carry out a fair punishment?
* some other purpose?

Which of the reasons do you agree or disagree with?

Cartoon by Bryan Reading

Photocopy Original © Hodder & Stoughton 2001

Unit 5: THE DEATH PENALTY

ACTIVITY 3
'Criminal' activities?

In pairs, go through the following list of crimes. Circle any activities which are not on your list of crimes. Which do you think should not be considered as crimes?

ARSON   ORGANISING PROSTITUTION   ADULTERY

MURDER   WRITING SLOGANS   BLASPHEMY

AIDING THE ESCAPE OF AN ARRESTED PERSON   RAPE

STEALING A BICYCLE   CHANGING YOUR RELIGION   HOMOSEXUAL ACTS

FRAUD   EXTORTION   TRAFFICKING WOMEN

WITCHCRAFT

TAX EVASION

ILLEGAL CURRENCY DEALING

BEING A MERCENARY

THEFT

EMBEZZLEMENT

TAKING BRIBES

PROFITEERING

TREASON

CONSPIRING WITH THE ENEMY

SODOMY

GETTING SOMEONE TO CHANGE THEIR RELIGION

HOARDING   SPYING

KIDNAPPING CHILDREN

CAUSING BREACHES OF MILITARY DISCIPLINE

SMUGGLING   DRUG TRAFFICKING

"I tried to form a trade union – and you?"
Len Spencer

PLANNING TO OVERTHROW THE GOVERNMENT   ROBBERY   SABOTAGE

CAUSING DAMAGE TO STATE PROPERTY   TERRORISM

SETTING UP AN INDEPENDENT TRADE UNION   OVERCHARGING

INCITEMENT TO LOOTING   HOOLIGANISM   FRAUD

Photocopy Original © Hodder & Stoughton 2001

FREEDOM!

ACTIVITY 4 BRIEFING SHEET
Death sentences and executions around the world

Over the past century the trend world-wide has been towards the abolition of the death penalty. In 1899 just three states in the world had stopped executions: Costa Rica, Venezuela and San Marino. By 1948 the death penalty had been abolished in eight countries, and by 1978 in 18. In 1999 a total of 98 countries had abolished the death penalty in law or no longer used it in practice. Of these, 67 were abolitionist states, 14 retained capital punishment only for exceptional offences such as wartime crimes, and the rest, while retaining executions in law, had not carried out capital punishment in practice for many years. 95 other countries retained and used the death penalty, but less than half of them actually executed prisoners in any one year. A few countries, including the Phillippines, re-introduced executions having previously abolished the death penalty.

In 1998 Amnesty International reported that 1,625 prisoners had been executed in 37 countries according to official statistics while 3,899 prisoners had been sentenced to death in 78 countries. Of the countries that still retain capital punishment in law, the number actually executing prisoners each year is smaller. In 1998 just five nations were responsible for more than 90% of the world's recorded judicial executions: China where 1,067 people were known to have been executed, several hundreds in Iraq, more than 100 in the Democratic Republic of the Congo, and 68 in both the USA and Iran. (The actual figures are believed to be much higher.)

In the 1990s six states are known to have executed prisoners who were under 18 years old at the time of the crime: Iran, Nigeria, Pakistan, Saudi Arabia, USA and Yemen. The majority of known executions of juvenile offenders took place in the USA (six since 1990).

In 1999, 67 juvenile offenders were under sentence of death in 13 states of the USA; all convicted of murders committed when they were 16 or 17 years old.

In the 1990s 19 countries carried out executions in public.

Sources: Juveniles and the Death Penalty: Executions World-wide since 1985, AI Index: ACT 50/05/95; Death Sentences and Executions in 1995, AI Index: ACT 51/01/97 AI Annual Report 1999

Photocopy Original © Hodder & Stoughton 2001

ACTIVITY 5 BRIEFING SHEET
Execution methods

Hanging and shooting are the most common methods of judicial execution today.

Hanging causes death by a shock of extreme violence, stopping first the breathing, then the heartbeat. The body is left with the neck stretched. Hanging appears to involve a period of extreme pain. Death does not always happen at the first attempt and is not instantaneous.

Death from **shooting** is virtually instantaneous if the person is shot at very close quarters through the skull. However, most executions are by a firing squad, from some distance. Although those firing will aim at the heart it is difficult to shoot a person dead at once by such a method.

Death by electrocution, gas and lethal injection are used in the USA alone.

In six US states execution takes place in a **gas chamber**. The prisoner is strapped into a metal chair with a perforated seat, a stethoscope is taped onto his chest so that a doctor outside the chamber will be able to pronounce death. A bowl is placed under the seat into which sulphuric acid is introduced. A gauze bag containing cyanide is lowered into the bowl. Hydrogen cyanide gas is generated in the chamber. This paralyses the heart and lungs of the prisoner. Giddiness and panic gives way to severe headache, followed by chest pains. The prisoner struggles vainly for breath, eyes popping, chest heaving, saliva bubbling between the lips, the tongue hanging thick and swollen from a drooping mouth. The face turns purple. The heart stops beating. Death takes as long as twelve minutes.

Lethal injections may not work effectively on diabetics or former drug users, whose veins may be hard to find. The arms may sometimes be cut open to find a deeper vein. It can be an extremely painful and brutal process.

Electrocution burns the body's internal organs. Witnesses always report a smell of burning flesh. In one case in 1983 it took three charges of electricity over 14 minutes before the prisoner was declared dead.

Beheading is used in five countries: it is done by sword – sometimes several blows are needed to sever the head, depending on the weight of the sword and the strength and accuracy of the executioner.

Stoning may be carried out by individuals throwing stones from a pile or by a lorry dumping the stones, or by a wall being collapsed onto the prisoner.

Sources: AI Annual Report 1999; Howard League for Penal Reform 'The Case Against Capital Punishment' 1991; AI Working for Freedom; AI USA etc. 'The Execution Protocol', Stephen Trombley 1993

Photocopy Original © Hodder & Stoughton 2001

ACTIVITY 6 POETRY 1
'Hang' by Hugh Lewin

'We have a very humane form of execution' (South African prison official during apartheid regime).

I once met a man
who was about to undergo
a mild form
of humane hanging

He was crossing the Reception Hall
to his last visit
looking up through the skylight
to the sun
outside
when we collided.
He looked down and apologised, smiling,
and left me embarrassed, silent

He was wearing regulation Condemned dress
khaki top and longs
without buttons
no laces, no ties, no belt
nothing to hang himself with
before he was hanged.

All steps possible
are taken to ensure
that a man about to suffer death
does not kill himself.

They came for him next morning
        a mild summer day
        the sun shining outside, already warm
they came at five
        the man still called the Sheriff
        and two lieutenants
        and three chief warders
        and four head warders
        and five section warders with keys
all relaxed and very attentive
        then the Commandant
        the doctor
        and the priest

continued

'Hang' by Hugh Lewin

allowed only so far as the double doors
where he stood helpless
waving a sort of blessing
> *as all the officials*
> *led the one man*
> *through the double doors*

the sun began to play through the skylight
> *into the room with the nice high windows*

They were all very nice
all of them murmuring
and he nodded back, dry-lipped
and patted hands with his section warder
as the hood was put over his head
> *everybody shuffling, silent,*
> *watchful*

Unsure of being part of the action
> *all so, as it were, common-place*
> *the recognisable faces and uniforms*

like wanting to speak aloud in a church service
> *with his feet squared in by the lines*
> *of the trap on the floor*

and he turned his head with its hood
> *looking for a noise*
> *as the trap*
>> *burst*
>>> *inwards*
>>>> *open*
>>>> *slip*
>>>> *fall*
>>>> *tight taut jerk*
>>>> *CRACK!*

A body is left to hang for twenty minutes
before the doctor declares it
> *finally*
> *totally*
> *officially*
> **finish and klaar***
> *a corpse.*

klaar = over (Afrikaans)

Hugh Lewin was a political prisoner held in Pretoria Central Prison, South Africa 1964 to 1972.

Photocopy Original © Hodder & Stoughton 2001

'The Ballad of Reading Gaol' by Oscar Wilde

*They hanged him as a
beast is hanged:
They did not even toll
A requiem that might
have brought
Rest to his startled soul,
But hurriedly they
took him out,
And hid him in a hole.*

*They stripped him of
his canvas clothes,
And gave him to the
flies:
They mocked the
swollen purple throat,
And the stark and
staring eyes:
And with laughter
loud they heaped the
shroud
In which their convict
lies.*

Excerpt from 'The Ballad of Reading Gaol' by Oscar Wilde, 1896

Photocopy Original © Hodder & Stoughton 2001

ACTIVITY 7 BRIEFING SHEET
International standards for a fair trial

Article 14 of the International Covenant on Civil and Political Rights (ICCPR) states that anyone facing a criminal charge has the right to:

- a fair and public hearing by a competent, independent and impartial tribunal
- be presumed innocent until proven guilty
- be informed promptly of the nature and cause of the crimes with which the defendant is charged
- have adequate time and facilities for the preparation of a defence
- communicate with counsel of the defendant's choosing
- free legal assistance for defendants unable to pay for it
- examine witnesses for the prosecution and to present witnesses for the defence
- have any conviction and sentence reviewed by a higher tribunal

"Have you anything to say before you are found guilty?"
Len Spencer

ACTIVITY 8 BRIEFING SHEET 1
Executions of the innocent

EXECUTION OF THE INNOCENT AROUND THE WORLD

As long as the death penalty is maintained, the risk of executing the innocent can never be eliminated.

350 people convicted of capital crimes in the USA between 1900 and 1985 were innocent of the crimes charged, according to a 1987 study. Some prisoners escaped execution by minutes, but 23 were actually executed.

In February 1994, authorities in Russia executed serial killer Andrei Chikatilo for the highly publicised murders of 52 people. The authorities acknowledged that they had previously executed the wrong man, Alexander Kravchenko, for one of the murders, in their desire to stop the killings quickly. Another innocent man suspected of the killings committed suicide.

In Japan, Sakae Menda had spent 33 years in prison for robbery and murder before he was finally acquitted and released in 1983. His alibi proved that he could not have been at the scene of the murders. He had been sentenced to death in 1950 but, year after year, appeals had postponed the carrying out of his sentence. 'My cellmates were executed one by one. I would become upset, my arms and legs turned rigid and I would have cold sweat on my back.'

EXECUTION OF THE INNOCENT IN THE UK

In 1952 Mahmood Hussein Mattan, a Somali-born seaman living with his family in Cardiff, was charged with the murder of a local shop-keeper. Mattan protested his innocence and had a clear alibi. After a trial strongly tainted by racism he was found guilty and executed in September 1952. His wife and children campaigned against Mattan's conviction for over 25 years. In February 1998 an appeal court overturned his conviction and he was 'posthumously pardoned'.

The court concluded that witnesses at the original trial were unreliable and that the prosecution had withheld evidence that a man similar in appearance to Mattan was more likely the actual murderer. In his ruling, the judge concluded that the case had shown that capital punishment was not a wise outcome for the criminal justice system which is human and therefore can make mistakes.

Photocopy Original © Hodder & Stoughton 2001

ACTIVITY 8 BRIEFING SHEET 2
Wrongful convictions in the UK

THE BIRMINGHAM SIX

Patrick Hill, Richard McIlkenny, Billy Power, Hugh Callaghan, John Walker and Gerard Hunter – the men who became famous as 'The Birmingham Six' – were convicted in 1975 for murders committed in two pub bombings in Birmingham. The IRA said that it had carried out the bombings in which 21 people died and 162 were wounded. The six men claimed that they had been held incommunicado and ill-treated during interrogation, as a result of which they made false confessions.

In 1987 the Court of Appeal upheld the decisions. The testimonies of fresh witnesses supporting the men's allegations of ill-treatment were dismissed by the judges as 'dishonest', 'mistaken' or 'irrelevant'. For 16 years the men's relations and friends campaigned alongside MPs, members of the public and Amnesty International and the European Parliament. After a further appeal hearing in March 1991, the six men were freed, their convictions overturned.

'We shouldn't have all those campaigns to get the Birmingham Six released. If they'd been hanged, they'd have been forgotten and the whole community would be satisfied.' Lord Denning, retired judge, on release of the Birmingham Six. He had turned down an earlier appeal by the Six. If the death penalty had been in force in 1975 the Birmingham Six would, in all probability, have been hanged.

THE GUILDFORD FOUR

In 1974, following terrorist bombings in Guildford and Woolwich, three men and a woman – who became known as 'the Guildford Four' were sentenced to life imprisonment. In 1989 their convictions were quashed after they had served nearly 15 years for crimes they did not commit.

'It's hard to avoid the conclusion that in the lynch-mob atmosphere of the time, someone – anyone – had to pay, and they happened to be the unlucky scapegoats.' Robert Harris, *Sunday Times* 22.10.89, on the release of the Guildford Four.

PADDY NICHOLLS

In 1975 Paddy Nicholls was jailed for life for the murder of a friend. He spent 23 years in prison, fighting his conviction. In 1998 he was cleared and released, aged 69. Evidence which showed that his friend had died of natural causes had been suppressed at his trial. In 1977 a journalist had written in the *Daily Express* 'Is this the murder that never was?' On his release Paddy Nicholls said: 'They've stolen a third of my life. … It's been a long haul but I always knew I would get out … You can always tell an innocent man in prison; there's an aura around them, something in the body language.' *The Guardian* 13.6.98

ACTIVITY 9 CASE STUDIES
State killings

In front of a crowd of thousands, Chidiebere Omuoha, aged 17, and five other prisoners were executed on 31 July 1997 in Owerri, southeast Nigeria. They had been sentenced to death by a special court directly appointed by the military authorities which allows no right of appeal to a higher or independent court. Chidiebere Onuoha was aged 15 years at the time of the armed robbery for which he was executed.

AI Death Penalty News, Sept. 1997

Public executions, Owerri, Nigeria, 1997

Girvies Davis was executed in Illinois on 17 May 1995 after spending 16 years on 'Death Row'. He was sentenced to death for the murder of an 89-year-old man in 1979.

Davis was first arrested for armed robbery. According to the police, ten days after his arrest he gave officers a hand-written note listing 11 murders he had committed. The police then took Davis on a tour of the crime scenes, during which he confessed to nine murders. However, Davis claimed that he was taken from his cell and driven to a deserted highway where he was offered the 'choice' of signing pre-written confessions or being shot 'while trying to escape'. Davis stated that he never saw the original confession note till it was held up as evidence in court.

According to records, Davis had dropped out of school, was illiterate and would have been incapable of writing the original confession. He had been diagnosed

continued

as having an 'organic brain disorder' and was 'mentally retarded'. The prosecution later conceded that at least three of the murders to which Davis 'confessed' were committed by other people.

Davis, who was black, was tried by an all-white jury following the prosecution's use of peremptory challenge (the right to exclude jurors without giving reasons) to remove all potential black jurors. The jury were not told that he could not have written his 'confession' note nor the other confessions he signed.

AI Report: USA, developments on the Death Penalty in 1995

Under an emergency 'crack-down on crime' introduced in China in 1996, defendants can be tried without warning, without being given a copy of the charges in advance and without notification of the trial being given to all parties concerned. This means, among other things, that defendants can be tried without the assistance of a lawyer and without knowing exactly what accusations they face until their trial.

Some people have been executed within a few days of the crimes they allegedly committed, after summary trials. In Jilin province, for example, three men were executed on 31 May for allegedly robbing a car loaded with bank notes on 21 May. According to an official newspaper, the three men, Tian Zhijia, Tian Zhiquan and Zhao Lian, were arrested on 24 May; they were tried and sentenced to death during an open meeting in the morning of 27 May – three days after their arrest. One of the defendants then appealed against the verdict to the provincial high court, the newspaper said. The high court heard the appeal and rejected it on 28 May, approving the death sentence for the two other defendants at the same time. The three men were executed by firing squad on 31 May – seven days after their arrest and ten days after the offence was committed.

Jilin Daily (Chinese newspaper) 1 & 6 June 1996. AI Index ASA 17/72/96

FREEDOM!

ACTIVITY 10 QUIZ SHEET
The death penalty in the UK

1. How many offences were punishable by death in 18th-century England?

under 10   over 50   over 200

2. Which of these English monarchs opposed the death penalty?

William the Conqueror   Henry VIII   Elizabeth I

3. Which of the following 'crimes' were punishable by death between 1600 and 1850 in England?

Being a traveller ('gypsy')
Stealing a loaf of bread
Stealing a handkerchief
Protesting about land enclosures
Highway robbery
Arson
Murder
Piracy
Trespassing on private property
Cutting down a cherry tree

Stephen Gardiner in his shroud making his dying speech at Tyburn

4. In what year was the last child executed for theft in the UK?

1700   1833   1901

5. In what year were public executions abolished?

1750   1811   1848

6. In what year was the death penalty abolished for pregnant women?

1850   1908   1931

7. In what year was the minimum age for the death penalty raised to 18 years?

1905   1948   1950

8. In what year was the last person hanged in Britain?

1935   1945   1964

9. In what year was the death penalty abolished for all crimes?

1968   1978   1998

Photocopy Original © Hodder & Stoughton 2001

ACTIVITY 10 FACT SHEET
The death penalty in the UK

In the Middle Ages 'felons' were at the mercy of the monarch. They could be put to death in a variety of ways or mutilated (e.g. by blinding or castration) instead. Not all monarchs were keen on the death penalty. In 1066 William the Conqueror decreed: 'I forbid that any person be killed or hanged for any cause.'

By the 13th century hanging was the usual standard punishment for all serious crimes, though Henry VIII favoured other methods too. During his 38-year reign (1509–1547) some 72,000 people were executed (hanging, beheading, disembowelling, even boiling to death). There were so many executions that Henry allowed them on Sundays – the only monarch to do so.

Henry's daughter Elizabeth I also used execution with enthusiasm not only to control crime but as an instrument of terror to maintain her power. In her reign there were over 800 executions a year.

In 1562 under Elizabeth I an Act was introduced to prevent bands of 'Egyptians' (travellers, originally from India, later known as Gypsies) from travelling around Britain. Foreign-born Gypsies were to be deported while any English-born people aged 14 or over who lived with them were to be executed. There are many records of large groups of Gypsies or vagrants being hanged over the next 100 years, the last time at Bury St Edmunds in the 1650s, when 13 were hanged.

During the 15th to 17th centuries 'witches' were attacked by the Christian Church. In the infamous 'witch-hunts' of the period women (often 'wise women' or healers, or assertive older women and widows) were denounced for witchcraft throughout Europe, including Britain. Many thousands of women were tortured and executed by hanging, burning, drowning or other methods.

From the 1690s new Criminal Codes made 100 offences punishable by death.

Throughout the 18th century more capital offences were added – by 1810 there were about 230, mainly for crimes against property and for acts of resistance such as opposing the enclosure of common land. Under the so-called 'Bloody Code' people could be hanged for minor offences such as stealing a loaf of bread, as well as more serious matters like arson, murder or highway robbery. In Chelmsford, in 1814, a man was hanged for cutting down a cherry tree.

Children between 7 and 14 could be hanged 'on strong evidence of malice'. Over 14 there was no restriction. In 1801 Andrew Brenning, aged 13, was hanged for stealing a spoon; in 1808 a seven-year-old girl was hanged.

Juries became reluctant to convict and death sentences were often not carried out. Nevertheless public hangings were a common spectacle – often with a public holiday and fair – at places like Tyburn (Marble Arch) in London.

continued

Photocopy Original © Hodder & Stoughton 2001

- 1833 the last juvenile was hanged in Britain – a 14-year-old thief in Newport.
- By 1835 reformers had removed some less violent offences from the capital list and by 1840 capital offences were reduced to 15.
- By 1861 the death penalty was only available for murder, high treason, piracy with violence and the destruction of public arsenals and dockyards.
- 1864 A Royal Commission recommended that murder be divided into two 'degrees' with the death penalty only to be used 'for all murders committed in or with a view to perpetration of any of the following felonies: murder, arson, rape, burglary, robbery or piracy'.
- 1868 public executions were abolished.
- 1908 the death penalty was abolished for persons under 16.
- 1931 the death penalty was abolished for pregnant women.
- 1948 the age limit for executions was raised to 18.
- 1952 Mahmood Mattan was hanged in Cardiff. He was later found to be innocent and 'posthumously pardoned' in 1998.
- In 1953 Derek Bentley, aged 19, was hanged for the murder of a policeman although the shot was fired by his 16-year-old accomplice. In 1998 Bentley's conviction was overturned posthumously.
- 1955 Ruth Ellis, aged 28, was the last woman to be hanged in the UK.
- 1964 Gwynne Evans and Peter Allen were the last people to be hanged in the UK.
- In 1965 the death penalty was abolished for murder under a private member's bill introduced by Sidney Silverman MP. It was retained for high treason and piracy.
- In 1998 the death penalty was fully abolished in UK for all crimes.

Derek Bentley

Sources: The Case Against Capital Punishment, *1991 Howard League for Penal Reform; AI Working for Freedom; Peter Linebaugh* The London Hanged *1991; Geoffrey Treasure* Who's Who in Hanoverian Britain *1997; Angus Fraser* The Gypsies *1992; E P Thompson* The Making of the English Working Classes, *1963*

Photocopy Original © Hodder & Stoughton 2001

ACTIVITY 11 INFORMATION SHEET

The death penalty in the USA – an impartial system?

SOME FACTS ABOUT THE DEATH PENALTY IN THE USA

- The death penalty was abolished in the USA in 1967 and resumed in 1977.
- In 2000 38 of the 50 US states provided for the death penalty in law; the death penalty is also provided under US federal military and civilian law.
- 366 prisoners were executed in the USA between 1977 and 1997.
- 45 prisoners were executed in the USA in 1996 and early 1997.
- Over 3,600 prisoners were under sentence of death in September 1999.

DISCRIMINATION AND THE DEATH PENALTY

'Capital punishment on Death Row USA means them as ain't got the capital, gits the punishment.'

Shabaka Waqlini, 14 years on Florida's death row. Released as innocent (1992).

Many studies of executions in the USA show that the death penalty is applied arbitrarily. Whether someone lives or dies is a lottery depending on factors such as plea bargaining and the competence of lawyers. Death row cells and the statistics of the executed rarely include millionaires. They are disproportionately filled with prisoners from impoverished and ethnic minority backgrounds – those least able to afford competent legal representation.

Those convicted of killing a white person are far more likely to be sentenced to death than if the victim is black. 82% of executions are for the killing of a white

Young Texans in vigil against the death penalty

continued

FREEDOM!

person though almost equal numbers of black and white people are victims of homicide. Every death sentence in Kentucky from 1976 to 1991 was for the murder of a white victim, although there had been 1,000 black homicide victims.

MENTAL HEALTH AND THE DEATH PENALTY

At least 11 prisoners executed in the USA during 1995 were reported to be suffering from a mental illness or 'mental retardation'. Frequently, information regarding the defendant's mental impairment(s) was not uncovered by defence counsel at the time of the trial, and not made known to the jury.

Varnall Weeks, executed in Alabama on 12 May 1993, had been diagnosed as being severely mentally ill and suffering from 'long-standing paranoid schizophrenia'. Psychologists testifying for both the prosecution and the defence agreed that he suffered from strange religious delusions. Weeks believed that he was God and that he would not die, but rather that he would be transformed into a tortoise and rule over the universe.

No evidence of his mental condition was introduced at his original trial in 1982. In a ruling on 25 April 1995 (after he had been on 'Death Row' for 13 years) an Alabama judge acknowledged that Weeks was 'insane' according to 'the dictionary definition of insanity' and what 'the average person in the street would regard to be insane'. However, the judge ruled that the electrocution could proceed because Weeks' ability to answer a few limited questions about his execution proved that he was legally 'competent'.

Sources: Amnesty International report AMR 51/01/96 February 1996. United States of America, Developments on the Death Penalty in 1995. Amnesty International Annual Report 1999. United States of America: Developments on the Death Penalty in 1996, AI Index: AMR 51/01/97

Photocopy Original © Hodder & Stoughton 2001

ACTIVITY 12 CASE STUDY
Wilburn Dobbs

Wilburn Dobbs, a black man, was sentenced to death in 1974 after a trial contaminated by racism. He was tried and found guilty of the murder of a white man, Roy Sizemore, during a robbery in December 1973. The offence occurred in the small, racially segregated community of Walker County, Georgia, with a 96% white population. At the trial, Dobbs was represented by a state-appointed attorney, who, on the morning of the trial, sought a delay stating that he was not prepared to go to trial and was in a better position to prosecute the case than defend it. The trial went ahead.

During the trial Dobbs was referred to as 'coloured' and 'coloured boy' by the judge and defence attorney. Two female jurors stated that they feared blacks and found them to be scarier than whites. Another juror stated: 'I would fear one [a black man] on the street … I think all white women would have that fear.' The judge had formerly served in the Georgia Senate and participated in an effort to prevent racial integration.

The jury was left unaware of the many mitigating factors in Dobbs' life. His mother was 12 when she gave birth to him. He never knew his father. Dobbs started life in an environment of alcohol consumption, prostitution and crime. Members of the black community where Dobbs grew up had no opportunity to speak.

The defence attorney presented no mitigating evidence as to why Dobbs should be spared the death penalty. At no time did he refer to Dobbs by name or even request that the jury return a verdict of life imprisonment.

He said blacks are less educated and less intelligent than whites 'because of their nature' or 'because my granddaddy had slaves'. He said that integration has led to deteriorating neighbourhoods and schools and referred to the black community in Chattanooga as 'black boy jungle'.

The Federal Court decided that the racial prejudice of the judge, prosecutor, defence lawyer and jurors in the case did not require that the death sentence be set aside. The Court of Appeals found that although certain of jurors' statements revealed racial prejudice, no juror stated that he or she viewed blacks as more prone to violence than whites.

26 years after his trial Wilburn Dobbs was still on death row. He has obtained permission to have his sentence reviewed. The death penalty could be re-imposed.

Source: Amnesty International 1998 'The death penalty in Georgia, USA'

Photocopy Original © Hodder & Stoughton 2001

ACTIVITY 13 INFORMATION SHEET
Death Row

'Death Row' is the name given to the cells in a prison where prisoners under sentence of death are held while they wait for execution or for clemency or a successful appeal. In the USA such prisoners are often held for many years – seven years is the average – sometimes much longer. 42% of the men on Death Row and 12% of the US population are black.

Most often, prisoners are kept in solitary confinement during this period. Often regarded as 'dead men', prisoners may suffer extreme psychological problems from the uncertainty of their position. Additional distress is caused to family and friends, who are powerless to relieve the prisoner's suffering. In 1998 an Amnesty International delegation, including Secretary General Pierre Sané, visited prisons in Texas. They found that many prisoners are held in terrible conditions for years while they wait to die:

- up to 23 hours a day locked up alone
- cells 1.5 × 2.7 metres, containing bed and toilet
- extreme heat – over 40 Celsius in summer
- food at 4am, 10am, and 4pm only

Pierre Sané said: 'We have witnessed how a deliberate policy aimed at dehumanising prisoners is implemented, coldly, professionally and heartlessly. The effect is such that it has also dehumanised their keepers. The condemned await their deaths in rows of tiny cages … their spirits are slowly broken.'

In 1991 prisoner Tim Davis said in Holman Prison, Alabama, 'I am approaching my 13th year of incarceration and it always brings me down. That and turning 30 about took all the wind out of my sails. Looking back over my life I feel emptiness. I haven't accomplished anything. It's as if I never existed. Plus it's lonely here, brother. I have my mom and stepfather but no lady friends who visit. I'll be all right. I go through these motions every so often and just keep on going on. Thirteen years is a long time to be confined in almost solitary confinement. This ole cage kind of weighs you down.'

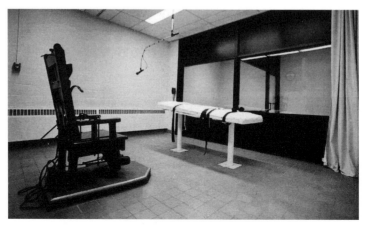

Electric chair and lethal injection gurney, Lucasville, Ohio

ACTIVITY 14 CASE STUDY
Ricky Ray Rector

The case of Ricky Ray Rector of Arkansas, USA, illustrates the complex forces involved in an execution. In 1981 Rector killed two men, then shot himself in the head damaging his brain and reducing his understanding to that of a small child, unable to grasp what was happening to him.

Under other circumstances, with a sympathetic state governor, Rector's chances of a reprieve would have been good. He was clearly no longer the same person who had shot two men dead. But the Governor of Arkansas was Bill Clinton, running for President and going through a bad patch in his campaign.

Clinton had run into trouble on the crime issue before. In 1979 he released a 73-year-old terminally ill murderer who had killed again before dying. Clinton lost the next election for governor. After that he reversed his position and supported the death penalty. At the next election he won back the governorship. Unfortunately for Rector, the execution became a test of Clinton's nerve. Would he permit the execution of a man with a severe brain damage? Clinton left the campaign trail and flew back to Arkansas to ensure that the punishment took place.

Rector spent his last hours as he had spent the previous ten years – alternately skipping, barking, laughing and howling. He left the dessert of his final meal, telling people that he could eat it when he returned from the execution chamber.

Bill Clinton told the civil rights leader Rev. Jesse Jackson, who made a personal appeal for clemency, that he could see no alternative to the execution, though he was 'praying about it'. Ricky Ray Rector's execution was a very long and gruesome process – his veins were too thin to take the lethal injection. A year later Clinton was sworn in as President of the USA.

A member of the state legislature, Jerry Jewell, was appointed Acting Governor of Arkansas as a temporary replacement for Bill Clinton. During the week that he was in office four death penalty cases passed across his desk. All four were saved from execution and Jewell expressed regret that he wasn't able to spare more. If Rector's case had come up in January 1993 instead of 1992, his chances of survival would have been much greater.

Source: Brian Dooley, Last Rights, *New Internationalist 244, June 1993*

ACTIVITY 15 INFORMATION SHEET 1
The deterrence argument: evidence from around the world

Some supporters of capital punishment claim that it is an effective deterrent. It deters people from committing murder. This argument assumes that murder is carried out in a calm, reasoned manner. Studies of the circumstances of murder suggest that this is not often the case. Statistics show that murders are most often committed:

- in moments of passion, when emotion overcomes reason – usually between people who are very close
- under the influence of drugs or alcohol
- by people who are mentally ill or confused
- in panic, upon discovery as a crime is being committed
- by professional criminals who believe that they will not be caught

A 1988 United Nations study of the relation between the death penalty and homicide rates, concluded that 'This research has failed to provide scientific proof that executions have a greater deterrent effect than life imprisonment. Such proof is unlikely to be forthcoming. The evidence as a whole still gives no positive support to the deterrent hypothesis.'

The study reviewed evidence from around the world on changes in the use of the death penalty and crime rates. The evidence showed 'that countries need not fear sudden and serious changes in the curve of crime if they reduce their reliance on the death penalty'.

The death penalty was abolished in Canada in 1976. The previous year, 1975, there were 701 homicides, in 1984 there were 668. In 1993, 17 years after the abolition, the homicide rate was 27 per cent lower than in 1975.

References: Roger Hood, The Death Penalty: A World-wide Perspective

A report by the US Death Penalty Information Center (based on telephone interviews with 386 randomly selected police chiefs in 48 states across the USA) showed that although police chiefs support the idea of the death penalty they do not believe it works in practice. Police chiefs rated the death penalty as the least cost-effective method of controlling crime, and ranked it last as a way of reducing violent crime. ... A majority also believe that murderers do not think about the possible punishments for the crime, that the death penalty does not sufficiently reduce the number of homicides, and that it is not one of the most important tools in fighting crime.

AI Report 'Death Penalty in the USA, 1995 Update'

Photocopy Original © Hodder & Stoughton 2001

Unit 5: THE DEATH PENALTY

ACTIVITY 15 INFORMATION SHEET 2

The deterrence argument: crime and capital punishment in the UK

'The number of offences (in the UK) initially recorded as homicide per 100,000 of the population was almost the same in 1989 as it was in 1857. The rate then was 1.26 and the rate for 1989 was 1.25 ... there is no evidence ... that the existence of the death penalty reduces murders or other crimes of violence.'

Kenneth Baker, Home Secretary, 17 December 1990, Criminal Justice debate, House of Commons

CRIME AND CAPITAL PUNISHMENT IN THE UK IN THE 18TH CENTURY

'Public executions were intended to act as a deterrent; but young apprentices, allowed a "Tyburn Fair" holiday, regarded victims as heroes, especially when they exited with a swagger. The procession from prison to gallows, Newgate to Tyburn (Marble Arch), would last about two hours; the carts stopped at taverns, and many condemned men were drunk by the time they reached their end – they would promise to pay for their drink "when they came back". ....

Public hangings proved counter-productive. "On Monday last eleven wretches were executed at Tyburn," commented Henry Fielding, "and the very next night one of the most impudent street-robberies was committed near St James's Square, an instance of the little force which such examples have on the minds of the populace. In real truth, the executions of criminals, as at present conducted, serve, I apprehend, a purpose diametrically opposite to that for which they were designed; and tend rather to inspire the vulgar with a contempt for the gallows rather than a fear of it." '

Roy Porter, London: a social history, (1994) pp. 153-4

Execution at Tyburn

Photocopy Original © Hodder & Stoughton 2001

Photocopy Original © Hodder & Stoughton 2001

ACTIVITY 18 RESOURCE SHEET
The humanitarian and moral arguments

'It was about forty yards to the gallows. I watched the bare brown back of the prisoner marching in front of me. . . . At each step his muscles slid neatly into place . . . his feet printed themselves on the wet gravel. And once, in spite of the men who gripped him by each shoulder, he stepped slightly aside to avoid a puddle in the path.

It is curious, but till that moment I had never realised what it means to destroy a healthy, conscious man. When I saw the prisoner step aside to avoid the puddle I saw the mystery, the unspeakable wrongness, of cutting a life short when it is in full tide. This man was not dying, he was alive just as we were alive. All the organs of his body were working – bowels digesting food, skin renewing itself, nails growing, tissues forming – all toiling away in solemn foolery. His nails would still be growing while he stood on the drop, while he was falling through the air with a tenth of a second to live. His eyes saw the yellow gravel and the grey walls, and his brain still remembered, foresaw, reasoned – even about puddles. He and we were a party of men walking together, seeing, hearing, feeling, understanding the same world; and in two minutes, with a sudden snap, one of us would be gone – one mind less, one world less.'

George Orwell, Collected Essays, Journalism and Letters, Penguin Books, 1968

'First, I am totally against the death penalty by any means. It is my belief that society should set the standard of non-violence and show by example its commitment to this. In saying this I accept that we have violent individuals in our midst who have to be dealt with. Indeed I am one. In 1967 I was sentenced to life imprisonment with a recommended minimum of 15 years. I was aged 23. At that time I was brutalised by prison staff and on three occasions almost lost my life. The situation became so bad that I was eventually kept naked inside a cell and given one book per week to read. I was kept like this for six-and-a-half years. This sort of treatment made me more resentful and filled me with hatred for prison officers and the public in general: the latter because they locked people like me up for being violent but turned a blind eye when prison officers brutalised prisoners.

This situation only erupted in further violence and made the situation worse. Having played the ultimate in the punitive line the authorities were left helpless. It was at this point that the prison authorities took another direction. They opened a place called the Special Unit and asked for volunteer staff. They were quite

Jimmy Boyle

continued

The humanitarian and moral arguments

courageous people who did not want violence – either to use it or have it used on them. As a result of this much more progressive regime I began to find I had other abilities and became a sculptor, a writer, and learnt a whole new set of skills. But more than this I learned a lot about me and why people get into trouble.

As a result of this I am now out working in the poverty ridden streets I came from and doing work that prevents many youngsters from getting into trouble. So if I had been hanged it would have been for a crime that I did not commit and second, perhaps many of the youngsters I work with and have helped may have ended up on murder charges.'

Jimmy Boyle, A Sense of Freedom

'Disappearance' and extrajudicial execution

6

UNIT AIMS

The aims of this unit are to enable pupils to:
- understand the concept of 'disappearance' and extrajudicial execution
- explore historical and current examples
- explore and express their feelings through poetry, narrative and drama
- empathise with the families of the 'disappeared'
- learn about how regimes involved in 'disappearance' and extrajudicial execution are being challenged

INTRODUCTION

'Disappearance' and 'extrajudicial execution' may be distressing subjects to you and your students, and will need sensitive handling. It is possible that students may have experience of 'disappearance' in their family. They may have lost a close family member either through sudden death or because a parent or sibling has suddenly left home. They may themselves be refugees from conflict or repression. It is, however, an important subject for students to learn about because of the prevalence of such abuses in today's world.

This section contains an activity on Turkey as a focus for exploring the issue of 'disappearance'. Other countries where 'disappearance' is also currently rife, such as Algeria, Colombia and Mexico, could equally well have been selected. It will also be important not to promote or reinforce the view that other countries and cultures are 'uncivilised' compared with Britain.

You could also make the following points,

or encourage groups to work them out for themselves:

- ever since the Crusades, Europe has 'demonised' Turkey, using it as a classic example of cruelty and barbarism
- Britain has its own record of internal and external human rights abuses. In many areas of the world, the legacies of slavery and colonialism have contributed to creating the conditions for conflict and oppression.

Activities explore the subject through information and case studies, media reports, personal accounts, poetry and literature. For Activity 4 travel brochures or advertisement posters on holidays in Turkey are needed. Students might also use the Internet to research other countries in which 'disappearance' and extrajudicial executions take place. Teachers will be able to prepare updates on the issues by visiting the Amnesty International website **www.amnesty.org.uk**.

In order to balance the disquiet which

learning about such violations may cause, activities encourage students to understand that in all of the countries where 'disappearance' and other abuses take place, many ordinary people are courageously working for human rights and democracy. Students can also find out how they can participate in challenging such abuses, through campaigns sponsored by international human rights organisations.

SUMMARY OF TOPICS

TITLE	CURRICULUM LINKS	PAGE
1. Role play on 'disappearance'	13+: Drama/English/ PSHE/Pastoral/RE	*175/—*
Citizenship	***Participation Skills:*** *use imagination to consider others' experiences*	
2. What is a 'disappearance'?	13+: PSHE/RE/English/History	*175/179*
3. The whys and wherefores of 'disappearance' and extrajudicial execution	14+: PSHE/RE/English/History/Law/Ethics/Economics and Business Studies/Media Studies/Sociology/BTEC National in Public Services: *e.g. Describe how human rights are violated in at least three countries*	*176/182*
Citizenship	***Knowledge and Understanding***: *legal and human rights, role of criminal justice system*	
4. Turkey – one country's 'disappearance'	14+: English/Politics/General Studies/Law/RE/History/Media Studies/Geography	*176/185*
5. Writing and drama on 'disappearance' in Turkey	14+: English/Drama/Theatre Studies/PSHE/RE	*176/—*
Citizenship	***Knowledge and Understanding***: *legal and human rights, role of business* ***Participation Skills***: *considering others' experiences*	
6. Researching 'disappearance'	14+: English/Drama/Theatre Studies/History/Geography/ Politics/General Studies/RE	*177/—*
7. Poetry on 'disappearance'	14+: English/Drama/RE/PSHE	*177/188*
8. Personal accounts of 'disappearance'	16+: English/Drama/Theatre Studies/RE/PSHE	*177/191*
9. Stolen children	14+: English/Drama/Art/PSHE	*177/195*
10. Impunity – getting away with murder?	14+: Law/Politics/English/Drama/Theatre Studies/General Studies/RE	*177/—*
Citizenship	***Knowledge and Understanding***: *legal and human rights and responsibilities, the criminal justice system* ***Key Skills:*** *communication, IT* ***Participation Skills***: *using imagination to consider others' experiences*	
11. A Long Way to Cherry Time	13+: English/Drama/RE/PSHE	*178/—*

ACTIVITIES: NOTES FOR TEACHERS

Activity 1: Role play on 'disappearance'

THE PLOT

Before the lesson take two young people aside so that they are not seen. Tell them that they are to be security police in plain clothes in the role play. They are to keep their identity secret. They are to mix in with the crowd, and at a given signal from you they are to silently but firmly arrest the newspaper seller and pull her/him quickly from the room.

THE ROLE PLAY

Tell the whole class that they are going on a journey by aeroplane. Ask them to suggest where they may be going, giving some steering (so that they choose a country in which 'disappearance' has taken place). Examples are Mexico, Colombia, the Philippines, Sri Lanka, Iraq, India, Turkey, Algeria, Indonesia.

Establish the setting: they are in a rural market in the chosen country. Ask them to suggest what the different stalls in the market might be selling in that particular country: fruit, vegetables, fish, tools, cooking equipment, livestock, second-hand clothing, music tapes, sweets. What sort of fruit, and vegetables? What music? And do not forget to have a stall with newspapers, books and magazines. What is the currency in the chosen country?

Stalls are then allocated amongst ten or so of the students. Everyone else is a shopper who will bargain with them.

Start the role-play. Get the stall-holders to shout out their wares loudly and the shoppers to really haggle.

When everyone is engaged, give the security guards the secret signal to act. 'Maria/Mario' (change the name as appropriate) the newspaper seller, is grabbed and quickly taken from the room.

Freeze the action and ask everyone else:

- What has just happened? Why did no one intervene? What do they feel about what happened? Who were the people who took her/him away? Why was s/he taken? Who knows her/him? What were the papers/books that s/he was selling? Is s/he a subversive selling opposition papers? Has s/he links with terrorists? What should people do now?

Now tell the group that Maria/o's parents, who are poor and uneducated, live up the hill. Suggest to the people in the market that a couple of them should go and see Maria/o's parents now to tell them what they saw, and to work out what to do.

Choose a couple of students to be the delegates from the market and two people to be the aged parents. Other students can suggest advice. Start the role play.

The market delegates tell the parents what happened in the market. Who could have taken Maria/o? Had anyone seen them before? Was one of them Maria/o's sweetheart? Did Maria/o owe someone money? Ask the class for suggestions. Explore them with the parents and the messengers. Ask them:

- What should they do now to find out what has happened?
- Where should they look – the hospital, the prison, mortuary?
- Who could help? The police? The army? The local religious leader? A lawyer? Anyone else?

You might role play what is happening to Maria/o and the captors, going into role yourself to interview them in the secret 'safe house' where Maria/o is actually being held in incommunicado detention. The military suspect Maria/o of links with a banned political organisation. They have heard there is a plot to explode a bomb in the town. Maria/o knows nothing. What are the options each has?

The action can again be frozen at relevant points to discuss what is happening and what might happen next.

Activity 2: What is a 'disappearance'?

Give out the fact and question sheets entitled: 'What is a "disappearance"?', 'Disappearance and extrajudicial execution' and 'Rights and wrongs of arrests and detention' for pairs to work on.

Pairs can share their thoughts, answers and questions as a whole class.

Activity 3: The whys and wherefores of 'disappearance' and extrajudicial execution

Hand out the exercise sheet 'Why does "disappearance" and extrajudicial execution take place?' for pairs or small groups to read and work on.

Then give out information sheet 'Where does "disappearance" take place?' and a blank map of the world. See Unit 4 on torture, page 107. Colour the map, show where 'disappearance' has taken place in recent years, select some examples from the exercise sheet and research other information to make an exhibition on 'disappearance'.

Activity 4: Turkey – one country's 'disappearance'

Give small groups the briefing sheet which has articles on 'disappearance' in Turkey, taken from a variety of sources. They can analyse the information to answer these questions:

- What evidence is there of state involvement in 'disappearance'?
- Who has taken what steps to highlight and challenge the issue of 'disappearance'?
- How effectively does each article convey its message information?
- What other approaches can they think of to publicise an issue?

Students can then find out about campaigns against 'disappearance' in Turkey and the Turkish Government's response. Use Amnesty International and Human Rights Watch websites at **www.amnesty.org.uk** and **www.hrw.org**.

Students can also research the background to the Kurdish conflict.

BACKGROUND INFORMATION

Turkey is one of the fastest growing new destinations for tourists from the UK. Most visitors want a cheap and pleasant break in the sunshine. Tourists don't usually know about Turkey's human rights record.

Although many of the profits from holidays in Turkey go to companies outside the country, tourism is big business in Turkey and a very fast-growing part of the economy.

- 7,083,000 people visited Turkey in 1995
- Tourism provided 10% of Turkey's employment in 1998 and continues to increase.

Give groups some marketing materials on holidays in Turkey (use travel brochures or posters from travel agent) and ask:

- What is the image of Turkey being presented?

Students can then design their own brochure or poster campaign for Amnesty International about 'disappearance' in Turkey using and subverting the image presented in travel brochures.

Activity 5: Writing and drama on 'disappearance' in Turkey

- Write a short article about 'disappearance' in Turkey for a children's newspaper.
- Write a play set in an airport lounge – a tourist off on holiday to Turkey meets a Turkish worker at the coffee bar with a 'disappeared' relative.
- Imagine that you are one of the Saturday Mothers organising the vigil each week. Write an open letter to other ordinary people around the world. Explain:
  - who you are;
  - who your 'disappeared' relative was;
  - what the vigil is for;
  - what you want as people around the world to do to put pressure on your government to end the human rights abuses.

Students may become involved in one of the campaigns against 'disappearance' and can research these on the Amnesty International website (**www.amnesty.org.uk**).

Activity 6: Researching 'disappearance'

Ask small groups to choose one country from Activity 3 to research the background of 'disappearance' and extrajudicial execution using the Amnesty International website. Create this as a drama piece and present it to other groups. This could include:

- background information given by a 'narrator', possibly the voice of a 'disappeared' person;
- personal testimonies of those involved e.g. child/parent of a 'disappeared' person, 'safe house' guard, member of armed forces, eyewitness, journalist;
- recreations of scenes and conversations between people;
- imagined conversations between the dead, living and those responsible.

After each group has presented their drama the rest of the class can ask questions to the characters who answer in 'role'.

In the de-briefing afterwards ask the players how it felt to play their role.

Activity 7: Poetry on 'disappearance'

Ask pairs to read the poem 'Will and Testament' by the Chilean writer Ariel Dorfman, and the lyrics of the song 'The Missing' by the Panamanian singer Reuben Blades. Discuss these questions:

Why is Dorfman's poem called 'Will and Testament'?

What will the authorities say about his 'disappearance'?

Why does he say 'don't believe them' three times at the end of the poem?

Who are the voices speaking through Reuben Blades' song?

What has happened to the people in the song?

Design a record cover for Reuben Blades' song 'Missing', featuring each of the stories he sings about, or design the cover for a book of poems on the 'disappeared' by Ariel Dorfman.

Activity 8: Personal accounts of 'disappearance'

Some very powerful literature and art has come of the experience of 'disappearance' including the moving short stories of Argentinian Alicia Portnoy's *The Little School* that her daughter illustrated and Mohammed Nadrani's *Kalâat M'gouna – Disappeared under the Roses (1995)*, with his own paintings now accessible on the Amnesty International website.

Hand out the testimonies of three survivors of 'disappearance' for the students to read.

Groups can research the background to 'disappearance' in Argentina, Chile, and Morocco and prepare a classroom exhibition of where the events took place, who were the victims, and the perpetrators, using the testimonies of the witnesses.

Activity 9: Stolen Children

Get students to read the testimonies of the Grandmothers of the Plaza de Mayo, and Father Jon de Cortina.

Get them to write a story or a play with the parents or grandparents searching for and discovering one of these stolen children, who will have grown up under a false name with another family. How will they prove the child's true identity? What will they do next?

Find out about Argentina in the 1970s and El Salvador in the 1980s where these events took place.

Design and make a poster for the Grandmothers' weekly protests in the Plaza de Mayo.

Activity 10: Impunity – getting away with murder?

Ask students to define the word 'impunity' or get them to look it up in a dictionary.

In pairs, students choose a country where 'disappearance' and extrajudicial execution has taken place in the past, but where those responsible have never been brought to justice (e.g. Argentina, Philippines, Haiti, Iraq, Morocco, Sri Lanka, Kuwait, Peru, Uruguay).

Students can use the keyword 'impunity' to search relevant websites on the Internet.

In many of these countries, such as Peru in 1995, special amnesty laws had been passed exonerating members of the security forces and civilian officials for their involvement in human rights violations.

The class can discuss such an amnesty law, and the reasons are against it, and what other options a country could consider (South Africa would make a good comparison here).

Then pairs can write a newspaper article or a speech arguing for the truth to be investigated, and those responsible for crimes to be brought to justice.

Activity 11: A Long Way to Cherry Time

Give students the illustrated children's story 'A Long Way to Cherry Time' (available on Amnesty International UK website: **www.amnesty.org.uk**) to read through and discuss. The letters can be read aloud as a radio play at an assembly or in a performance to a Year 7 class about 'disappeance' and the work of Amnesty International.

- Groups can recreate a scene in which Djamila's parents discuss what has happened, what they might do, their fears and what they will tell Djamila about the 'disappearance' of Uncle Latif.

Read the whole of Abdel Latif Labbi's poem. What are the metaphors he uses? What are the feelings and thoughts the writer is describing?

- Role-play a scene where the Director of Intelligence is talking to another member of the state police about the 'disappearance' and torture of Uncle Latif and discussing how to deal with Djamila's letter.
- Why does Uncle Latif describe himself as Prisoner number 3823, Cell 379, Provincial Jail?
- What difference does it make that he has become an 'official' prisoner? Why does Uncle Latif say 'Latif Nobody has become Mr Abdellatif Somebody?
- Imagine you are Uncle Latif. Write a diary from the time you were seized by the police up until the visit from Djamila. Describe your thoughts and feelings.

ACTIVITY 2 FACT SHEET

What is 'disappearance'?

An enforced 'disappearance' is the seizure of a person by government authorities or their agents, who then deny that the victim is in their custody.

Enforced 'disappearance' is not a new form of repression. A well-known example of 'disappearance' being deliberately used to intimidate and repress a population was in occupied France during the Second World War. The head of the German High Command, Field Marshal Wilhelm Keitel, signed the 'night and fog' decree ('*Nacht und Nebel'*) in an attempt to crush the French Resistance. It was designed to inspire terror and to counter insurgency. Arbitrary targets among the population were selected for enforced 'disappearance' in response to acts of resistance against the German occupiers. The 'disappeared' were transferred to concentration camps in Germany under cover of darkness, with the authorities denying knowledge of their arrest, whereabouts or fate.

Field Marshal Keitel said:
'Intimidation can only be achieved by capital punishment or by measures by which the relatives of the criminal and the population do not know his fate.' He was found guilty of crimes against humanity in Nuremberg after the war.

Thirty years later, 'night and fog' methods began to be used in Guatemala, Brazil, Chile and Argentina. Many other countries have since used, or are using, the same sinister methods.

Field Marshall Keitel on trial at Nuremberg

- Write down some words that the term 'night and fog' suggests to you.
- Write down three things that you consider especially disturbing about 'disappearance'.
- Why do you think that those in authority have used this method rather than imprisonment or execution?
- List countries where enforced 'disappearance' is taking place today.

Photocopy Original © Hodder & Stoughton 2001

ACTIVITY 2 QUESTION SHEET 1
Disappearance and extrajudicial execution

HOW DOES 'DISAPPEARANCE' HAPPEN?

Enforced 'disappearance' is illegal abduction. Most cases happen in secret and suddenly – at night from people's homes, from work or simply in the streets. Those who make the 'arrests' are usually in plain clothes with no identification.

WHAT HAPPENS TO THE 'DISAPPEARED'?

From the moment of their abduction, the 'disappeared' are helpless. They are held 'incommunicado' where no one can contact them. No one knows why they have been taken or where they have gone. Usually those arrested or kidnapped are driven away, blindfolded, to a secret prison or detention centre. They are almost always tortured for information about their associates, families, friends and acquaintances. In many cases they die under torture.

WHAT IS EXTRAJUDICIAL EXECUTION?

Extrajudicial execution is illegal killing that is carried out by agents of the state – i.e. outside any judicial process of trial, sentence and punishment. The citizens are deemed to be a threat to their security. Such execution may be carried out, systematically, by repressive regimes on an extensive scale.

WHO IS RESPONSIBLE FOR 'DISAPPEARANCE' AND EXTRAJUDICIAL EXECUTION?

Governments are responsible for almost all cases of 'disappearance' and extrajudicial execution. They use their security forces, often in disguise (the military or secret police) or paramilitary groups (which may be clandestine) to carry out these illegal activities on their behalf. 'Disappearance' is planned and carried out by paid agents of the state. The weapons, the vehicles used, the 'safe houses', etc. where the 'disappeared' are taken are all paid for by the authorities.

ACTIVITY 2 QUESTION SHEET 2

Rights and wrongs of arrest and detention

There are times when the police or the authorities may wish to hold suspects 'incommunicado' for a period, during which nobody – lawyer, doctor, family – can contact them.

Write down three reasons police or authorities might give for holding someone incommunicado.

1)

2)

3)

Human rights lawyers want laws on arrest to be respected in order to protect the rights of the arrested person. Write down four reasons they might give for wanting tighter rules to control on arrest and detention and to limit incommunicado detention.

1)

2)

3)

4)

Photocopy Original © Hodder & Stoughton 2001

Photocopy Original © Hodder & Stoughton 2001

Why does 'disappearance' and extrajudicial execution take place?

The main motivations for 'disappearance' and extrajudicial execution (political killings) are:

1. To defeat and control political opposition
2. To retain power and control
3. To pursue a religious or ideological idea
4. To 'control' the poor and 'criminal' elements
5. To deal with minorities
6. To prevent trade union and human rights activity

Look at the following examples of 'disappearance' and extrajudicial execution. Next to each, write down the main motivation that you think those responsible had for these acts.

A. Hundreds of babies and small children are seized from their parents by the security forces. The parents may then be 'disappeared' or killed. The children's origins are disguised. They are then secretly given away to childless couples often connected to the armed forces or police. (Argentina 1976 to 1983, El Salvador 1980s)

B. In July 1998, the fate of two nuns, who were 'disappeared' in 1977, is finally revealed by a former member of a 'death squad': their bodies had been put in a sealed drum and dumped in a river. It is estimated that 30,000 people were 'disappeared' or extrajudicially executed in the 'dirty war'. (Argentina, 1976 to 1983)

C. Many fair-haired, blue-eyed children are taken away from their parents by the occupying army and given away for adoption to childless couples. (Nazi-occupied Poland, 1942 to 1945)

D. At least 110 people, mostly ethnic minority villagers from the South East, but also journalists and members of political parties, are 'disappeared' in the name of 'state security'. (Turkey, 1993 to 1995)

E. Members of peasant organisations, indigenous peoples, students and teachers are 'disappeared' during counter-insurgency and anti-narcotics operations by the military. (Mexico, 1998)

F. More than 700 people are 'disappeared' as reprisal for attacks on the military by armed opposition groups. (Sri Lanka, 1996)

G. Thousands of people including monks, students, doctors, peasants supporting a democratically elected but subsequently banned political party are killed on the street by the military. (Myanmar, 1988)

continued

Why does 'disappearance' and extrajudicial execution take place?

H. Tens of thousands of civilians are massacred, 'disappeared' by security forces, state-armed militias and armed opposition forces calling themselves 'Islamic groups'. (Algeria, 1990s)

I. In the years after the genocide, thousands of civilians have been 'disappeared' or murdered with the complicity or involvement of the Army. (Rwanda 1996 to 1999)

J. More than 1,500 citizens, many of them active members of student, labour, religious, political and human rights organisations, were 'disappeared' by military and paramilitary groups under the military dictatorship and under democracy because of their suspected involvement in opposition groups. (Philippines, 1965 to 1992)

K. A Roman Catholic priest and his parents are among more than 27,000 people from religious and ethnic minority communities targeted for elimination, 'disappeared' or murdered by one of the armies in the conflict. (Bosnia-Herzegovina, 1995 to 1996)

L. Thousands of civilians from an ethnic minority community are 'disappeared' or killed by state military forces. (Albanians in Kosovo, Yugoslavia, 1998–9)

M. Hundreds of street children are murdered per year, many at the hands of the police. (Brazil, 1990s)

Tamil villagers in Sri Lanka in protest against 'disappearance'

Photocopy Original © Hodder & Stoughton 2001

Photocopy Original © Hodder & Stoughton 2001

ACTIVITY 3 INFORMATION SHEET
Where does 'disappearance' take place?

Amnesty International listed reports of enforced 'disappearance' in the following countries in its annual reports between 1993 and 1998.

Afghanistan	Iraq
Algeria	Kuwait
Angola	Libya
Argentina	Mexico
Bangladesh	Morocco
Bosnia	Mozambique
Brazil	Nepal
Burundi	Pakistan
Cambodia	Palestine
Chad	Papua
Columbia	Peru
Costa Rica	Philippines
Congo	Romania
Dominican Rep	Rwanda
Ecuador	Senegal
Eritrea	Sri Lanka
Ethiopia	Sudan
Gambia	Syria
Georgia	Tadjikistan
Greece	Togo
Guatemala	Turkey
Haiti	Uruguay
Honduras	Uzbekistan
India	Venezuela
Indonesia	Yemen
Iran	Yugoslavia

ACTIVITY 4 BRIEFING SHEET
Turkey – one country's 'disappearance'

1. TURKEY – WORLD LEADER FOR 'DISAPPEARANCE' IN 1994

In 1995 the United Nations Working Group on Enforced and Involuntary Disappearances stated that Turkey had been the country with the highest number of reported 'disappearances' in the world in 1994.

Turkey has tense relations with all its neighbours. The country has a long-standing dispute with Greece over Cyprus and has been occupying Northern Cyprus since 1974. Successive governments have engaged in violent conflict with the Kurdish population living within Turkey. Abuse of human rights in Turkey is well documented. Torture in custody is commonplace. Arbitrary detention is widespread. In 1994, 4,041 people lost their lives as a result of armed clashes and political killings by unknown assailants; in 1995 this figure was 4,576; in 1996, 3,440. Between November 1991 and mid-1995, the number of political prisoners soared from 900 to 10,000. Between 1992 and 1997 the number of 'disappearances' attributed to Turkish security forces is reported to have reached 500. Four out of five of the people who have 'disappeared' in custody have been Kurds.

Source: Campaign Against the Arms Trade Report 1997

2. AMNESTY INTERNATIONAL NEWS BRIEFING, 8 JUNE 1998

8 June 1998

TURKEY: Still no proper investigation into 'disappearances'

Amnesty International has received no reply from the Turkish Government concerning the 'disappearance' of Neslihan Uslu, Hasan Aydogan, Metin Andaç and Mehmet Mandal, who were last seen in Izmir on 31 March. This case was raised by Amnesty International Secretary General Pierre Sané on 27 April in a letter to the Turkish Prime Minister, Mesut Ylmaz, urging that reports of their 'disappearance' be promptly and impartially investigated, and that findings be made public. Amnesty International also submitted the case to the United Nations (UN) Working Group on Enforced and Involuntary Disappearance.

Amnesty International fears that the four have 'disappeared' are heightened by the fact that they are known to the police and have reportedly been threatened with death and 'disappearance' on numerous occasions. Their lawyers have made inquiries in person to Izmir State Security Court, Izmir State Prosecutor, Police Headquarters and local gendarmerie stations, but were told that the four persons are not held in any of these places. Their names are also not on the registers of Buca and Bergama prisons.

continued

FREEDOM!

3. THE STATE'S RESPONSE TO CAMPAIGNS AGAINST 'DISAPPEARANCE' IN TURKEY AND THE CONTINUING VIGILS

On 20 December 1996 the Turkish government established the 'Bureau for the Investigation of Disappearances'. It appeared, however, that its real purpose was not to establish the fate of the 'disappeared' but to discredit those concerned organisations and people whose call for thorough investigation along the lines indicated by the UN Declaration on the Protection of All Persons from Enforced Disappearance is an enduring embarrassment to the authorities.

Less than a month after its foundation the Bureau has published its findings on scores of allegations of 'disappearance', but these findings consist of one or two lines of official denial that the individual was ever detained. No serious investigations seem to have been carried out. For example, the report mentioned that Tevfik Kusun, who 'disappeared' on 29 November 1996 after being taken from the building site where he worked, was not held in police custody; but failed to mention that his body was found by a local highway on 7 January 1997. Similarly, the report stated that police archives had no record that Mahmut Mordeniz, who 'disappeared' on 28 November 1996, was detained but failed to note that family and others witnessed his detention by people who introduced themselves as police, that a local police unit confirmed that he had been detained, and that his wife also 'disappeared' the same day.

Such gross omissions, of which these are typical examples, confirm that the Bureau is no more than a publicity exercise.

Source: Amnesty International Press Release, June 1998

4. 1997 REUTERS INFORMATION SERVICE

Mothers in Istanbul demand word of missing persons

ISTANBUL (April 12, 1997) – For the 100th week, Turkey's 'Saturday Mothers' stood vigil in an Istanbul plaza, continuing their demand for an account of missing loved ones, a symbol of the country's record of human rights abuses.

About 200 people gathered on Saturday in the European heart of Istanbul, holding aloft black and white photographs of sons, daughters, fathers and brothers last seen in the hands of the security forces.

They have met there every Saturday since May 1995, and vow to carry on until the disappearances stop and their relatives are accounted for.

'We will come here each week until the missing are found', said the father of Hasan Ocak, whose body was later found in a municipal grave.

'We must find the bones of all the "disappeared".'

Turkey's Human Rights Association says it is investigating 792 reports of disappearances from 1992 through 1996. Amnesty International says *its* investigators have solid documentation of at least 135 cases.

continued

Photocopy Original © Hodder & Stoughton 2001

Turkey – one country's 'disappearance'

However, experts say many 'missing' go unreported altogether in nine restive eastern provinces, which remain under emergency rule restrictions.

Most are believed dead, either at the hands of the security forces or right-wing death squads. Rights workers say they have found some bodies that still bore the ink from police fingerprinting.

The authorities report they have no records of most of those said to be missing, suggesting many have joined outlawed guerrilla groups, such as the Kurdistan Workers Party, or are already in prison. Poor record-keeping complicates the search.

'Human dignity will defeat torture', chanted the Saturday Mothers. 'If you stay silent, they'll come for you next.'

Hasan Ocak's mother in protest of the 'Saturday Mothers', Istanbul, June 1998

Photocopy Original © Hodder & Stoughton 2001

188

FREEDOM!

ACTIVITY 7 POETRY
'Will and Testament'
by Ariel Dorfman

When they tell you
that I am not a prisoner,
do not believe them.
They will have to acknowledge
it sometime.

When they tell you
that they let me free
do not believe them.
They will have to acknowledge
that it was a lie
sometime.

When they tell you
that I betrayed the Party,
do not believe them.
They will have to acknowledge
that I was loyal
sometime.

Don't believe them,
don't believe
anything they tell you
anything they swear to you
anything they show you
don't believe them.

And when finally
the day will arrive
when they will ask you to come in
to recognise the corpse
and you see me there
and a voice will say
'we killed him
he faded out in the torture
he is dead'
when they tell you
that I am
entirely absolutely definitely
dead
don't believe them
don't believe them
don't believe them.

Mothers of the 'disappeared', Buenos Aires, Argentina

Photocopy Original © Hodder & Stoughton 2001

ACTIVITY 7 SONG
'The Missing' by Ruben Blades

Somebody tell me if they've seen my husband
His name is Ernesto;
He is 40 years old
He works as a watchman
Where they sell cars
He was wearing a dark shirt
Light pants
He left two nights ago
And has not returned
And now I don't know what to think
Because this has not happened before

I have been searching for my sister
These past three days
Her name is Altagracia
After her grandmother
She left work to go to school
She was dressed in jeans
And a white blouse
Her boyfriend has not seen her
He is in his house
They don't know of her at the police
Nor in the hospital

Someone tell me if they have seen my son
He is a student of pre-medicine
His name is Agustin
And he is a good boy
Although sometimes obstinate
In his opinions
He has been detained
I don't know by which force
... white-pants, striped shirt ...
It happened day before yesterday

She is a woman of God
She bothers no-one
Yet she has been taken away
As a witness
For a matter that has to do
only with me

Photocopy Original © Hodder & Stoughton 2001

continued

FREEDOM!

'The Missing' by Ruben Blades

I gave myself up this afternoon
And now nobody knows where she is

Last night I heard explosions
Shots from a shotgun and revolver
Speeding cars
Brakes screeching, screams
The echo of boots in the street
A door was beat upon ...
Moans, begging, broken dishes
It was time for the soap opera on television,
So nobody looked outside

Where have the missing gone?
Look in the water and in the bushes
Why is it they are missing?
Because we are not all equal
When is it they return?
Each time our thoughts bring them back.

Panama 1990

Translated by Dan Jones

Photocopy Original © Hodder & Stoughton 2001

ACTIVITY 8 TESTIMONY 1
Adriana Borquez

Adriana Borquez (1936–) was educated at the University of Chile and trained as a teacher. She became involved in community work among shanty-town dwellers, and took up adult literacy work. As a devout Christian she wished to share their experiences, in 1975 under the military regime of General Pinochet, she was abducted and became a 'desaparecido' (disappeared person). She was first tortured in a Santiago prison, then in a notorious secret 'safe house' of Colonia Dignidad, in a large house which had been converted into a detention centre. She escaped by a subterfuge after being held for three months, and clandestinely fled the country.

'To be free is to have the ability and the opportunity of choosing at decisive moments in your life. I know that very well. I realised it with intensity for the first time in my life at the Colonia Dignidad. It was when I was tied to the grid and received the first electric shocks which shook my body. During these moments I chose and that made me free forever. I could have talked, and so betrayed my friends, fellows and the organisation to which I belong, and by doing so deny my struggle and my principles. Or I could have assumed the responsibility of my convictions, my values, my actions and my words and confronted torture without denunciation, without accusation, without escaping behind the shield of someone else's orders. At this moment I chose to be faithful to the direction of my life, not to drag others into the hell that I was suffering, not to put them on the tracks which would have led to the destruction of the organisation. I chose to die there if it were necessary. I freed myself then because I felt bound to the principles of honour and decency, and because I felt afraid of the idea of having to assume the shame of treachery. On the other hand, I also realised that never again would I be able to give myself completely, unreservedly to people, because this act of freedom of mine has put a barrier between the others – as I can't know how they will choose at any given time – and me, who chose the way of freedom (and loneliness). We, the "disappeared ones" are exactly that, "disappeared". Without any known existence, without even the right to be able to do anything, because to do something is a way of recapturing your own identity. The reality is that in some way we are nothing. We have no reference, we are not here, and yet we do exist, with great intensity, and we are here.'

Photocopy Original © Hodder & Stoughton 2001

ACTIVITY 8 TESTIMONY 2
Mohammed Nadrani

Mohammed Nadrani was one of the hundreds of left-wing students, workers and intellectuals who were arrested in Morocco during a wave of government repression between 1974 and 1976. Many of those arrested were sentenced to long terms of imprisonment. But Nadrani, like scores of other Moroccans, and many hundreds of Sahrawi detainees from the Western Sahara, was never officially arrested and never brought to trial. He was simply 'disappeared'. He was held in a secret centre in Rabat where he was tortured. He was held under guard in a small cell for 16 months continually blindfolded and handcuffed day and night. In 1977 they took him to clandestine jails in Agdz, and in Kalaât-M'Gouna, that were also used to house many Sahrawi 'disappeared' detainees whose existence was denied by the Moroccan authorities. He was kept in a cell in total isolation for 18 months. Finally, after nine years as a 'disappeared' prisoner in secret detention he was released without charge on 31 December 1984.

'The secret police came for me, I was one of those who "disappeared". Time stood still. In the darkness my body felt as if it had been seized by a gigantic wave and swept down into an abyss. The shouting of my torturers seemed to come from some distant depths. I'd never felt so close to death. My torturers continued pouring water over my head. They beat the soles of my feet, my thighs, my whole body. I could only think of one thing: I was going to die, drowned, suffocated. I struggled to remove the cloth which covered my face and was stopping me from breathing. But it was too strong a system meticulously planned by the malevolent spirit of the torturers.

Regaining consciousness, I found myself lying on the floor. I didn't know how long I'd been lying there, unconscious, inert. My torturers hovered around me, trying hard to revive me. I couldn't stop vomiting. My whole body was trembling. I was very cold.

Someone had redressed me in my trousers and red shirt. As I was no longer able to walk, they carried me to my cell. I continued to shake under a blanket. I tried not to think about them, but it was impossible.

They had brutally forced themselves into my life. They came into my house confiscated my keys, my watch, my papers. From this time on, my body belonged to them. My present and my future was in their hands. They fiercely and unrelentingly tried to extract the details of my past.

I recalled the faces of my companions and the smile of my beloved. Why won't they let me die? I heard approaching footsteps in the corridor. My entrails rose to my throat, I was sick to my stomach. Curled up, I was contorted with pain. I

continued

Photocopy Original © Hodder & Stoughton 2001

am thirsty. I want to drink, I said, without thinking, to a man who had come to pull me off of the campbed.

All the water which you swallowed wasn't enough? Alright, we will start again, he replied.

Never will I forget the nightmare of the complex at Rabat, the hell of the prisons of Agdz and Kalâat M'Gouna. Never will I forget those who told us, "You are here to die". Never will I forget the martyrs, victims of the blind oppression of Morocco's MAKHZEN.'

Mohammed Nadrani, Kalâat M'gouna – Disappeared under the Roses *Amnesty International 1995*

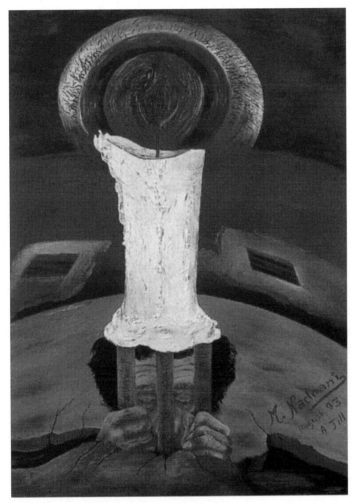

Painting by Mohammed Nadrani

Photocopy Original © Hodder & Stoughton 2001

FREEDOM!

ACTIVITY 8 TESTIMONY 3
Alicia Partnoy

Alicia Partnoy (1955–) was born in Argentina and was among up to 30,000 Argentinians who 'disappeared' after the military junta came to power in 1976.

She was a student, active in the Peronist Youth Movement.

'On January 12, 1977, at noon, I was detained by uniformed Army personnel at my home, Canada Street 240, Apt. 2, Bahia Blanca; minutes later the same military personnel detained my husband at his place of work. I was taken to the headquarters of the 5th Army Corps and from there to a concentration camp, which the military ironically named The Little School *(La Escuelita)*. We had no knowledge of the fate of Ruth, our daughter. From that moment on, for the next five months, my husband and I became two more names on the endless list of "disappeared" people. When it rained, the water streamed into the rooms and soaked us. When the temperature fell below zero, we were covered with only dirty blankets; when the heat was unbearable, we were obligated to blanket even our heads. We were forced to remain silent and prone, often immobile or face down for many hours, our eyes blindfolded and our wrists tightly bound. We went without food for 18 consecutive hours daily. We were constantly hungry. We ate our meals blindfolded, sitting on the bed, plate in lap.

When we were thirsty, we asked for water, receiving only threats or blows in response. For talking, we were punished with blows from a billy jack, punches, or removal of our mattresses. The atmosphere of violence was constant. The guards put guns to our heads or mouths and pretended to pull the trigger. After three and a half months I was transferred from The Little School to another place where I remained "disappeared" for 52 more days. The isolation was complete and the risk of being killed the same. By June 1977, my family was informed of my whereabouts. I "re-appeared" but remained a political prisoner for two and a half more years. I could see my daughter, and I knew that my husband had also survived. I never discovered why the military had spared my life.'

Alicia Partnoy, The Little School – Tales of Disappearance and Survival in Argentina, *Virago Press 1988*

Photocopy Original © Hodder & Stoughton 2001

ACTIVITY 9 TESTIMONY 1
Grandmothers of the Plaza de Mayo

We work for our children and for all of the children of future generations in the world, in order to preserve their identity, their roots and their history, the fundamental basis for human dignity.

The Grandmothers of the Plaza de Mayo (May Square) is an organisation of relatives of the victims of 'disappearance' in Argentina. Their aim is to locate their grandchildren who were stolen from their daughters in the secret prisons of Argentina under the military dictatorship. The daughters were then 'disappeared'. The grandmothers aim to restore the stolen children to their legitimate families, to create the conditions in which such abuses will never occur again, and demand punishment for all those responsible.

Grandmothers' protest, Plaza de Mayo, Buenos Aires

ABDUCTED CHILDREN IN ARGENTINA

When in 1976, the armed forces seized control of the government of Argentina, they began to implement a systematic plan of destruction and of violation of the most fundamental human rights. Among the 30,000 'disappeared' were hundreds of children, kidnapped along with their parents or born in the secret detention centres where their pregnant mothers had been taken. Many of the children were fraudulently registered as children of members of the military; others were abandoned, or left in institutions as children whose identity was unknown, depriving them of their rights, their freedom and their natural families. In 20 years of uninterrupted search we have been able to localise 58 'disappeared' children, of whom eight had been assassinated, 31 are living with their true families. The others are in close contact with their grandparents, or in the process of adaptation, having been recovered their true identity and the true story of their lives. Some of these cases are still in process in the Justice Department.

Photocopy Original © Hodder & Stoughton 2001

ACTIVITY 9 TESTIMONY 2
Father Jon de Cortina

THE 'DISAPPEARED' CHILDREN OF EL SALVADOR

A Jesuit priest working in El Salvador since 1968, Father Jon de Cortina is co-founder of the Association in Search of 'Disappeared' Children. Working with the Boston-based human rights group Physicians for Human Rights, Father Jon's group is trying to trace the many Salvadorean children who were abducted from their families by the military during the 12-year civil war in El Salvador. They have managed to trace over 200 of these children already. The stolen children's ultimate destinations have included the United States, Europe, Honduras and urban El Salvador. Many of those traced have been adopted by middle-class or wealthy families who had been told the children were war orphans.

Salvadorean soldiers seized the children from their families in the conflict zones, and took them away in helicopter gunships, or sometimes brought in babies and school-age children by the carload telling relief workers the children had been abandoned, or their parents had been killed. US officials and workers in international rescue agencies had reason to suspect that some of the children had been stolen – to terrorise civilians into submission or to be sold for adoption. The US Embassy granted 2,354 visas for Salvadorean children adopted during the war. The majority may have not been kidnapped, but Father Jon has listened to enough anguish from Salvadorean parents to know that some are, and that his search is justified.

'Our objective is to find the children. We do not want to take them away from their adoptive families or create problems for them, but the youngsters have a right to know who they are; their identity should be fulfilled. Their families have a right to know how their own children are.'

Photocopy Original © Hodder & Stoughton 2001

Genocide

7

UNIT AIMS

This unit aims to:

- explain the term 'genocide' and other related terms
- explore some historical examples of genocide
- outline some examples of genocide in the 20th century and examine their causes
- examine the process of establishing a permanent International Criminal Court
- enable students to explore their own experience of 'difference' and diversity

INTRODUCTION

This unit looks at intolerance, racism and genocidal behaviours. Some students may have experience of genocide as refugees or within their family history (which will clearly need to be taken into account in the selection of materials for use); while to other students genocide may seem incomprehensible, something that only happens somewhere else in the world.

This unit attempts to make links between:

- the ideology of 'race' and extreme nationalism
- imperialism and genocides past and present
- intolerance and scapegoating on a personal, local scale and genocidal behaviours on a larger scale.

Throughout this unit, students are asked to consider the individual's responsibility for society's actions and to think about these issues as they relate to their lives.

The material and information provided is necessarily selective. The unit is divided under three linked headings: *What is genocide?* explains the terminology, and explores the genocides commited by colonial powers and some of the major genocides of the 20th century: the Holocaust, East Timor,

Srebrenica, Rwanda and Burundi; *The worst crimes in the world* examines the purpose and potential effectiveness of establishing an International Criminal Court; *Difference* asks students to explore their own experience of being 'different' or of excluding others. It looks at how something potentially positive, like a strong sense of identity, can become exclusive and therefore dangerous. Racism in the UK, and the way in which refugees are treated, are considered here.

Many other examples of genocide are suggested which could be further researched by students; Sven Lindqvist's *Exterminate All the Brutes*, is an excellent and accessible source of further information and analysis.

You may also want to go back to Unit 1 and use the section on the United Nations to explore the role, responsibility and behaviour of the international community in response to recent genocides.

Finally, Unit 7 aims to encourage students to reflect on our inter-connectedness; our individual uniqueness and yet our common humanity; our need to belong; our potential to recognise what we share, to value the differences in each other and to promote inclusion and celebrate diversity.

SUMMARY OF TOPICS

TITLE	CURRICULUM LINKS	PAGE
PART 1: WHAT IS GENOCIDE?		
1. Some definitions of genocide	14+: English/PSHE/Pastoral/History: e.g. KS4 – Racism, citizenship and treatment of minorities, persecution of the Jews/Law/RE	*199/205*
Citizenship	**Knowledge and Understanding:** *legal and human rights and responsibilities*	
2. History of genocide	14+: PSHE/Pastoral/History: e.g. 'A' level History – Africa, economic and strategic considerations behind imperialism . . . the role of the press and the Boers/Geography/English/RE	*199/209*
3. Genocide in the 20th century	14+: PSHE/Pastoral/Sociology/History: e.g. KS4 – Hitler, Nazism and Nazi beliefs/English/RE	*199/211*
Citizenship	**Knowledge and Understanding:** *Challenges of global interdependence and responsibility, legal and human rights* **Key Skills:** *IT* **Enquiry Skills:** *researching evidence from different sources*	
4. Survivors – witness accountsof genocide	14+: PSHE/Pastoral/Sociology/History/Geography/English/Drama/Theatre Studies	*200/220*
Citizenship	**Knowledge and Understanding:** *legal and human rights, operation of criminal justice system* **Enquiry Skills:** *critical approach to evidence, contemporary issues* **Key Skills:** *IT*	
PART 2: THE WORST CRIMES IN THE WORLD		
5. International Criminal Court	16+: PSHE/Pastoral/Sociology/History/English/Law/Theatre Studies/Drama	*201/226*
PART 3: DIFFERENCE		
6. Identity	13+: PSHE/Pastoral/Sociology/English/Drama/Theatre Studies/RE	*201/—*
Citizenship	**Knowledge and Understanding:** *origins and implications of diverse national/ethnic identities in the UK, need for mutual respect and understanding* **Participation Skills:** *considering others' experiences, reflecting on process of participation* **Enquiry Skills:** *contributing to group discussion*	
7. Groups	13+: PSHE/Pastoral/Sociology/English/Drama/Theatre Studies/RE	*201/—*
8. Outsiders	13+: PSHE/Pastoral/Sociology/English/Geography/History/Drama/Theatre Studies/RE/Art/Media Studies	*202/—*
9. What is racism?	13+: PSHE/Pastoral/Sociology/History/Geography/English/Drama/Theatre Studies/Art/RE	*202/228*
Citizenship	**Knowledge and Understanding:** *origins and implications of the diverse national, ethnic identities in the UK, need for respect and understanding* **Key Skills:** *communication, IT* **Participation Skills:** *critically evaluating ideas that are not their own*	

ACTIVITIES: NOTES TO TEACHERS

Part 1: What is genocide?

Activity 1: Some definitions of genocide

Ask students to work in small groups to share what they know about these words:
● race ● ethnicity ● genocide ● ethnic cleansing ● nationalism.

Ask them to discuss the contexts in which they have heard these terms being used.

Give students the definitions on the four fact sheets to read. The whole class can then discuss:

● Do you consider that you are a member of an 'ethnic group'? Do you think there are distinct 'ethnic groups' in society? What are the possible benefits and dangers of making such distinctions?

● Has the term 'genocide' been devalued by over-use for propaganda in recent conflicts?

● What message does the term 'ethnic cleansing' convey? What other euphemisms do you know (e.g. 'collateral damage' for civilian casualties of bombing)?

● Is pride in your nationality the same as nationalism?

Activity 2: History of genocide

Give students the fact sheet 'History of genocide'.

Ask pairs to share their initial thoughts and feelings. Small groups can make a list of the key factors which led to the genocides described. They can then discuss:

● What do you think the writer Sven Lindqvist means by saying 'Colonial massacres like this and many others led the way to the Holocaust'?

● Why has the scale of massacres in the 20th century been so vast?

● Could America have existed without genocide?

FURTHER ACTIVITIES

● Write a poem of lament for the Guanches or Hereros.

● Create a drama or piece of art called 'Voices of the ghosts of genocide'.

● Research the history of some other pre-20th century genocides, and how these communities have fought for their rights and survival in the 20th century, e.g. Aborigines in Australia, indigenous peoples in the Americas.

Activity 3: Genocide in the 20th century

Give students the fact sheet 'Factors which make genocide more likely'. They can read the four different case studies. They may want to discuss their thoughts and feelings. Groups can use the information to investigate these questions.

● Why do you think this genocide happened?

● Which factors from the fact sheet apply in this case? Were there other factors?

● Was the country's government involved and if so, why?

● Can you think of any steps which might have been taken to stop the genocide occurring?

● Could genocide happen in any country in the world? Could it happen here?

● Brainstorm your ideas about the most important factors in preventing the growth of racial/ethnic hatred.

FURTHER ACTIVITIES

Find East Timor on the map. Research its natural resources.

● Visit the Amnesty International website (**www.amnesty.org/ailib/aipub**) to find out the current situation in East Timor.

- Find out about the 'Seeds of Hope – East Timor Ploughshares', a peace action group in the UK. In July 1996 four women were tried for damaging British Aerospace Hawk aircraft that they said were to be used by the Indonesian military in East Timor. In the trial all four were acquitted after arguing that they had used justifiable force to prevent genocide. Make a poster about their action. Devise a short play in which the women defend their action.
- Write a song commemorating the hundreds of young people massacred by the Indonesian military at a funeral service at Santa Cruz, Dili in 1991 (featured in the Amnesty International film *A Small Window*).
- Find out more about the UK's sale of weapons. Find out UK government policy on arms sales and exports. Hold a debate on the statement 'It is not arms which kill people, it's people who kill people', with witness testimonies from various people in role (e.g. an arms trader, an employee who makes tanks, a member of the UK Government, a diplomat and a victim of repression from the country that received the weapons).
- Research and discuss the reasons why the international community took no action on the invasion of East Timor in 1975 in contrast to its action when Iraq invaded Kuwait.
- In case study 4, 'Genocide in Rwanda and Burundi', what is meant by the statement that the international community did not protest 'lest condemnation lead to action'? Why do you think the international reaction to the genocidal behaviour in Kosovo in 1999 was different?
- Go to the website of Human Rights Watch: www.hrw.org/ and find the full text of the report on Rwanda, 'Leave None to Tell the Story'.
- Investigate other genocides and 'ethnic cleansings' of the 20th century: Armenians in Turkey; Cambodia 1974; Tibetans in China; Tartars in the Soviet Union; Kurds – in Turkey, Iran, Iraq; The Marsh Arabs in Iraq; Bangladesh and Pakistan in 1971.

Activity 4: Survivors – witness accounts of genocide

Give students 'Barbara's story' to read. Ask students to share their initial reactions. Then ask:

- Why did Barbara think the female guards were worse than the men?
- What physical and mental scars might the survivors of such inhumane treatment have to bear? What might they need to be able to carry on surviving?
- What reasons can you think of to explain how vast numbers of ordinary people actively participated in the death camps and genocide?

Give students the poem 'If this is a man' by Primo Levi (case study 2) to read. Pairs can discuss: What is the central message of the poem? Do you think the poem is purely about the Holocaust? What do you notice about the language or imagery?

Put the paragraph starting 'there is no rationality in the Nazi hatred . . .' into your own words.

In 1958 Primo Levi said 'It will not happen to us a second time'. In 1978 he said 'what happened can happen again'. Do you think he changed his mind? Why?

Give students 'Stories from Rwanda' to read. Ask:

- What reasons are given about factors which led to the genocide?
- What most saddens each person he talks to?
- What does Joseph mean when he says 'the country is empty'?
- What signs of hope for Rwanda does the writer describe?

FURTHER ACTIVITIES

- Find out about the Holocaust from: Holocaust Education Foundation (**www.holocaust-trc.org**); The Anne Frank Educational Trust UK (**www.afet.org.uk**); The US Holocaust Memorial Museum (**www.ushmm.org/education**).
- Write a poem or drama script to commemorate the courage of the Rwandan schoolgirls.
- Write an essay exploring why genocide has continued since the Holocaust, despite the international community's resolve never to let it happen again.
- What steps could be taken when there is a danger of genocide in a country?

Part 2: The worst crimes in the world
Activity 5: International Criminal Court

Discuss what is meant by 'the worst crimes in the world'.

Give out the fact sheet. Ask students to list points for and against a permanent International Criminal Court (ICC). Discuss:

- What about the countries which argue they are responsible for their own internal affairs?
- Do those who try international criminals have to be blameless?
- 'I was only obeying orders' – is this a valid defence?

Students can then choose a scenario to role play and present to the rest of the class:

- United Nations delegates from Senegal and the United States debate the US refusal to ratify the statute of the International Criminal Court.
- A meeting between a family member of a Nazi war criminal who argues he is too old to be tried and a person whose family perished in the Holocaust.

FURTHER ACTIVITIES

- Find out (from Amnesty International website: **www.amnesty.org.uk**) how many nations have ratified the Statute of the International Criminal Court.
- Research the history of the International War Crimes Tribunals at Nuremberg and Tokyo, and the ad hoc Tribunals for Rwanda and Former Yugoslavia in the 1990s.

Part 3: Difference
Activity 6: Identity

Before the session, ask students to bring in photographs, personal momentoes and other materials to make a collage about themselves and their identity. What is their name, what does it mean, where did it come from, important relationships, their heritage, groups they are a part of, qualities/abilities they are proud of, where they live, countries they have links with, things that are important to them, significant events in their lives, aspirations for the future.

Ask individual students to write down five words which describe their identity. Share these in pairs; discuss choices, similarities and differences in the words they have chosen.

They can share these in small groups.

Give each student a list of names of the other students in the class. See if they can match one aspect of their own identity with something from each other person in the class. Then discuss:

- What aspects of identity did they share with others? Did any of the matches surprise them?
- What aspects of identity were unique to them as individuals?
- What are the things that are immediately obvious about each individual's identity?
- Have other people ever made prejudiced assumptions about them because of aspects of their identity, e.g. looks/clothes, gender, race, nationality, religion, disability?
- Did they/could they challenge the prejudice?
- Do they think race and nationality are important aspects of their identity? If so, what are the benefits and dangers of this?

Activity 7: Groups

Ask individuals to make a list of all the groups they belong to. In pairs, they can then discuss one or more of the important groups listed, using the following questions to aid discussion:

- How/why you're a member of this group – did you choose to belong to it?
- What do you like about being a member of this group? What do you dislike?
- Can anyone join this group or is it 'exclusive'? What criteria are there?
- Does this group have 'rules', rituals, codes of behaviour? What do you think of these?
- Is there a 'leader' in your group? How does s/he influence the group?
- Are there things about the group you'd like to change?
- What happens when your group comes into contact with a different group?
- Do you, or other people in the group, behave differently when all the group members are there compared to when only two or three of you are together?

- Have you ever done something as a member of a group that you have regretted later? Why do you think this happened?

As a whole class, discuss the following questions:

- What are the important groups that almost everyone has identified?
- What are the benefits of being a member of a group?
- Are there limitations or drawbacks of belonging to certain groups?
- Do other people stereotype any of the groups you belong to? If so, why?
- Have many people put down the racial group they belong to? Why/why not?
- Why do human beings need to belong to groups? Can belonging to a group be dangerous?
- What are the benefits and dangers of having a strong leader in a group?
- What makes some groups very powerful whilst other groups are relatively powerless?
- Which groups use patriotism to define themselves? When is this positive?
- Why is local or national identity important to football team supporters?
- What can you do about groups which exist and which you think are dangerous?

Activity 8: Outsiders

Ask individuals to think of a time when they have been made to feel like an 'outsider', that they didn't 'belong' or were in some way 'different' and inferior. Ask pairs to discuss the experience, using the following questions if they wish:

- What was said or done to make you feel like an 'outsider'?
- How did you feel at the time? How do you feel about it now?
- What do you think the people involved felt about excluding you? Why do you think they behaved like this? Do you think they were strong or weak?
- What could you say or do in a similar situation now?

As a class, brainstorm examples in the past or present, of groups of people in society who have been, or are, treated as being 'different', inferior, 'outsiders'. Ask small groups to choose one of the examples from the past to research. They can then create a short drama in which they tell the stories of different individuals belonging to this group, for example:

- French Huguenot refugees coming to England in 1685
- Irish settlers escaping the Great Famine in 1845
- People with mental and physical illnesses locked up in 'lunatic asylums' (18th to 20th century)
- People from South Asia, Italy, Cyprus, the Caribbean, China, Ireland invited to Britain to fill job vacancies in the 1950s
- Unmarried women locked up in mental institutions for having babies (early 20th century)
- Gay men and lesbians given electric shock treatment to 'cure' them (20th century)

Discussion questions:

- Why do you think a society needs or wants to define some of its members as 'outsiders'?
- What problems are there for which societies want to find 'scapegoats'? What are the reasons for scapegoating? Which groups are most vulnerable to being scapegoated?
- What are the effects of this on the individuals scapegoated? On the whole society?
- Do you think there is such a thing as 'Britishness'? If so, is it inclusive or exclusive?
- Is there an English national identity? How is it different from Welsh, Scottish or Irish?
- Which groups of people in Britain feel a stong regional identity? Why?
- Norman Tebbit MP, a Conservative politician, said that the test of whether you were British or not was which nation's cricket team you supported. Do you agree or disagree with this?

Activity 9: What is racism?

Ask small groups to write a short definition of racism. The whole class can then read information sheet and share examples that they have heard about, witnessed or experienced.

Give groups the quiz sheet, and then look at the answers sheet as a whole class. They can discuss their reactions: did anything surprise them?

Groups can brainstorm ways of preventing racism, and design posters.

FURTHER ACTIVITIES

- Find out about the racist murder of Stephen Lawrence, the trials and the enquiry. (Stephen Lawrence Family Campaign: **www.blink.org.uk/campaign/stevelaw/slmain.htm**) Research the findings of the MacPherson Report. What progress has been done to implement the recommendations? Visit **www.bbc.co.uk**
- Paint a picture or write a poem in memory of Stephen Lawrence or other people in the UK who have been murdered just because of their 'race'.
- Visit the Runnymede Trust's website: **www.britkid.org** for more quizzes, games and information on challenging racism in Britain.

Activity 10: The Roma – welcome to Britain?

Ask small groups to brainstorm phrases they associate with the word 'gypsy'. Divide these words into negative, and positive.

Ask:

- Are the words mainly positive or negative?
- Where do you think your ideas/images came from?
- What do you know to be factually true about the culture/lifestyle/history of 'gypsies'?
- Are there 'travellers' who aren't 'gypsies'? What ideas/images do you have about 'travellers'? Why might people want to adopt a travelling lifestyle?

Give students the fact sheet 'The Roma: 'Welcome to Britain?' to read in pairs. Ask them to make notes on:

- Feelings and thoughts about what they have read.
- Do they find anything surprising?
- Which articles of the UDHR are breached by the treatment of Roma in Central Europe?
- Do they think it matters what names are used to describe a group of people?
- What words would they use to describe the attitudes of settled people over the centuries to the Roma? What feelings do they think lie behind these attitudes?

Give groups the following statements to discuss and to agree a diamond rank order from 'most agree' to 'most disagree'. They can then share their decisions, and discuss their ideas as a whole class.

- The media is responsible for the racist attacks against Roma in Britain.
- Asylum seekers shouldn't be made too comfortable.
- All societies need to scapegoat some groups as 'outsiders'.
- People seeking asylum should do everything they can to 'fit in'.
- Racist behaviour is the same as genocidal behaviour.
- Genocidal behaviour could never happen in Britain.

FURTHER ACTIVITIES

- Research the 1999 Asylum and Immigration Act and the current treatment of asylum seekers in Britain (visit The Refugee Council **www.refugeecouncil.org.uk**). Write an essay on immigration controls.
- Find out more about the experiences of Roma people in Europe from:
  - Minority Rights Group: **www.minorityrights.org**
  - Romnews Network of the Roma National Congress: **www.romnews.com**
- Write a short play in which a Roma family moves next door to a British Asian family.
- Find out about English words with Romani origins. Or any place names in your area which show that 'gypsies' have lived there in the past (such as Gypsy Hill in South London).
- Find out about your local council's provision for travellers.
- Find out about 'gypsy' music and how it is connected to other forms of world music.
- Design a poster which shows that asylum seekers are welcome.
- Find out about the cricket knowledge test which fans travelling from Asia had to pass before being granted British visas to see the World Cup in May 1999 (no restrictions were applied to South African, Australian and New Zealand fans). Write a short comedy sketch about this.

204

Activity 11: I did not speak ...

Ask students to read the poem by Martin Niemoller and then in pairs:

- Sum up the central message of this poem in a sentence.
- Who is 'they' in the poem?
- Do they find the poem effective?
- Think of some everyday situations in which people do not speak out against oppression or injustice. Role-play the situations, with one student giving reasons for not speaking out, and the other putting forward reasons to speak out.

ACTIVITY 1 FACT SHEET 1
Genocide

Raphael Lemkin – whose whole family was murdered because they were Jews in Poland – created the term 'genocide' in 1944. He used it to describe the mass murder of millions of Jews, Slavs, gypsies and others in the parts of Europe occupied by the Nazis. Lemkin's definition of genocide was 'the destruction of a nation or an ethnic group'. The word is made up of *genos* from Greek, meaning a race or tribe, and *cide* from Latin *caedere*, to slay.

Genocide involves:

1. the deliberate intention to annihilate an entire ethnic group;
2. very large numbers of people killed.

When there is clearly an attack on an ethnic group but on a less overwhelming scale, the international community uses the term 'genocidal behaviour'.

'After the defeat of Nazi Germany in 1945, the newly created United Nations Organisation set out to make "genocide" illegal. In December 1948 it drew up the UN Convention on the Prevention and Punishment of the Crime of Genocide, which declared that "genocide whether committed in time of peace or in time of war, is a crime under international law".

The Convention describes genocide as acts "committed with intent to destroy, in whole or in part, a national, ethnic, racial or religious group". Genocide is defined not only as the killing of members of a particular group but also:
- causing them serious bodily or mental harm
- inflicting conditions of life on them that might lead to death
- trying to stop them having children
- taking their children away and giving them to another group to bring up.'
From: R. G. Grant, Talking Points: Genocide, *Wayland, 1998*

Some organisations consider the definition of genocide too narrow as it does not include the mass killing of people due to their social, economic or political group. Millions were murdered on such grounds in the Soviet Union under Stalin, in China in the Cultural Revolution, and in Cambodia under the Khmer Rouge. Another wider definition of genocide includes 'cultural genocide' – the destruction of a way of life, resulting in the disappearance of a distinct group. This has happened to many 'first peoples' in the world, such as the Kayapo in the Brazilian rainforest, or aboriginal peoples in Australia.

ACTIVITY 1 FACT SHEET 2
Race

The term 'race' when applied to people means a group with common genetically transmitted physical characteristics, such as skin colour, which distinguish them from others. The idea that human beings can be divided into separate and distinct biological races is rejected by biologists. It is now generally accepted that all people in the world belong to one race and have a common ancestor who lived in Africa some 200,000 years ago. The physical differences in people around the world are caused by their adaptation over thousands of years to different environments.

'Scientific' explanations of racial difference were put forward by 19th-century Europeans who drew up lists and hierarchies of 'race'. These were used to justify the European conquest of most of the world. These 'scientists' also suggested that producing children of 'mixed race' was dangerous and must be prevented by keeping racial groups 'pure'. In 1835 the French diplomat Joseph Arthur Gobineau wrote an influential essay, 'The Inequality of the Human Races', claiming that the 'Aryan Race' (which he defined as white Europeans of the blond Nordic type) was a superior race. (Aryan is an Indian Sanskrit word meaning 'noble'.) In 1850 the Scottish anatomist Robert Knox argued, with no scientific evidence, that 'the dark races' were 'inferior' and destined for 'extinction'. Such ideas of 'scientific racism', 'eugenic' theories, and an obsession with the myth of 'higher and lower races' led to the Nazi ideas of blood and racial purity and to the murder of six million people in the Holocaust.

The United Nations Education, Science and Cultural Organisation (UNESCO) asked leading geneticists in the 1950s to undertake a study of human beings and the realities of biological 'race'. They found that:
- the idea of 'racial purity' was myth;
- there are no distinct 'races' of people with different internal, biological capacities, in brain power, body functions and natural abilities;
- there are no harmful biological effects of 'mixed race' parentage;
- 'race' is less a biological than a social fact;
- the genetic differences between members of the same 'race' (such as 'caucasians' like Scandinavians and Greeks) are often greater than those between members of different 'races'.

Although 'race' is an invention without biological meaning, physical difference does still have very real social meaning. Racial identity may be something in which many people take pride. However, even in a multi-racial society, people are oppressed, excluded, attacked or killed, because of racially defined difference.

ACTIVITY 1 FACT SHEET 3
Ethnicity

'Ethnic' literally means the same as 'racial'. The term is derived from the Greek word *ethnos* meaning 'race'. The term 'ethnicity' is often used instead of 'race' because it is used to refer to cultural and social as well as physical characteristics. An 'ethnic group' is any group of people (whether a minority or not) with a distinct culture or way of life, expressed for instance through language, music, religion, food, customs and attitudes. 'Ethnic minorities' are groups of people in a community whose culture or cultural origin is in some way distinct from those of the majority of society. This kind of 'labelling' can be a source of pride but also can exaggerate and strengthen divisions between people. While everyone has an ethnic identity, the word 'ethnic' has been used in a derogatory way by white people to refer to black people, often to suggest differences that are inferior, quaint, curious.

After the collapse of the Soviet Union, there have been many revivals of separate 'ethnic identities' expressed in nationalism in European Europe. In the 1990s, for instance, the Federal Republic of Yugoslavia, a country whose peoples were an extraordinarily complex mixture of different religions and to some extent different cultures and ethnic origins, began to splinter into separate smaller states constructed around 'ethnicity'.

'ETHNIC CLEANSING'
In order to try to get control of as much territory as possible the different cultural groups in Yugoslavia started to push minority groups out of 'their' areas to keep them 'pure'. Because communities had lived together for many generations and intermarried, many families have members with different 'ethnic origins'. It was impossible for them to see themselves as part of one or another group and they were caught in tragic situations.

The term used to describe such mass expulsion of minorities is 'ethnic cleansing' (based on the term 'racial cleansing' used by the Nazis). Such expulsions are not the same as genocide, although in many cases they were also accompanied by patterns of genocidal behaviour as whole communities were massacred in Bosnia-Herzegovina and Kosovo. The term 'ethnic cleansing' is now commonly used to describe large-scale attacks on minorities, such as the expulsion and murder of people of Chinese origin from areas of Indonesia in 1998.

The ideas behind ethnic cleansing and genocide are linked. The word 'exterminate' comes from the Latin word *exterminare* meaning historically to 'drive over the border'.

ACTIVITY 1 FACT SHEET 4
Nationalism

'Nationalism' is an ideology that seeks to make the political boundaries of a state the same as the area where a particular 'nation' lives. Nationalists consider 'nations' as distinct because their people belong to a distinct ethnic group, or have their own language, culture or religion. But few areas of the world have a 'pure' population, because throughout human history people have moved around.

'Nationalism' involves a strong sense of national identity, and pride in and devotion to one's nation and its interests. To be a nationalist means being loyal to the 'people' (the ethnic, cultural or linguistic group with which one identifies) and wanting the country where one lives to have a separate identity.

Historically, nationalism has been the driving force behind anti-colonial liberation movements. At the turn of the 21st century, nationalism has again become a very important one. As the world becomes more and more dominated by global communications, global finance and international laws and institutions, small nations are asserting their right to separate identity. They are determined to run their own affairs in the way which is right for them.

But nationalism is an idea which has two faces. It can be a very dangerous ideology, leading to conflict and oppression. Because of its association with ideas of 'purity', nationalism has often led to the persecution of minority groups within a country. Extremist racist organisations often seek to put the word 'national' in their titles (e.g. the British National Party in the UK, or the Front National in France). Extreme nationalism as state policy has also often led to genocidal behaviour.

ACTIVITY 2 FACT SHEET
History of genocide

The Canary Islands, now a popular tourist destination, were the scene of genocide 500 years ago. The 80,000 Guanches who lived there – an advanced, Berber-speaking Stone Age community of African origin – became the first people to be destroyed by European expansion.

In 1478 the rulers of Spain sent an armed force to Grand Canary to seize the island from the Guanches. They soon captured the plains, but the Guanches held out in the mountains for five years. The 600 warriors and 1,500 women, children and old people who surrendered were all those left alive from a once numerous population.

'Las Palmas was defeated in 1494. Tenerife held out until 1496. Finally, one lone native woman signed to the Spaniards to come closer. "There was no-one left to fight, no-one to fear – all were dead." Neither guns nor horses decided the outcome of the war. Bacteria were victorious. . . . Of Tenerife's 15,000 inhabitants, only a handful survived. . . .

Those who survived the diseases instead died of actual subjugation – loss of relatives, friends, language, and lifestyle . . . In 1541 there was one single Guanche left, 81 years old and permanently drunk. The Guanches had gone under.'

After destroying the population of the Canaries and taking their land, the Europeans moved to the Americas and the Caribbean. Millions of people they encountered died of the 'disease, hunger and inhuman labour conditions' which they brought with them.

'In Mexico alone, there may have been 25 million people when the Europeans arrived in 1519. Fifty years later, the number had fallen to 2.7 million. Fifty more years later there were 1.7 million indians left. Over 90% of the original population had been wiped out in 100 years.'

In the late 19th and early 20th centuries the powerful European nations were dividing up the territory of Africa between them in the so-called 'Scramble for Africa'. The British, French, and Belgians had all carried out genocidal massacres of peoples who stood in their way.

'In 1904 in Southwest Africa (now Namibia), the Germans demonstrated that they too had mastered an art that Americans, British, and other Europeans had exercised all through the 19th century – the art of hastening the extermination of a people of "inferior culture".

Following the North American example, the Herero people were banished to reserves and their grazing lands handed over to German immigrants and

continued

Photocopy Original © Hodder & Stoughton 2001

FREEDOM!

colonisation companies. When the Hereros resisted, General von Trotha gave orders in October 1904 for the Herero people to be exterminated. Every Herero found within the German borders, with or without weapons, was to be shot. But most of them died without violence. The Germans simply drove them into the desert and sealed off the border. . . .

When the rainy season came, German patrols found skeletons lying around dry hollows, 24 to 50 feet deep, dug by the Hereros in vain attempts to find water. Almost the entire people – about 80,000 human beings – died in the deserts. Only a few thousand were left, sentenced to hard labour in German concentration camps.'

Colonial massacres like this and many others led the way to the Holocaust. They were based on the assumption that less 'developed' people or those who were not 'settled' could legitimately be exterminated to make room for 'superior' people (Europeans) who would make 'proper use' of agricultural and mineral resources.

Source: Sven Lindqvist, Exterminate All The Brutes, *Granta, 1997*

Killing of Hereros

'America was founded on genocide, on the unquestioned assumption of the right of white Europeans to exterminate a resident, technologically backward, colored population on order to take over the continent'.

Source: Susan Sontag, Styles of Radical Will, *1966*

Photocopy Original © Hodder & Stoughton 2001

ACTIVITY 3 FACT SHEET
Factors which make genocide more likely

- historical grievances
- colonial legacies
- territorial aggression
- exploiting hatred
- dehumanization of those who are 'different'
- ill-treatment and isolation of minority
- elite 'killing squads'
- authoritarian governments

R. G. Grant, Talking Points: Genocide, *Wayland, 1998*

Photocopy Original © Hodder & Stoughton 2001

ACTIVITY 3, CASE STUDY 1
'The Final Solution'

The Holocaust was the organised genocide of six million Jews by the Nazi regime and their collaborators during the Second World War.

In 1933 approximately nine million Jews lived in the 21 countries of Europe that were to be occupied by Germany during the war. By 1945, two out of every three European Jews had been killed or starved to death. In addition, a quarter of a million Roma (gypsies), 250,000 mentally and physically disabled people, tens of thousands of homosexuals, Communists, socialists, trade unionists and anti-Nazis were also murdered. Over three million unarmed Soviet prisoners of war were also annihilated because of their nationality. Almost two million Poles and other Slavs were worked to death in Nazi slave labour camps.

Jews have lived in Europe for nearly 2,000 years, since their exile from Palestine during Roman times. Jewish people have made many important contributions to European society, but at times throughout history Jews have been excluded, expelled, and persecuted because of their distinctive culture.

In the 1920s and 30s Germany, like many other countries, was in the grip of an economic crisis. This was exploited by Adolf Hitler's National Socialist German Workers Party, NSDAP, the Nazi Party. The Nazis came to power through an election in 1933, and quickly moved to seize total power, banning other political parties and trade unions and putting all news media, education and professions under their control.

The Nazis developed their project of creating a German 'master race' to dominate the world. In their plan, Jews, Gypsies and 'subhuman Slavs' were 'inferior races' of which Germany had to be 'cleansed', made racially 'pure'. The Nazis dreamed of a 'Greater Germany' expanding to the East with the return of 'lost territories' and more space – 'living room' (*Lebensraum*) – where 'pure race' German Aryans could live.

Their persecution of Jews started with isolation and exclusion. Jewish shops were labelled and boycotted. Jews were expelled from teaching and public service. Books by Jewish writers were publicly burned. Thousands of Jews fled abroad. Under the 1935 'Nuremberg Laws', all intermarriage with Jews was banned. Jews were made second-class citizens. Jewish businesses had to be sold. Jews could not live, or even walk, in certain parts of German cities. The new laws defined Jews not by their religion or by how then wanted to identify themselves, but by the so-called 'race' of their grandparents, even if the grandparents had converted to Christianity. There were even categories of 'mixture', and special laws for the treatment of someone with one Jewish grandparent.

Following the invasion of Czechoslovakia, the start of the Second World War and

continued

the rapid Nazi conquest of Poland and much of Europe in a short period, 'Greater Germany' contained millions of Jews. The Nazis began a programme of mass murder.

In January 1942 Nazi leaders held a secret meeting at Wannsee near Berlin to plan what they called *'Endlösung'* – 'the final solution of the Jewish question' – the systematic killing of all the 11 million Jews in Europe. They listed the numbers of Jews in each country of Europe that were to be killed (including 300,000 in Britain) and decided that Europe was to be 'combed from east to west' until there were no more Jews alive.

Over the next four years the plan was put into operation, with the active support of many local people in the countries that the Nazis occupied. Systematically Jews, Roma and all the other peoples whom the Nazis planned to eliminate, were rounded up.

Two million Jewish women, men and children were killed in their towns and villages, or taken to be shot or beaten to death at mass-murder sites near their homes, mostly by special SS units (*Einsatz Gruppen*) – murder squads that followed the German Army. Many others were forced to live in closed ghettoes until they died of starvation.

At least four million others were forced to leave their homes and taken by train in cattle trucks from all over Europe to their deaths in distant concentration camps, where they were murdered by being worked to death, starved to death, beaten to death, shot or gassed.

The genocide continued until the war ended in 1945. The Holocaust was unique in human history, not only in its horrific scale but also in its methodical planning and the scientific way in which it was carried out.

After the war the most important Nazi leaders were put on trial at the International War Crimes Tribunal at Nuremberg. The United Nations was formed. New legal principles were drafted to prevent such atrocities in the future. The Universal Declaration of Human Rights was proclaimed, and the international community promised that such a thing as the Holocaust could never happen again.

Sources: Martin Gilbert, The Holocaust, *1989 &* The Holocaust, maps and pictures, *1978; Stuart Hood & Lisa Jansz,* Fascism for Beginners, *1993; US Holocaust Memorial Museum; Lindquist 1999; New Internationalist 196*

ACTIVITY 3 CASE STUDY 2
East Timor

East Timor is part of an island in the Pacific Ocean, a small territory of some 600,000, located between Australia and Indonesia, populated by the Maubere people. It had been a Portuguese colony from the 16th century to 1975, when the East Timorese people declared their independence. Less than a month later, Indonesia – a military dictatorship since the mid-1960s under President Suharto, and the world's fifth largest nation – invaded the territory by air and sea. Indonesia has no legal or historical claim on the territory. Apart from the natural resources it hoped to exploit, Indonesia, over-populated and over-crowded, also wanted to seize the land space for Indonesians.

The invasion took place only hours after the US President Gerald Ford and Secretary of State Henry Kissinger met with President Suharto in Indonesia. The United States then doubled its military aid to Indonesia and blocked the UN from taking effective enforcement action. Since 1975, the United States has sold more than $1.1 billion worth of weaponry to Indonesia. Throughout the 1980s and 1990s, the United Kingdom has been the largest arms supplier to Indonesia. Australia and other Western nations have also made huge profits through economic contracts with Indonesia and the exploitation of East Timor's natural resources.

It is estimated that the Indonesian invasion and occupation led to the deaths of over 200,000 East Timorese people: one-third of the population. Indonesia's occupation has been condemned in a series of United Nations resolutions calling for Indonesia's withdrawal without delay. It was only recognised by Australia. But the UN has not taken any further action.

In the 25 years since 1975, the Indonesian military was responsible for the destruction of East Timorese villages, the elimination of families and systematic murders, political killings, enforced 'disappearances', torture and rape. There were reports of enforced sterilisation, forced labour camps and numerous other genocidal behaviours. The 'Indonesianization' of East Timor involved the imposition of the Indonesian culture and language and the enforced resettlement of 80% of East Timorese villagers to make way for Indonesian settlers. In 1998 20% of the population in East Timor was Indonesian.

In November 1991 up to 400 peaceful Timorese demonstrators, mostly school students and young people, were shot or 'disappeared' by Indonesian troops in a massacre at the Santa Cruz cemetery in Dili, the capital of East Timor. The killings were captured on film. Only after that did Western nations start to condemn Indonesia's actions more consistently. However, the same countries have continued to sell arms to Indonesia.

There was armed Timorese opposition to the Indonesian occupation for 25 years.

continued

Photocopy Original © Hodder & Stoughton 2001

Xanana Gusmao, the leader of the Fretilin resistance movement from 1981, eluded capture for more than a decade. The Indonesians used a tactic known as 'the fence of legs' to try and trap the resistance fighters. Thousands of elderly Timorese, women and children were forced to march through the jungle, 'sweeping' the undergrowth, and calling on the resistance to surrender. Guerrillas heard the East Timorese call out warnings to flee and encouragements. Eventually, Xanana Gusmao was captured in 1992 and sentenced to life imprisonment. He continued to campaign for his country's freedom from inside jail.

In 1996 the Nobel Peace Prize was given jointly to the Catholic Bishop Belo of Dili and to Jose Ramos Horta, Fretilin spokesman, for their campaigns for human rights and their proposed peace plan.

Indonesia's President Suharto was forced out of office in May 1998 by student-led demonstrations. In August 1998, the new President, B. J. Habibie, proposed a referendum of the people of East Timor to decide if the territory should be part of Indonesia or have autonomy. In February 1999 Xanana Gusmao was released from jail and placed under house arrest.

A ballot on autonomy was held in August 1999. In the run up to the referendum Amnesty International reported intimidatory attacks, threats and killings of pro-independence Timorese Indonesian militias, heavily armed groups, mostly Indonesian settlers, equipped and trained by the Indonesian Army. More than 90% of the adult population took part in the referendum which was far from peaceful. The vote was overwhelmingly for independence.

In the weeks that followed an orgy of destruction took place throughout East Timor, with the militias, supported by the Indonesian Army and Police, razing towns to the ground and driving out the people from their burning homes, with widespread reports of torture, rape, killings and 'disappearances'. The UN compound in the capital Dili was attacked and destroyed, and local members of UN staff murdered. A third of the population of East Timor fled to the hills or were forcibly deported to West Timor and other parts of Indonesia. In October 1999 the UN Security Council, with the agreement of Indonesia, sent in an international peace-keeping force to restore order. Gradually many of the refugees returned. The Indonesian armed forces and the militias left. A Commission of Enquiry began to investigate crimes against humanity and war crimes in East Timor. The UN took over as the transitional authority as East Timor began to take the first steps towards independent self-government.

Sources: Amnesty International News Releases April 1998, East Timor International Support Center website; Past, Present and Future website, East Timor Action Network website, Community Aid Abroad website, Hidden Agendas, John Pilger, 1998, Vintage

Photocopy Original © Hodder & Stoughton 2001

ACTIVITY 3 CASE STUDY 3# Srebrenica

Bosnian Muslim refugees, Srebrenica 1993

The Kingdom of Yugoslavia came into being in 1929, bringing a number of smaller territories together as one single country. The people included: Muslims (parts of Yugoslavia had been part of the Turkish Empire and many people had converted to Islam in the 15th century); Serbs, whose traditional religion is Orthodox Christian; Croats from a Catholic Christian religious tradition; and many other communities. During the Second World War – in which two million Yugoslavs were killed – some Croats supported the Nazis in their policy of extermination against Serbs and Muslims, while others joined the anti-Nazi resistance.

After the war the resistance leader, Marshal Josip Broz Tito, became the president of the post-war Communist state of Yugoslavia. Under his leadership the complex Yugoslav Federation of six republics and two autonomous provinces held together. After Tito's death in 1980, growing tensions between the different ethnic communities and increased nationalist demands were exploited by ambitious political leaders. With the collapse of the Soviet system, Yugoslavia faced financial chaos and did not receive the economic aid which it hoped for from the West.

In 1991 the Federation began to crumble. The republics of Slovenia and Croatia declared their independence, followed in 1992 by the republic of Bosnia Herzegovina. The Serb community in Bosnia wanted to remain within the

continued

Photocopy Original © Hodder & Stoughton 2001

Unit 7: GENOCIDE

Yugoslav Federation. Although the Bosnian government promised that the rights of all minorities would be assured and Bosnia would remain a multi-cultural country, Bosnia's Serbs proclaimed their own separate republic and a civil war began. 200,000 people – 5% of the population – died in the war. All sides in the war were responsible for abuses of human rights, but Serb forces carried out most. Abuses included: massacres; the enforced 'disappearance' of up to 20,000 people; torture; mass detention without charge; trials in 'concentration camps'; and campaigns of 'ethnic cleansing' driving non-Serb people out of their homes to create 'pure' Serb territories. According to UN figures, 40,000 women were raped in the war – mainly in specially created Serb 'rape camps'.

In 1993 the United Nations sent peace-keeping troops into Bosnia Herzegovina to create 'safe havens', including one round the town of Srebrenica. Here, the local Muslim population was joined by some 25,000 other Muslims, refugees fleeing the civil war. Yet UN soldiers protecting the enclave did not defend the town. Instead they drove away and the Serbs moved in.

'The defenceless Muslim population was subjected to what has been called the worst single atrocity in Europe since the end of the Second World War. The Serbs loaded Muslim men onto trucks and drove them to a killing ground where they were shot. The bodies were buried in mass graves. The number of dead is estimated at between 6,000 and 8,000.' Grant, *Genocide*, Wayland 1998

A BBC TV report described the massacre at Srebrenica as 'scenes from hell, written on the darkest pages of human history.'

Peace in Bosnia was negotiated under the Dayton Accord of 1996, which divided Bosnia into two autonomous regions, one a Serb area and the other a Croat and Muslim area. Friends and neighbours were divided and 'mixed' families faced many problems.

Source: R. G. Grant, Talking Points: Genocide*, Wayland, 1998; NI 'World Guide 1999–2000'; AI reports.*

Photocopy Original © Hodder & Stoughton 2001

ACTIVITY 3 CASE STUDY 4
Genocide in Rwanda and Burundi

More than a million Hutus fled Rwanda following the 1994 genocide.

The neighbouring countries of Rwanda and Burundi lie in the heart of Africa, surrounded by mountains, forests, rivers and great lakes. Since ancient times the land has been inhabited by Hutu people, who traditionally live by growing crops, and a small number of Twa people, traditionally hunters and potters. In the 15th century Burundi and the highlands of Rwanda were invaded by Tutsi people, traditional cattle breeders who migrated south from Ethiopia and Uganda to find fresh pastures. Because of their warrior culture and their more sophisticated weapons, the Tutsi minority were able to dominate the Hutu majority. The two communities lived together peacefully, sharing languages and religions. There was some intermarriage so that some people were of mixed descent.

In the late 19th century the area was colonised by Germany. It was then taken over by Belgium after the First World War. The European rulers supported Tutsi domination, which helped them to control the majority people. The Belgian rulers also reinforced the difference between the Tutsi and Hutu communities, issuing identity cards which stated a person's ethnicity.

In 1962 both Burundi and Rwanda became independent states. In Burundi the new government was controlled by Tutsis. After a series of violent uprisings, the Tutsi-dominated army massacred 350,000 Hutus in 1971. During the 1980s there was a gradual growth in democracy and rights for Hutus. The first Hutu president was elected in 1988. But further massive killings in 1988 and 1993 built up an atmosphere of terror and violence spread between communities.

continued

Photocopy Original © Hodder & Stoughton 2001

Genocide in Rwanda and Burundi

In Rwanda, independence came through a bloody civil war. The new government, dominated by Hutus, abolished the power structure which had favoured the Tutsis. Tensions between the communities continued. Nearly 60% of Rwanda's Tutsis left the country, mainly going to Burundi.

In April 1994 the presidents of Rwanda and Burundi, both Hutu, were killed when their plane was shot down on their way back from peace talks in Tanzania.

In Rwanda – an extremely poor country with a rapidly growing population – a small Hutu elite chose genocide to control the country. The resources and authority of the state were used to incite tens of thousands of Rwandans to murder the Tutsi minority. Within 100 days they massacred 800,000 Tutsi men, women and children and moderate Hutus opposed to 'Hutu Power'. Three-quarters of the Tutsi population of Rwanda were hunted down and slaughtered in their homes, schools, churches, workplaces – often hacked or bludgeoned to death with machetes and clubs. The murders were well planned, led by organised Hutu 'militias' (many of them very young men) that had been prepared for their role by the government. Ordinary civilians – including women, children and priests – joined in the murder of their neighbours and former friends.

The international community did not intervene to stop the massacres, although French troops were sent in to oversee the evacuation of French citizens.

In July 1994 Tutsi-led rebel forces gained control of Rwanda. More than a million Hutu refugees fled to neighbouring countries. Most returned to their homes by the end of 1996 but violence continued.

Twenty-two of those presumed responsible for the genocide were executed in 1998 without a proper trial, in spite of appeals from the Pope and the UN Secretary-General. Amnesty International called the executions 'a brutal parody of justice which . . . will perpetuate the cycle of violence.'

In Burundi, growing conflict between Hutus and Tutsis became a civil war in which, by 1998, more than 250,000 people had died. Intercommunal violence between Tutsis and Hutus spread to the neighbouring Democratic Republic of the Congo, where it played a part in the major civil conflict.

In its report on the Rwanda genocide, Human Rights Watch states: 'France, the US, Belgium and the UN failed to heed the warnings of coming disaster and refused to recognise the genocide when it began. They withdrew the troops which could have saved lives and made little protest about the genocide, lest condemnation led to action.' This 'international indifference' was more tragic when 'even feeble censure caused changes in the genocidal programme'. The report asks: 'What might have been the result had the world acted promptly and firmly cried "Never Again"?'

Sources: NI 309; 'The World Guide' 1999–2000' NI 1999; 'Leave None to Tell the Story: Genocide in Rwanda' Human Rights Watch 1999; R. G. Grant, Talking Points: Genocide, Wayland, 1998; Yahya Sadowski 'What really makes the world go to war' Foreign Policy journal 111 Summer 1998

Photocopy Original © Hodder & Stoughton 2001

ACTIVITY 4 CASE STUDY 1
Barbara's story

Barbara Richter was born into a Roma (Gypsy) family in 1929 in Bohemia, which is now part of the Czech Republic. The ancestors of the Roma had migrated to Europe from India over 1,000 years ago. They were regarded, like the Jews, as outsiders. Some had dark hair and skin. They spoke their own language and had their own customs.

The gates of Auschwitz

At the start of the Second World War, 700,000 Roma were living in Europe. The Nazis regarded them as subhuman. Anyone with at least two Roma great-great-grandparents was considered Roma under the Nazi race laws. In Germany Roma were sterilised. Many were sent to Buchenwald and Dachau concentration camps. In 1940 surviving German Roma were sent to Poland and forced to live in special ghettoes. Nazis soon began to round up and execute Roma in all the countries they occupied, or deport them. In 1942 a Nazi decree ordered all the Roma of Europe to be sent to the concentration camp at Auschwitz in Poland.

Barbara was 14 when, in 1943, she was caught and put on a cattle truck to the death camp. When she arrived she experienced 'selection'.

'The prisoners were immediately inspected by a doctor . . . He divided them into two groups. Those who looked old or sick or who had young children were made to stand on one side of the road, the rest on the other. Barbara was placed in the second group while the family who had sheltered her [while she was hiding from the Nazis in Prague] went into the first. Barbara never saw them again because their group was marched away to the gas chambers, where they were put to death.

Those who were allowed to live were put into a special Gypsy section of the new camp at Birkenau. This was immediately alongside the older Auschwitz camp, most of whose inmates were Jews. Not far away were the dreaded gas chambers and the crematorium where the bodies of dead prisoners were burned, so that the air was always tainted with charred flesh. It made Barbara and the other inmates feel sick at first, but after a time they became used to it.

The other thing that happened to them was that they were given a badge to denote which "racial" group they came from. Gypsies wore a brown triangle. [Jews wore a yellow star, homosexuals a pink triangle.] They were then branded

continued

Unit 7: GENOCIDE

on the wrist with their prison number: Barabara's was Z1963. The marking was permanent and was still visible on her wrist more than 50 years later.

The guards . . . seemed to take delight in being cruel to the prisoners. Some of the younger ones started off by being kind and approachable but they were soon affected by the attitude of the others and began to taunt and mistreat the inmates like the rest.

In Barbara's experience, the female guards were even worse than the men. She remembers one incident when four Gypsy children were scraping out the pot at the end of lunch [thin soup of turnips, water and salt]. A female guard took out her pistol and shot the children . . .

. . . The work they were made to do was hard but pointless. One of the main tasks was breaking stones and carrying large loads of them from one place to the next . . . One day Barbara was among a group breaking stones when the woman next to her collapsed and died. Barbara noticed a lump of bread fall from her hand and instinctively went to pick it up. It may seem heartless to take food from a dead woman but in the desperate atmosphere of the camp an extra piece of bread could mean the difference between your own life and death. She had no hesitation in taking it.

But a guard had seen her do it. He rushed up, took the bread from her and struck her so hard that she fell to the ground. She was stunned and in pain but she knew that if she did not get up the guard would kick her until she was senseless. So she rose to her feet and when she was knocked over again she got up again. Her punishment was 25 lashes and three days in confinement on a starvation diet.

In the last months of the war, Barbara and the few hundred surviving Roma prisoners were moved between different camps. Now nearly 16, she was often sexually assaulted. At the last camp in Austria, desperate to escape from assault, she jumped out of a window on to a truck, whose driver helped her to get out of the area.

For days she walked, keeping off the main roads so that she would not be seen, living off food from the woods and fields, terrified that an army patrol would find her and notice the Auschwitz number tattooed on her arm. By trying to burn it off, she made her arm sore and infected, but the number would not disappear. Barbara found her way to Prague, where she hid with other Roma till the war ended and she was reunited with her mother, who had also survived the death camps.'

Michael Leapman, Witnesses to War, *Viking, 1998*

Photocopy Original © Hodder & Stoughton 2001

ACTIVITY 4 CASE STUDY 2
Primo Levi

IF THIS IS A MAN
You who live safe
In your warm houses,
You who find, returning in the evening,
Hot food and friendly faces:
Consider if this is a man
Who works in the mud
Who does not know peace
Who fights for a scrap of bread
Who dies for a yes or no.
Consider if this is a woman,
Without hair and without name
With no more strength to remember,
Her eyes empty and her womb cold
Like a frog in winter.
Meditate that this came about:
I commend these words to you.
Carve them in your hearts
At home, in the street,
Going to bed, rising;
Repeat them to your children,
Or may your house fall apart,
May illness impede you,
May your children turn their faces from you.

Primo Levi was born into a Jewish family in Turin, Italy in 1919. He trained as a chemist but was banned by anti-Jewish laws from working in his profession. In 1943 he joined the partisan resistance. He was arrested in 1944 and sent to Auschwitz concentration camp where he survived until liberation in 1945 and was sent with other Italians to White Russia before finally returning home. His Holocaust experiences have been the subject of his acclaimed books of memoirs, stories and poetry. In his writing Primo Levi constantly re-examines the meaning of the Holocaust for humanity, and the meaning of survival for himself.

In his early books Levi expressed his belief that the world had learned the lessons of Auschwitz:

'If there is one thing sure in this world, it is certainly this: that it will not happen to us a second time.'
Survival in Auschwitz, 1958

Primo Levi died in 1987, apparently by suicide. By then, the world had seen the

continued

mass murder of millions in Cambodia, mass slaughter by the French military in Algeria, the horrors of apartheid in South Africa. Levi knew that the lesson had not yet been learned.

Shortly before his death he tried to answer a frequent question posed by his readers: 'How can the Nazis' fanatical hatred of the Jews be explained?' He wrote:

'. . . there is no rationality in the Nazi hatred . . . we cannot understand it, but we must understand from where it springs, and we must be on our guard. If understanding is impossible, knowing is imperative, because what happened could happen again. Conscience can be seduced and obscured again – even our consciences.

. . . We must remember that these faithful followers [of the Fascist leaders], among them the diligent executors of inhuman orders, were not born torturers, were not (with a few exceptions) monsters, they were ordinary men . . .

. . . the memory of what happened in the heart of Europe, not very long ago, can serve as support and warning.'

'The Author's Answer to his Readers' Questions', 1987, Primo Levi.

Primo Levi

Photocopy Original © Hodder & Stoughton 2001

ACTIVITY 4 CASE STUDY 3
Stories from Rwanda

'Rwanda is spectacular . . . Gashes of red clay and loam mark fresh hoe work; eucalyptus trees flash silver against brilliant green tea plantations; banana trees are everywhere. On the theme of hills, Rwanda produces countless variations: jagged rain forests, round-shouldered buttes, undulating moors, broad swells of savannah, volcanic peaks as sharp as filed teeth. During the rainy season, the clouds are huge and low and fast, mists cling in highland hollows, lighting flickers through the nights, and by day the land is lustrous.

. . . One day, when I was returning to Kigali from the south, the car mounted a rise between two winding valleys, the windshield filled with purple-bellied clouds, and I asked Joseph, the man who was giving me a ride, whether Rwandans realise what a beautiful

Tutsi survivor of the genocide

country they have. "Beautiful?" he said. "You think so? After the things that happened here? The people aren't good. If the people were good, the country might be OK." Joseph told me that his brother and sister had been killed, and he made a soft hissing click with his tongue against his teeth. "The country is empty," he said. "Empty".'

***

'Every Rwandan I spoke to seemed to have a favourite, unanswerable question . . . For Francois Xavier Nkurinziza, a Kigali lawyer, whose father had been Hutu and whose mother and wife were Tutsi, the question was how so many Hutus had allowed themselves to kill. Nkurunziza had escaped death only by chance as he moved around the country from one hiding place to another, and he had lost many family members. "Conformity is very deep, very developed here," he told me. "In Rwandan history, everyone obeys authority. People revere power, and there isn't enough education. You take a poor, ignorant population, and give them arms, and say, 'It's yours. Kill.' They'll obey. The peasants, who were paid or forced to kill, were looking up to people of higher socio-economic standing to see how to behave. So the people of influence, or the big financiers, are often the big men in the genocide. They may think that they didn't kill because

continued

they didn't take life with their own hands, but the people were looking to them for their orders. And in Rwanda an order can be given very quietly."

As I travelled around the country, collecting accounts of the killing, it almost seemed as if, with the machete, the *masu* – a club studded with nails – a few well-placed grenades, and a few bursts of automatic-rifle fire, the quiet orders of Hutu Power had made the neutron bomb obsolete.

"Everyone was called to hunt the enemy," said Theodore Nyilinka, a survivor of the massacres. . . . "But let's say someone is reluctant. Say that guy comes with a stick. They tell him, 'No, get a *masu*.' So, OK, he does, and he runs along with the rest, but he doesn't kill. They say, 'Hey, he might denounce us later. He must kill. Everyone must help to kill at least one person.' So this person who is not a killer is made to do it, and the next day it's become a game for him. You don't have to keep pushing him."

***

I cannot count the times I've been asked, "Is there any hope for Rwanda?" I like to quote a Hutu hotel manager, Paul Rusesabagina, who told me after the genocide, "with my countrymen – Rwandans – you never know what they will become tomorrow." Although he didn't mean it that way, this struck me as one of the most optimistic things a Rwandan could say after the genocide.

But I'll leave you to decide if there is hope for Rwanda with one more story. In 1997, Rwandan television showed footage of a man who confessed to being among a party of *genocidaires* who had killed 17 schoolgirls and a 62-year-old Belgian nun at a boarding school. . . . The prisoner . . . explained that the massacre was part of a Hutu Power liberation campaign. . . . The students, teenage girls who had been roused from their sleep, were ordered to separate themselves – Hutus from Tutsis. But the students had refused. They said they were simply Rwandans, so they were beaten and shot indiscriminately. . . . Might we all take some courage from those brave Hutu girls who could have chosen to live but chose instead to call themselves Rwandans?'

Extracts from: Philip Gourevitch 'We wish to inform you that tomorrow we will be killed with our families', Stories from Rwanda, Picador, 1999

FREEDOM!

ACTIVITY 5 FACT SHEET
International Criminal Court

PUTTING MASS MURDERERS ON TRIAL

1945. After the Second World War, international war crime tribunals were set up by the Allied powers: the United Kingdom, France, the Soviet Union and the United States; in Nuremberg, Germany and in Tokyo, Japan. In the dock in Nuremberg were some of the key German leaders facing charges of 'crimes against humanity', including genocide. Although there had been genocide and war crimes through history these were amongst the first of such trials.

Eleven of those found guilty at Nuremberg were sentenced to death. However, most of those responsible for carrying out the genocide were never tried and returned to their everyday life. The international tribunals were temporary and were dissolved when the trials ended. They were criticised for being victors' courts conducted against the vanquished by the victorious nations.

International War Crimes Tribunal, Nuremberg, 1945

1948. The Genocide Convention was agreed at the UN. UN lawyers first studied the feasibility of a permanent International Criminal Court (ICC).

1950. Lawyers made their report, but the proposal for an ICC was blocked during the Cold War. No international action was ever taken against the genocidal Khmer Rouge in Cambodia or the Pakistan Army in Bangladesh acts.

1989. Trinidad & Tobago suggested at the United Nations that the work of setting up a permanent international criminal court should be revived.

1990. UN General Assembly instructed lawyers to start the project.

1993–1995. Temporary International Criminal Tribunals were set up by the UN Security Council to try those accused of crimes against humanity in Rwanda and Former Yugoslavia. Every member state of the UN was obliged to co-operate for instance by not sheltering those who are wanted for trial.

1996. The UN Commissioner for Human Rights said: 'We must rid this planet of

continued

Photocopy Original © Hodder & Stoughton 2001

International Criminal Court

the obscenity that a person stands a better chance of being tried and judged for killing one human being than for killing 100,000.'
1998. The Statute of the International Criminal Court was adopted at Rome (120 states in favour, 7 against, 21 abstentions).

WHAT IS THE ICC?

The International Criminal Court (ICC) will be a permanent international criminal court for the 21st century to bring to justice those responsible for the worst crimes in the world: genocide, other crimes against humanity and war crimes. The first responsible to act is still with national authorities. The ICC will act if national authorities are unable or unwilling.

It will be different to other war crimes courts because:
1. it is a permanent court, rather than one set up for a particular occasion;
2. it is international, not just set up by the victors in a war.

The ICC Statute:
- states that genocide, other crimes against humanity and war crimes (including rape and sexual abuse) 'must not go unpunished';
- recognises 'the duty of every State to exercise its criminal jurisdiction over those responsible for international crimes';
- guarantees justice for women and children;
- guarantees the right to a fair trial;
- excludes the death penalty even for the worst crimes in the world.

However the Statute has limitations:
- restricted authority to conduct trials for war crimes;
- restricted authority to try crimes committed in the territory of a state party or by its nationals. Thus dictators who are accused of crimes against their own people would have to give permission for themselves to be put on trial;
- broad defences to crimes are possible, e.g. 'I was obeying orders';
- the UN Security Council can delay an investigation for 12 months renewable;
- no prosecutions for crimes which took place before the ICC was set up;
- not all countries support it.

The world's most powerful country, the USA, opposes the ICC because:
- the Pentagon fears US servicemen being arrested and tried for war crimes;
- the US considers it unacceptable for an American citizen to be tried in a foreign court;
- there is a fear of 'frivolous and political prosecutions';
- some influential politicians in the US are very hostile to the UN.

Amnesty International 1999

Photocopy Original © Hodder & Stoughton 2001

ACTIVITY 9 INFORMATION SHEET
Racial prejudice and racism

Racial prejudice is the belief that differences in physical or cultural characteristics (e.g. skin colour, religious beliefs, dress) are directly linked to differences in intelligence, ability, personality or morality. Someone who is racially prejudiced may believe that they are better than another 'racial' group, or will dislike or even hate another 'racial' group because they are believed to be 'different'. Racial prejudice can be held by members of any group against another.

Racism is more than just racial prejudice, because inequality and discrimination, based on the false idea of a superior white 'race', has been built into political, social and economic institutions over centuries, giving white people the most economic, political and social power. (This is often referred to as 'institutionalised racism'). For example, a black person is still more likely to be unemployed and less likely to get a job than a white person, even when they have better qualifications than the white person.

Racism is also seen in the behaviour of white people who are racially prejudiced: examples range from acting on a belief that white people are 'better', to verbal abuse and physical violence. Organised racism promotes the false theory of the 'racial superiority' of white people, and then acts this out in racist violence.

However, there is really no such thing as a white British, or white European race. Apart from the fact that all human beings share a similar genetic and biological make-up, people from all over the world have been settling in Britain from 15,000 BC to the present day.

Unit 7: GENOCIDE

ACTIVITY 9 QUIZ SHEET
Racism in Britain

1. What is racial discrimination?

2. If a black person has the same or better qualifications as a white person, are they more likely to be unemployed? If yes, how much more likely.

3. Is it more likely that you will be arrested by the police if you are a young black man? How much more likely?

4. Are you more likely to be a victim of crime if you are black or white?

5. If you are a black Londoner, are you twice or four times as likely to be homeless as a white Londoner?

6. How often are serious racial attacks reported to the police; once a week, once a day, once every half hour?

7. Are black people more likely to be targets of racial attack than white people? If yes, how many times more likely?

8. Out of every three immigrants into Britain, how many are white?

9. How long have black people lived in Britain?

10. What percentage of black people in the UK were born in Britain?

11. How much more likely is it that a young person will be detained under the Mental Health Act in comparison with a young white person?

12. Is it more likely that a black pupil will be suspended from school for the same misbehaviour as a white pupil?

13. Can you name any organisation that exists to fight racial discrimination?

Photocopy Original © Hodder & Stoughton 2001

FREEDOM!

Racism in Britain

1. RACIAL DISCRIMINATION

The Race Relations Act of 1976 makes it unlawful to discriminate against anyone because of their race, colour, nationality (including citizenship), ethnic or national origins. It applies to employment, training, housing, education and services, e.g. health service, pubs, banks.

There are two kinds of discrimination; direct and indirect:

Direct discrimination happens when someone is treated worst or differently to others because of their 'race', colour, nationality, or ethnic or national origins. E.g. if an Asian woman does not get a job in a company because she won't 'fit in' with the staff who are all white, she has been directly discriminated against.

Indirect discrimination is when everyone seems to be treated the same way, but because of certain conditions or requirements, one group of people are put at a greater disadvantage. This can be intentional or unintentional. E.g. a Liverpool store manager told a careers office that he didn't want applicants from certain postal districts. These were areas where there was a high percentage of black residents. The law found him guilty of indirect discrimination.

In Bradford in 1999, three friends, one white, one black and one Asian, won their case of racial discrimination at an Industrial Tribunal. The white man had refused the job after the employer turned his friends down saying they were a problem, 'you know what I mean'. It is the first time that a white man has won a case of racial discrimination for sticking by his black colleagues.

Inciting racial hatred is a criminal offence, and includes: threatening behaviour, abuse and insults, publishing anything that is likely to cause racial hatred. The Crime and Disorder Act of 1998 created nine new racially aggravated offences carrying sentences of up to two years more than was previously the case.

Despite the law, racial discrimination, racial harassment and violence are widespread. Institutionalised racism is not legally recognised. It is difficult to prove that discrimination has occurred.

2. EMPLOYMENT

Black people are twice as likely to be unemployed in the UK as white people, even when they are better qualified.

- In 1994/5 there were 1,365 industrial tribunal claims against employers on the grounds of racial discrimination.

Photocopy Original © Hodder & Stoughton 2001

continued

Unit 7: GENOCIDE

- 11% of black people with degrees and 6% of Asians with degrees were unemployed compared with only 3% of white degree holders.

3. JUSTICE

A young black man is five times more likely than a young white man to be arrested and is also more likely to be charged (rather than cautioned).

- In 1997/8, 38% of stops and searches in London were of black and ethnic minorities.
- 5.5% of the total UK population are black and ethnic minorities. In 1997, 18% of male prisoners and 25% of female prisoners were from ethnic minorities.
- There were 358 complaints about racial discrimination or assault by police officers in 1997/8. There were disciplinary charges in two of these cases.
- Out of 510 circuit judges, five are black.

Cartoon from Newham Monitoring Project (NMP)

4. CRIME

The British Crime Survey of 1996 shows that black and ethnic minorities are more likely to be victims of crime than white people. People of Pakistani and Bangladeshi origin are at greater risk in almost every category of crime.

5. HOUSING AND HOMELESSNESS

Black people are four times more likely to be homeless in London than whites. Additionally:

- One in five accommodation agencies discriminate against black people.
- The London Housing Survey 1993 found that Asian council tenants with children are most at risk of racial attack.

6 AND 7. RACIAL INCIDENTS AND VIOLENCE

On average, a racial attack occurs every half hour. Black and Asian people are 60 times more likely than white people to be targets. Asian people, particularly women and children, experience the highest number of attacks.

continued

Photocopy Original © Hodder & Stoughton 2001

FREEDOM!

Photocopy Original © Hodder & Stoughton 2001

- A 1994 report by the Home Affairs Select Committee on Racial Attacks and Harassment said that the number of reported racial attacks rose from 4,383 in 1988 to 7,793 in 1992 (an increase of 78%).

- In 1994 the United Nations Human Rights Commission condemned Britain for failing to do enough to halt the significant increase in racial incidents; over the last five years racial incidents had soared by over 50%. In November 1994, the Commission therefore announced that it would be carrying out a full investigation into racial discrimination and violence in Britain.

- The 1994 Anti-Semitism World Report documented a 20% rise in anti-Jewish attacks in the UK in the previous year, including serious assaults, threats, the desecration of cemeteries and synagogues and the widespread distribution of anti-Semitic literature.

- Figures from British Crime Survey 1996 estimate the true number of racially motivated crimes to be around 382,000 a year, but only 13,878 racial incidents were reported to the police in 1997/8.

- In an eight-week study in Burley, Leeds, in 1994, Leeds University researchers recorded 84 incidents of racial harassment, ranging from verbal abuse and stone throwing to stabbings, all perpetrated by children. The average age of the culprits was seven.

8. IMMIGRATION

Two out of every three immigrants coming to the UK are white.

- Before 1962, all people from former British colonies were British subjects, with the right to live and work in Britain. The government encouraged immigration because of labour shortages. The 1962 Immigration Act, and laws since then, made it much more difficult for people from the New Commonwealth (countries like Pakistan, India, Ghana, Nigeria) to come to Britain than people from the Old Commonwealth (countries like Australia, New Zealand and Canada). The laws therefore specifically discriminated against black people. Since 1973 black and Asian immigration has been mainly limited to dependants of those who have already settled here.

- More people have emigrated from Britain than come into Britain over the past decade. In 1991, 11,000 more people left the UK than entered it.

9 AND 10. BLACK AND BRITISH

Records show that there have been black British people at least since the end of the 15th century. The first black Britons almost certainly came to Britain with the Romans, 2,000 years ago, long before the Angles or the Saxons arrived. Roman records refer to soldiers, described as 'Moors', from northern Africa, defending Hadrian's Wall. Ironically, this wall was built as a barrier to keep the Scots out.

More than 50% of Britain's black population was born in Britain (1991 census analysis). More than 75% of them are British citizens. 86% of black people in Britain under 16 years of age were born in the UK and approximately 15% of white people were born outside Britain.

continued

11. HEALTH

Compulsory detention under the Mental Health Act in the UK is 25 times more likely for young black people than for young white people.

1991 census analysis shows that black people face widespread discrimination in employment, access to housing and health services. Black and Irish children have higher rates of long-term illness than any other group, while young Bangladeshi adults are twice as likely to have long-term illnesses.

12. EDUCATION

Research by the Commission for Racial Equality found that African-Caribbean pupils are four times as likely as white pupils to be suspended from school for the same kinds of misbehaviour. 1997 DfEE statistics show that Black Caribbean pupils are five times more likely to face permanent exclusion than white pupils.

- In 1989, there were fewer than 20 black headteachers in Britain.
- A 1994 study by Norwich and Norfolk Racial Equality Council, and previous research in the West Country and Wales, has revealed that whilst black people make up less than 1% of rural communities, almost all black people living in rural areas have experienced racial harassment, taunts, discrimination and violence. Primary as well as secondary school playgrounds produced some of the worst and most frequent examples.
- An extensive research study at the Institute of Education, Warwick, in 1994, showed that black pupils, and African-Caribbean pupils in particular, are outperforming pupils of all other races at the age of five and stay in the lead until at least the age of seven. By 16, African-Caribbean pupils are the least educationally successful.

13. FIGHTING RACIAL DISCRIMINATION

There are many organisations, both locally and nationally, who are actively fighting against all forms of racial discrimination. National organisations include the Commission for Racial Equality, the Runnymede Trust, The Institute of Race Relations.

Photocopy Original © Hodder & Stoughton 2001

Photocopy Original © Hodder & Stoughton 2001

ACTIVITY 10 FACT SHEET
The Roma – welcome to Britain?

Visitors arriving in Britain are used to seeing signs saying 'Welcome to Britain'. But some are less welcome than others. The Roma people – often called Gypsies – have experienced that lack of welcome for hundreds of years. Laws made under Henry VIII described them as 'Europe's most unwanted race'. People were tortured, expelled and even hanged just for being 'Egyptians' – for having dark skin and hair, speaking their own language, travelling rather than living in houses.

The name 'Egyptian', shortened to 'Gypsy', dates from the first arrival of the travelling people in Europe in the 11th century, when they were believed to come from Egypt. Their origins are now known to be in India – Romani is recognised as one of the languages of India and aspects of Roma culture still reflect India. They probably moved westwards as travelling musicians and performers. Roma are still famous for their unique music – an exciting fusion of East and West which has given them a leading role in the spread of 'world music'. The community call themselves by various names: Roma in Eastern Europe, Sinti in Germany, Romanies or Travellers in Britain, Manouches in France (the Romani/Hindi word 'manush' meaning man). Some have also 'reclaimed' the insult names – Gypsy, Gitane, Zigeuner – and use them with pride. There are now 12 to 15 million Roma around the world, 80% in Europe, mainly in the Balkans, especially Romania, Central Europe and the former Soviet Union.

For hundreds of years the lives of Roma people in Europe have been dominated by 'two brute historical facts: enslavement (particularly in Eastern Europe) and attempted genocide (particularly in Western Europe).' [Thomas Acton, Britain's first Professor of Romani]. In Romania, the Roma were legally slaves until 1864. Across Europe from the 15th to 18th centuries there were oppressive laws similar to those in Britain: thousands were hunted down, branded, beaten, hanged or expelled, just because they lived a nomadic life.

These murderous attitudes persisted into the 20th century. The Nazis classified 'Gypsies', like Jews, as unwanted outsiders 'of foreign blood'. At least 200,000 Roma were systematically murdered for being 'different'.

After the war, government policies in Central and Eastern Europe tried to 'end the Romani problem' by forcing them to settle. In Czechoslovakia (now the Czech Republic and Slovakia) a policy of 'dispersal and transfer' was developed to try to spread Roma thinly around the country and break up large communities. Roma women were pressurised to be sterilised.

With the collapse of Communism, racism against Roma people came out into the open again, especially in Romania, Slovakia and the Czech Republic. They are mistrusted and scapegoated for many social problems, especially crime. They face

continued

exclusion and discrimination in education, health, employment and housing. In Romania whole Roma villages have been burned and the people forced to flee. In the Czech Republic nearly 75% of Roma are unemployed, compared with a national rate of 6%. A survey in Prague in 1996 showed that 24 out of 40 restaurants refused to serve Roma. One town in the Czech Republic proposed to build a wall around the Roma area to keep the community cut off from the rest of the town.

Many Roma were murdered and thousands violently attacked in Europe in the 1990s. In the Czech Republic 1,250 racially motivated attacks on Roma were documented between 1991 and 1997, with at least 28 murders. Helena Bihariova drowned after white men beat her and threw her into the River Elbe. The Czech state attorney declared that those who called this a racial incident were 'hysterical'. The family and friends of 18-year-old Tibor Danihel, murdered by an armed skinhead gang in 1993, had to campaign for six years before the killers were brought to trial.

Under such threats, some Roma families from East and Central Europe have come to Britain, to seek a safe haven. Instead they found themselves under attack from sections of the media. With exaggerated stories about 'hordes of gypsies' arriving at Dover and Folkestone. In fact, during 1997, about 500 Roma applied for asylum. Heads of families were usually kept in prison while waiting for their asylum claim to be assessed.

The Dover Express, in October 1998, described Roma asylum seekers as 'the scum of the earth' targeting 'our beloved coast-line' and complained 'we are left with the backdraft of a nation's human sewage and no cash to wash it down the drain'. Racist organisations organised marches and public meetings against asylum seekers in Dover and Folkestone. Families of refugees had lighted rags and fireworks pushed through their letter-boxes and bottles thrown through their windows. The words 'We will burn you out' were painted on one house.

The Daily Mail asked how the government would 'stem the tide' of Gypsy migrants and printed the address of one asylum-seeing family in Dover. The family's home was attacked and windows smashed.

Almost all the asylum claims of Roma families were refused. The government's position was that East European Roma were not refugees but economic migrants, attracted by the UK's generous benefits system. In May 1998 an Appeals Adjudicator overturned the Home Office's rejection of the claims of four asylum-seeking Slovak Roma families, saying that 'their fear of persecution on return to Slovakia was well-founded'.

'Briefing on Czech and Slovak Roma' The Refugee Council October 1998; Campaign Against Racism and Fascism Journal 48 February/March 1999 & April/May 1999; Roma National Congress website; Angus Fraser, The Gypsies, *Oxford 1992; Martin Gilbert,* The Holocaust, *1989*

ACTIVITY 11 POETRY
'I did not speak ...'
by Martin Niemoller

First they came for the Communists,
*   and I didn't speak up,*
*   because I wasn't a Communist.*
Then they came for the Jews,
*   and I didn't speak up,*
*   because I wasn't a Jew.*
Then they came for the workers,
*   members of the trade unions;*
*   I didn't speak up because I wasn't a trade unionist.*
Then they came for the Catholics,
*   and I didn't speak up,*
*   because I was a Protestant.*
Then they came for me,
*   and by that time there was no one*
*   left to speak up for me.*

Dachau, 1942

Pastor Martin Niemoller was a Protestant minister and an outspoken critic of the Nazi regime and was active in promoting resistance. He was arrested in 1937 and imprisoned in Sachsenhausen and Dachau concentration camps until the end of the war on the direct orders of Hitler.

After the war, Niemoller was instrumental in producing the 'Stuttgart Confession of Guilt', in which the German Protestant churches formally accepted guilt for the horrors of the Nazi regime.

Martin Niemoller travelled widely as an advocate of peace and reconciliation. He died in Germany in 1984, at the age of 92.

Amnesty International as a campaigning organisation

8

UNIT AIMS

The aims of this unit are to enable pupils to

- understand the role and the work of pressure groups and charities
- investigate the work of Amnesty International
- look at how human rights research is conducted
- introduce the history of the organisation
- outline how Amnesty International works for change and how it gets its message across

INTRODUCTION

This unit looks in detail at Amnesty International as an organisation – its role, its history, its structure, its democratic procedures, its methods of influencing decision makers and its ways of working. Some of this unit will be of particular interest to business students.

Activities examine the role of human rights organisations and other pressure groups in highlighting human rights abuses, promoting human rights and making a real difference to the world we live in. The important story of the birth of Amnesty International, which is explored through role play, highlights the way in which one person's anger about injustice and

oppression, and their determination to do something, has saved the lives of thousands of people and has motivated many more to join campaigns for human rights.

The constraints and benefits of operating as a business are examined. This includes consideration of Amnesty International's ongoing need to campaign and fundraise so that its work can continue and develop. The structure and mandate of Amnesty International as an organisation and how these have evolved are explored.

Finally, students are asked to consider the part that they can play in challenging human rights abuses and in promoting freedom.

SUMMARY OF TOPICS

TITLE	CURRICULUM LINKS	PAGE
1. Putting on the pressure	13+: English/PSHE/Pastoral/Art and Design	*238/242*
2. 'Freedom!'	13+: PSHE/Pastoral/History/Drama/Theatre Studies	*239/245*
Citizenship	***Knowledge and Understanding:*** *opportunities for individuals and voluntary groups to bring about social change*	
3. The Amnesty researcher	14+: PSHE/Pastoral/Law/English/RE	*239/247*
Citizenship	***Participation Skills:*** *critically evaluating views* ***Enquiry Skills:*** *analysing information from different sources* ***Knowledge and Understanding:*** *human rights issues*	
4. Is this a case for Amnesty International?	14+: PSHE/Pastoral/Law/English/RE	*239/248*

ACTIVITIES: NOTES FOR TEACHERS

Activity 1: Putting on the pressure

Ask groups to try to define these words:

- Charity
- Campaign
- Pressure group
- Non-governmental organisation

Share their definitions.

Give students information sheet 1 on pressure groups
- Divide the following campaigning organisations among groups of students. Ask them to find out what they can about them (aims, addresses, etc.) and report back.

TAPOL
MENCAP
Anne Frank Memorial Trust
Charter 88
Stonewall
Greenpeace
Oxfam
Forward
Survival International
Liberty
Change
Inquest
Article 19
Antislavery International
Index on Censorship
Romany Guild
International PEN
Southall Black Sisters

- Ask students to list any local pressure groups in your area. Are they sectoral or promotional pressure groups?
- Hand out information sheets 1 and 2. Ask students to find out what each organisation campaigns for.

- Which are the least effective/least recognised logos?
- What image is each logo trying to convey?
- Why does an organisation have a logo?
- Ask groups to design a new logo for Amnesty International or for another pressure group of their choice. It must be simple, easy to reproduce and immediately recognisable.

Activity 2: 'Freedom!'

Ask the students to read the information sheets 'How Amnesty International began' and 'Who runs Amnesty International?'.

ROLE PLAY

Ask two students to role-play two 60-year-old Portuguese men meeting for a drink one evening in August 1999 in that very same bar where, in 1960, they had toasted freedom ('*Liberdade*!') as students, had been arrested for subversion and thrown into jail.

As they raise their glasses to drink another toast to 'Freedom!' two more of your students, playing foreign visitors, enter the bar. What they are doing in Portugal?

They are delegates to Amnesty's International Council Meeting that is taking place nearby. The two Portuguese men buy them a drink. What is this organisation? The two men may have vaguely heard of it. What does it do? How you wish such an organisation had been around when they were in trouble. They tell the visitors what happened to them in this very bar in 1960 when they toasted 'Freedom!' and talk about their unfair trial, the Secret Police and the bad things that happened to them in prison.

They ask how Amnesty International started. How amazed they are to learn for the first time about what grew out of that drink to 'Freedom!'

RULES ON A PAPER NAPKIN

Peter Benenson, Louis Blom-Cooper, and Eric Baker wrote the first version of Amnesty International's working rules, the Mandate, on paper serviettes over a meal in the White Swan pub in the Strand.

Get small groups to set out their own ground rules for the new organisation on a small piece of paper, using the information sheet: 'How Amnesty International began'.

Activity 3: The Amnesty researcher

Give out the information sheet 'Amnesty International and its research'.

- Ask why Amnesty International places so much emphasis on the accuracy and impartiality of its reports.
- Ask small groups to draw up a 60 to 80 word job advertisement to recruit a new researcher for Amnesty International's Research Department to work on Korea. The advert will need to explain briefly what Amnesty International does, and the sort of work that researchers undertake. What skills and qualities might Amnesty be particularly looking for (e.g. languages, knowledge of human rights, research skill, writing ability, local knowledge)?

Activity 4: Is this a case for Amnesty International?

AMNESTY INTERNATIONAL'S MANDATE AND THE UDHR

Give pairs of students a copy of fact sheet 1 'What Amnesty International does – the Mandate', a copy of the UDHR and a large sheet of paper, folded lengthways down the middle.

Ask them to write headings of the main areas of Amnesty International's Mandate on the left-hand side of the paper. On the right-hand side they should write down the corresponding numbers of Articles in the UDHR.

Do any areas of Amnesty International's Mandate not appear in UDHR Articles? Which are they? Why do your students think this is?

HUMAN RIGHTS SCENARIOS

Hand to groups the fact sheets 'What Amnesty International does – the Mandate', 'A typical year's work for Amnesty International' and 'Human rights scenarios'.

The cases in 'Human rights scenarios' are all imaginary, but bear similarity to the sort of cases Amnesty International is dealing with each day.

Groups take on the role of Amnesty International researchers. They must carefully consider the information in each case and answer these questions:

- Does the case fall within Amnesty International's Mandate – if so, which part of the Mandate applies?
- Is further information needed?
- What action might Amnesty International consider taking in this case?

When groups have reported back on their findings, share these probable responses of Amnesty International researchers if these were actual cases.

1. AZERBAIJAN

Amnesty International would:

- Oppose the legislation criminalising same sex relations between consenting adults.
- Consider adopting Vladimir and Asghar as prisoners of conscience and campaigning for their immediate release.
- Call for impartial investigations into allegations of brutality and excessive use of force by the authorities against the peaceful demonstration by the Baku Pink Triangle.
- Not consider the ANYF detainees as prisoners of conscience.

Amnesty International Membership Actions likely to be considered:

- Adoption of Vladimir and Asghar by local Amnesty International groups as prisoners of conscience.
- Possible international awareness-raising campaign on the persecution of sexual minorities.

2. IRAQ

Amnesty International would:

- Oppose the execution of Dr Aziz and all other executions.
- Consider that his trial as a political prisoner would appear to have been grossly unfair.

Amnesty Membership Actions likely to be considered:

- Organise an Urgent Action appeal with Amnesty International members world-wide writing to the Iraqi authorities against the execution, raising questions about the fairness of the trial and calling for impartial investigation into the alleged use of torture to obtain his confession.
- Issue an international press release on the Aziz case and its background.

3. THAILAND

Amnesty International would:

- Oppose the deportation of U John Win to China on the basis of his well-founded fears of persecution if forcibly returned to Burma.
- Not support the case of Daw Ma Thin.

Amnesty Membership Actions likely to be considered:

- Appeals by Amnesty Thailand and Amnesty's International Secretariat to the Thai authorities against Win's deportation.
- International Press Release on the background to the Win case.
- Letter writing campaign by Amnesty International groups in other countries working on human rights in Burma.

4. SRI LANKA

Amnesty International would:

- Not consider these prisoners as prisoners of conscience.

It would:

- Call on the Sri Lankan authorities to arrange immediate and impartial investigations into the allegations of torture, drugging and sexual abuse of the women prisoners.

- Research the situation further.

Amnesty Membership Actions likely to be considered:

- Letter writing campaign by Amnesty International groups in other countries working on human rights in Sri Lanka calling for an inquiry into the allegations.

FURTHER ACTIVITIES

- Visit Amnesty International's website for the latest Amnesty International Urgent Action appeals (perhaps those issued in the past two weeks) on behalf of recent real victims of human rights abuse round the world.
- Ask students in pairs to draft their own personal appeal letters to one of the authorities named in the appeal or to the country's Ambassador in the UK.

Letters should always be courteous, well-informed and short and requesting action.

Groups look at the letters that have been drafted, discuss how they might be made more effective, make any necessary improvements, write the letters out and, where appropriate, send them off by fax or post.

ACTIVITY 1 INFORMATION SHEET 1
Pressure groups

Pressure groups and campaigning organisations have an important part to play in any **democracy**. They are voluntary organisations that provide an effective way for people to give voice to their concerns, stand up for their values, and take action to change things.

Citizens in a democracy not only have the right to make their views heard but have a **responsibility** to do so. This responsibility is especially important when dealing with **human rights** and their violations.

A pressure group is a set of people who have come together with a common aim, who have organised themselves to defend their interests, to promote their ideas and to try and influence political decisions. There are two main types of pressure groups:

- Sectoral groups: represent their members' professional, or personal identity or interest (e.g. a trade union, the Women's Institute, the British Medical Association, The Confederation of British Industry, the British Legion, the Automobile Association, a tenants' association, or a students' union).
- Promotional groups represent a cause that their members support (e.g. the League Against Cruel Sports, Oxfam, the Lord's Day Observance Society, green campaigns like Friends of the Earth, the World Wildlife Fund and Greenpeace, political reform movements like Charter 88, and human rights groups like Amnesty International, Liberty or the Child Poverty Action Group.

Pressure groups are independent voluntary organisations. They are often known as non-governmental organisations. There are very large numbers of them, from small local organisations to huge national and international movements. Many are registered charities.

These groups usually campaign for the aims of their organisation by:

- Building support for their ideas amongst the public
- Attracting interest and coverage in the media
- Lobbying elected representatives (trying to influence the decisions of elected representatives, such as Councillors, and Members of Parliament)

Under UK law registered charities may not become directly involved in political campaigning, although there is sometimes confusion about the exact meaning of the term 'political'. Many non-governmental pressure groups in the UK have both a 'charitable arm' and a 'non-charitable arm'. The Amnesty International Charitable Trust funds those parts of Amnesty's work that are considered charitable: research work, human rights education and relief work for the victims of human rights abuse. Amnesty International UK undertakes the work

continued

of the organisation that is not considered charitable: including political lobbying and campaigning for the release of prisoners of conscience, against unfair political trials, and for the abolition of the Death Penalty.

HUMAN RIGHTS GROUPS

These promote human rights and try to stop their abuse. Today there are thousands of human rights groups around the world. Many concentrate their efforts in order to be more effective. Some, like TAPOL (Indonesia) and the Burma Action Group, concentrate their efforts on human rights in a particular country. Others concentrate on the rights of a particular group in society, such as children (like Save the Children Fund or Casa Alianza) or jailed writers (like International PEN), or on a particular human right, such as freedom of expression (Article 19) or death in custody (Inquest).

Amnesty International is one of tens of thousands of voluntary organisations that are involved in campaigning. Amnesty International's structure, aims, and ways of working are unique. A look at the way it functions will nonetheless give an idea of the way many other non-governmental organisations operate to achieve their goals.

Photocopy Original © Hodder & Stoughton 2001

Organisations and their logos

Organisation	Purpose of organisation	Logo
The Campaign for Nuclear Disarmament		
Save the Children Fund		
Oxfam		
Christian Aid		
The Royal Society for the Protection of Birds		
Amnesty International		

Photocopy Original © Hodder & Stoughton 2001

ACTIVITY 2 INFORMATION SHEET 1
How Amnesty International began

In 1960, Peter Benenson, a 40-year-old British lawyer, read a newspaper article on his way to work. It described how two Portuguese students in a Lisbon bar had raised their glasses to drink a toast to 'Freedom!'

Portugal at the time was under the fascist dictatorship of General Salazar. The newspaper report said that the students had been arrested and had been sentenced to seven years' imprisonment for the crime of 'subversion'.

Incensed by this, Peter Benenson began to consider ways in which the Portuguese authorities – and other governments – could be persuaded to release such victims of injustice. His idea was to bombard governments with letters of protest at the imprisonment of what he called prisoners of conscience, and to call for their release.

Together with the Quaker Eric Baker, and lawyer Louis Blom-Cooper, Peter Benenson launched his 'Appeal for Amnesty 1961'. The editor of the *Observer* newspaper gave Peter a whole page of his paper to publicise this idea, and editors in other countries ran the same article.

On 28 May 1961 Peter Benenson's article 'The Forgotten Prisoners' appeared, telling the stories of six people who were in prison simply because of their ideas. Two Roman Catholic bishops and one philosopher were prisoners in communist countries in Eastern Europe; one was a priest jailed for opposing the colour bar in the USA; one was a communist seaman jailed for his trade union activities in Greece. The sixth was Agostinho Neto, an African doctor and poet held without trial in Portugal, a political prisoner who was later to become the President of Angola.

The article received a tremendous response: letters of support and money arrived, details of many more prisoners were sent in, and volunteers eager to work for the release of prisoners of conscience came forward in many countries. Within eight weeks the first international meeting had taken place. Amnesty International had begun. In its first year, national Amnesty International Sections had been set up in seven countries.

Within twelve months, the new organisation had sent delegations abroad to make representations on behalf of prisoners and had taken up hundreds of cases. It established its principles of political impartiality. Its concerns were the human rights involved in each prisoner's case, not the political or religious ideas either of the prisoner or of the imprisoning state. Its members campaigned on prisoner cases, policies and actions agreed internationally. Amnesty International members took action only on cases abroad, not in their own countries.

Who runs Amnesty International?

Today Amnesty International has over a million members and supporters world-wide in over 150 countries. There are Amnesty International sections and local groups in over 70 countries around the world, with many thousands of Amnesty International groups in schools and colleges.

Amnesty International is a democratic organisation. Its policies and activities are decided and carried out by its members. Its governing body is its International Executive Committee (IEC) of nine members from round the world, eight are volunteers elected at Amnesty International's policy-making conference, the 600-strong International Council Meeting (ICM) held every two years to decide policies and draw up plans. Each Amnesty Section can propose changes to the organisation's structure, goals, methods, investigations and action.

Amnesty International's policies have evolved and changed over the years, in response to changing patterns of human rights violations round the world. Today, for example, the world no longer sees the 'show trials' and large numbers of political prisoners that marked the Soviet Gulags and the prisons of South Africa in the 1960s. Amnesty International's targets and methods have also developed as the organisation has grown in size and sophistication.

In recent ICMs, Amnesty International has decided to expand its work to include campaigning against human rights abuses by armed opposition groups, to work against the trade in torture equipment, to act against the persecution of sexual minorities, and to work against Female Genital Mutilation.

Amnesty International has sections in 70 countries with their own offices and full-time staff to organise Amnesty's members and campaigns. The British section, Amnesty International United Kingdom (AIUK), is one of the largest.

Photocopy Original © Hodder & Stoughton 2001

ACTIVITY 3 INFORMATION SHEET

Amnesty International and its research

From small beginnings in 1961 Amnesty International has grown into the world's largest international organisation dealing with human rights.

In 1999 Amnesty International's world headquarters, the International Secretariat, (IS), was based in 1 Easton Street, London WC1, an address known all over the world. It employed more than 340 paid staff and 100 volunteers from over 50 countries, most of them working in its Research Department. The organisation is headed by a Secretary General. In 1999 this was Pierre Sané from Senegal.

Amnesty International's reputation depends on the credibility of its research information. Its publications are widely trusted and quoted by journalists, human rights campaigners, scholars, and governments around the world.

All the research is carried out by highly skilled country specialists, who are experts in their countries, their languages, history, religions, and politics. Before Amnesty International takes any action, each piece of information is meticulously checked for accuracy. Researchers must seek additional independent external sources of information to confirm each story, and to verify the reliability of their informants. Translations are carefully examined. The work of Amnesty International's research staff is backed up by the knowledge of experts in the law, medicine, media work and technology.

Amnesty International's information comes in from many sources. Some is obtained through the monitoring of the world's news broadcasts, newspapers, and its official documents and books. Much comes in letters, phone calls, faxes and reports from prisoners or their lawyers and relatives, from human rights groups, trade unions, religious figures, refugees, tribal organisations, political groups, writers. Some is conveyed to Amnesty in secret, on small scraps of paper smuggled from clandestine prisons by bribed guards, or taken out of 'closed countries' at great peril to the witnesses.

ACTIVITY 4 FACT SHEET 1
What Amnesty does – the Mandate

Amnesty International is a human rights organisation that promotes all the rights in the Universal Declaration of Human Rights, but limits its campaigning work to tackling some of the gravest violations of individual civil and political rights. This is laid down in what is known as Amnesty International's **Mandate**, which is primarily based on Articles 3, 5, 9, 10, 18, and 19 of the Universal Declaration of Human Rights.

Amnesty International seeks:

- **The release of prisoners of conscience.** These are men, women, and children detained anywhere for their beliefs, religion, ethnic origin or race, language, or sex, who have neither used nor advocated violence. (Amnesty International's 2000 Annual Report recorded confirmed or possible prisoners of conscience in the jails of 61 countries.)

- **Fair and prompt trials for all political prisoners.**
  In recent years Amnesty International has highlighted up to a quarter of a million prisoners held in administrative detention in the world, detained with no charge, trial or the right to challenge their imprisonment. (In 2000 Amnesty drew attention to grossly unfair trials in 51 countries.)

- **An end to torture** and other cruel, inhuman, or degrading treatment or punishment of all prisoners. (Although the physical or mental torture of prisoners is banned under international law, and is illegal in almost all legal codes, in 1999 Amnesty International reported torture in more than 110 member states of the United Nations.)

- **An end to 'disappearance' and extrajudicial executions.**
  Amnesty opposes enforced 'disappearances' and political killings. (In 1999, there were reports of enforced 'disappearances' in 37 countries and political killings at the hands of the state in 38 countries.)

- **An end to the Death Penalty**
  Amnesty International opposes capital punishment anywhere in all circumstances. (In 1999, executions were carried out in 31 countries, and prisoners under sentence of death were waiting on 'death row' in 63 countries.)

- **Fair treatment for refugees**
  Amnesty International opposes the forcible return of refugees to their country of origin if they are at risk of imprisonment, torture, execution, or persecution. It calls for fair treatment within the country of refuge. (Estimates of the number of refugees world-wide totalled 27 million in 1997, the vast majority of whom were women and children.)

Photocopy Original © Hodder & Stoughton 2001

ACTIVITY 4 FACT SHEET 2

A typical year's work for Amnesty International

1998 was the 50th anniversary of the Universal Declaration of Human Rights. During the year Amnesty International highlighted its importance and collected over 17 million signatures round the world for the rights enshrined in the Declaration. These were presented to the United Nations in Paris on Human Rights Day, 10 December 1998. Amnesty International highlighted the situation of dozens of human rights defenders at risk because of their beliefs and human rights activity.

In 1998 Amnesty International successfully lobbied for the establishment of an International Criminal Court to bring to trial those responsible for criminal human rights abuses.

In 1998, the Research Department of Amnesty International published over 100 major country and theme reports in the four languages of the movement – French, Spanish, Arabic and English – and organised campaigning activity on these reports. Amnesty issued over 550 different emergency appeals on different cases like torture, 'disappearance' and execution that were taken up by participants in Amnesty's 100,000 Urgent Action network round the world.

In 1998, as in other years, Amnesty International lobbied the United Nations in Geneva and New York, and was present at countless intergovernmental conferences and meetings.

During 1998 Amnesty International issued literally hundreds of press briefings on human rights stories.

In 1998 Amnesty International published its 400-page Annual Report highlighting human rights abuses in over 150 countries round the world. Human Rights injustices were identified in widely differing countries, large or small, across the political spectrum, from China to USA. During the year the organisation had to respond very quickly to massive human rights violations, such as massacres in Algeria and murders and ethnic cleansing in Kosovo.

In 1998 the organisation sent international delegations on over 150 research or diplomatic missions, trial observations, and prison visits to more than 70 countries to conduct on-the-spot research on the human rights situation, and to talk about the organisation's concerns to government representatives.

At the beginning of 1998, local group members of Amnesty International from more than 4,000 local groups around the world were working on 1,500 Action files, for over 4,000 victims of human rights violations in over a hundred countries. Action Files on cases such as prisoners of conscience and

Photocopy Original © Hodder & Stoughton 2001

continued

A typical year's work for Amnesty International

'disappearance' are often long-standing, and can last for many years, often until the case is solved (e.g. a prisoner is released).

In 1998 the United Kingdom Section of Amnesty International organised its own campaigns in the UK on Refugees and on Children's Rights. It pressurised the UK Government to take action to prevent the export of arms and equipment to states where they could be used to abuse human rights.

Amnesty International UK rejoiced at the final removal of the Death Penalty from UK law. The organisation took an active part in compiling evidence for an extradition case against the former dictator of Chile, General Pinochet, and worked to establish the principle that no one can grant themselves impunity from punishment for criminal acts.

Amnesty demonstration during Pinochet hearing, House of Lords, 1999

Photocopy Original © Hodder & Stoughton 2001

ACTIVITY 4 FACT SHEET 3
Human rights scenarios

1. AZERBAIJAN

Vladimir Shirokin, 20, has been found guilty of having homosexual relations with his friend, Asghar Ahmed, 21, a fellow student at the Engineering School of Baku University. In Baku High Court yesterday they were sentenced to five years jail under Article 113 of Azerbaijan's Legal Code.

Two protest demonstrations took place outside the court. A peaceful picket organised by the Baku Pink Triangle Society with placards calling for homosexual equality was violently broken up by police armed with clubs. Several demonstrators were arrested and charged with breaching the peace. There were a number of injuries amongst the protestors. The Pink Triangle claimed excessive use of force by the authorities.

A protest march was staged by the Azerbaijani Nationalist Youth Front (ANYF) with placards saying that AIDS was an Armenian plague, and all queers should be gassed. ANYF supporters threw stones and rocks at the other demonstrators – several of whom were injured. Yadigar Malik, President of ANYF, was arrested. He said this was a denial of his freedom of speech.

2. BASRA, IRAQ

Dr Muhammad Aziz, a surgeon from Basra Teaching Hospital, and a leading lay figure in the Shia religious community in Southern Iraq, was sentenced to death this afternoon in the Military Court for 'planning terrorist acts with the armed opposition, bomb-making and conspiring to undermine the security of the State'. The trial lasted seven minutes. The only evidence produced was a signed confession by Aziz admitting to being a terrorist.

His sister, who was in the public gallery, said Aziz did not speak in the trial. He looked drawn and was walking unsteadily with a limp. He had no lawyer to represent him. He seemed confused. She said her brother had been arrested immediately after he refused to carry out military orders to cut off the left ears of Shia army deserters and to brand crosses on their foreheads.

Under Iraqi law there is no appeal. The execution is due to take place within a few days.

continued

FREEDOM!

3. BANGKOK, THAILAND

Two Burmese asylum seekers who had come here by air via China to seek asylum will be returned to China tomorrow. The Chinese authorities are likely to return them immediately to Myanmar.

U John Win is a Karen teacher, a Christian from Maniplaw in the East of Myanmar. He claims to have escaped from a secret place of detention, a house where he had been held by Tatmadaw, the Burmese military, and severely tortured for four weeks. He had been arrested as a suspected member of the armed opposition. He had refused to take part in forced labour to lay a pipeline through his village. A doctor from the Thai Centre for the Victims of Torture examined the Karen leader yesterday and said his body bore four scars that suggested he had been hung up by his arms for extensive periods and severely whipped with steel cables.

Daw Ma Thin is a young singer from Mandalay who has said she wants to perform classical opera for the King of Thailand as there are few opportunities in Myanmar for her to develop her remarkable musical and dancing skills.

4. COLOMBO, SRI LANKA

Kayankaddu Ratnaweera, a leading figure in the armed opposition group, the Tamil Tigers, and a number of other women detainees who are Tiger suspects, are being held without charge or trial in a Sri Lankan prison. They have gone on hunger strike in protest at their ill treatment. A press release, smuggled out of Nittambuwa Jail claimed that Tiger suspects were being ill-treated and subjected to daily strip searches in front of male guards allegedly looking for concealed weapons. Several of the detainees claimed they had been injected with drugs that resulted in severe pain. Two women said they had been raped by Sinhalese guards. A government spokesman said the alleged press release was simply not credible. Anyway these women terrorists had been responsible for a series of brutal murders and a savage attack on a prison guard.

Photocopy Original © Hodder & Stoughton 2001

Resources

SOME USEFUL ADDRESSES:

Amnesty International UK
Education/ Youth and Students/ Junior Urgent Actions/ Information
99/119 Rosebery Avenue, London EC1R 4RE
Tel: 020 7814 6200 Website: **www.amnesty.org.uk**

N. Ireland Office: 80a Stranmillis Road, Belfast BT9 5AD Tel: 028 90 666 216
Scottish Office: 11 Jeffrey Street, Edinburgh EH1 1DR Tel: 0131 557 2957
E. Midlands Office: 23 King John's Chambers, 13 Bridlesmith Gate, Nottingham NG1 2GR
Tel: 0115 948 1991

The Anne Frank Educational Trust UK
PO Box 11880, London N6 4LN Tel: 020 8340 9077 Website: **www.afet.org.uk**

Anti-Slavery International
Thomas Clarkson House, The Stableyard, Broomgrove Road, London SW9 9TL
Tel: 020 7501 8920 Website: **www.antislavery.org**

Article 19
Lancaster House, 33 Islington High Street, London N1 9LH Tel: 020 7278 9292 Website:
www.article19.org

British Red Cross
9 Grosvenor Crescent, London SW1X 7EJ Tel: 020 7235 5454 Website:
www.redcross.org.uk/news.asp

Casa Alianza UK
(rehabilitation, care and legal aid for street children in Central America)
The Coach House, Church View, Grafton Underwood, Northamptonshire NN14 3AA
Tel: 01536 330 550 Website: **www.casa-alianza.org**

Catholic Fund for Overseas Development (CAFOD)
Romero Close, Stockwell Road, London SW9 9TY Tel: 020 7733 7900
Website: **www.cafod.org.uk**

Campaign for Freedom of Information
Suite 102, 16 Baldwins Gardens, London EC1N 7RJ Tel: 020 7831 7477 Website:
www.cfoi.org.uk

Charter 88
18A Victoria Park Square, London E2 9PB Tel: 020 8880 6088
Website: **www.charter88.org.uk**

Christian Aid
35–41 Lower Marsh, London SE1 7RL Tel: 020 7620 4444
Website: **www.christian-aid.org.uk**

Citizenship Foundation
Ferroner's House, Shaftesbury Place, Aldersgate Street, London EC2Y 8AA Tel: 020 7367 0500
Website: **www.citfou.org.uk**

Photocopy Original © Hodder & Stoughton 2001

FREEDOM!

Commission for Racial Equality
Elliot House, 10–12 Allington Street, London SW1E 5EH Tel: 020 7828 7022
Website: **www.cre.gov.uk**

Development Education Association (DEA)
3rd Floor, 29–31 Cowper Street, London EC2A 4AT Tel: 020 7490 8108
Website: **www.dea.org.uk**

Education International
5 boulevard du Roi Albert II (8), 1210 Brussels, Belgium
Tel: 0032 2 224 0611 Website: **www.ei-ie.org**

Equal Opportunities Commission
Arndale House, Arndale Centre, Manchester M4 3EQ Tel: 0161 833 9244
Website: **www.eoc.org.uk**

Forward
6th Floor, 50 Eastbourne Terrace, London W2 6LX Tel: 020 7725 2606
Website: **www.forward.dircon.co.uk**

Human Rights Watch
33 Islington High Street, London N1 9LH Tel: 020 7713 1995
E-mail: **hrwuk@hrw.org** Website: **www.hrw.org**

Index on Censorship (INDEX)
Lancaster House, 33 Islington High Street, London N1 9LH Tel: 020 7278 2313
Website: **www.indexoncensorship.org**

Inter Parliamentary Union (IPU)
Place du Petit-Saconnex, P.O. Box 4381211, Geneva 19, Switzerland Tel: 0041 (0)22 9194150
Website: **www.ipu.org**

International Alert
1 Glyn Street, London SE11 5HT Tel: 020 7793 8383
Website: **www.international-alert.org**

International PEN
9/10 Charterhouse Blds, Goswell Road, London EC1M 7AT Tel: 020 7253 4308
Website: **www.oneworld.org/internatpen**

Liberty (National Council for Civil Liberties)
21 Tabard Street, London SE1 4LA Tel: 020 7403 3888
Website: **www.liberty-human-rights.org.uk**

Minority Rights Group
379 Brixton Road, London SW9 7DE Tel: 020 7978 9498
Website: **www.minorityrights.org**

National Library of Women (Fawcett Library)
London Guildhall University, Calcutta Street, Old Castle Street, London E1 7NT
Tel: 020 7320 1189
Website: **www.lgu.ac.uk/fawcett**

National Union of Teachers
Hamilton House, Mabledon Place, London WC1H 9BD Tel: 020 7388 6191
Website: **www.teachers.org.uk**

Oxfam
274 Banbury Road, Oxford OX2 7DZ Tel: 01865 311311
Website: **www.oxfam.org.uk**

Photocopy Original © Hodder & Stoughton 2001

Panos Institute
9 White Lion Street, London N1 9PD Tel: 020 7239 7622
Website: **www.panos.org.uk**

Parliament
House of Commons Information Office
House of Commons, London SW1A 2TT Tel: 020 7219 4272
Website: **www.parliament.uk**

Peace Child International
The White House, Buntingford, Herts SG9 9AH Tel: 01763 274 459
Website: **www.peacechild.org**

Refugee Council
3 Bondway, London SW8 1SJ Tel: 020 7820 3000
Website: **www.refugeecouncil.org.uk**

Save the Children Fund
17 Grove Lane, London SE5 8RD Tel: 020 7703 5400
Website: **www.savethechildren.org.uk**

Scottish Education and Action for Development (SEAD)
167–171 Dundee Street, Edinburgh EH11 1BY Tel: 0131 477 2780
Website: **www.sead.org.uk**

Stonewall
46–48 Grosvenor Gardens, London SW1W 0EB Tel: 020 7881 9440
Website: **www.stonewall.org.uk**

Survival International
6 Charter House Buildings, London EC1M 7ET Tel: 020 7687 8700
Website: **www.survival.org.uk**

UNICEF
Africa House, 64–78 Kingsway, London WC2B 6NB Tel: 020 7405 5592
Website: **www.unicef.org.uk**

United Nations
Website: **www.un.org**

United Nations Association UK
3 Whitehall Court, London SW1A 2EL Tel: 020 7930 2931
Website: **www.oneworld.org/UNA_UK**

Womankind Worldwide
3rd Floor, 5–11 Worship Street, London EC2A 2BH Tel: 020 7588 6096
Website: **www.womankind.org.uk**

SOME USEFUL HUMAN RIGHTS EDUCATION MATERIALS

Order all asterisked materials from: Amnesty International, PO Box 4, Rugby, Warks, CV211
RH (Tel: 01788 545553) quoting the product code.

Education packs
Amnesty International: *Just Right**
CD ROM and Teachers' Pack on the Rights of the Child 1999 KS3/4 £10.00 quoting **Product
Code: CC 005**

Burr, Margaret: *We Have Always Lived Here*
The Maya of Guatemala Education Pack 1991 £10.75 Minority Rights Group

Photocopy Original © Hodder & Stoughton 2001

FREEDOM!

Charter 88: *Have I the Right?*
Pack on the Human Rights Act and its importance for young people 1998

Fountain, S.: *It's Only Right*
Learning about the Convention on the Rights of the Child UNICEF 1993

Amnesty International: *Why Human Rights? 2*
Interactive video education pack on Amnesty International 1996 £39.50

Why Civil Liberties?
Team Video 7 unit video pack on civil rights in the UK 1993 £39.25
Order from Team Video, 222 Kensal Road, London W10 5BN Tel: 020 8960 5536

Videos

Amnesty International: *Use Your Freedom**
20 minute video about Amnesty International (1996) KS2, KS3 £7.00. **Product Code: VR 185**

Amnesty International: *The Small Window**
20 minute video on Amnesty International's campaigning work (1995) KS4 £7.00 from
Amnesty International, PO Box 4 Rugby, Warks CV21 1RH (Tel: 01788 545 553) quoting
Product Code: VR 186

Amnesty International: Animated cartoon film of the Universal Declaration of Human Rights
(1988) £5.00* **Product Code UD 213**

Channel 4 Schools: *Off Limits: Human Rights* (1998) £12.99
Young people explore the UDHR. Two 25 min video films, teacher's notes. KS3/4
Order from Channel 4 Schools, POB 100, Warwick CV34 6TZ Tel: 01926 436 444

Books

Freire, Paulo: *Education: The Practice of Freedom*
Writers & Readers Publishing Coop 1976

Freire, Paulo: *Pedagogy of the Oppressed*
Penguin 1976

Osler, Audrey and Starkley, Hugh: *Teacher Education and Human Rights*
David Fulton Pubs 1996

Rutter, Jill: *We Left Because We Had To*
Refugee Council, 1996 £7.00

Seager, Joni: *State of Women in The World Atlas* Penguin Books 1997

Selwood, Sara: *Free Expressions**
(1991) Art and Human Rights. KS4
Product Code YA 095

Starkley, Hugh: *The Challenge of Human Rights Education*
Cassell 1991

Supple, Carrie: *From Prejudice to Genocide*
Trentham Books 1993 £16.50
Invaluable material for Holocaust studies KS4 +

Wright, Peter: *The Maths and Human Rights Resource Book**
Amnesty International (£5.00)
Product Code ED 085

Human Rights: Guidance for Key Stages 2 and 3
24 pp Handbook on teaching and learning about Human Rights £5.00
ISBN 19001090 50. DEA /EIHRN

What do We Mean By Human Rights?
Six illustrated background readers for students of KS2, KS3 on different human rights topics:
46 pp £10.99 each 1977 Franklin Watts, 90 Leonard Street, London EC2A 4RH

The Progress of Nations. UN Human Development Report: State of the World's Children
World ranking of achievements and statistics in civil, political, economic and social rights,
education, nutrition, women's rights. Produced annually. UNICEF

State of the World Population report UNPFA

World Guide
Facts, figure on development worldwide. Updated annually. New Internationalist

BIBLIOGRAPHY

Amnesty International: *Human Rights Education Resource Notebook on Gay and Lesbian Rights* AI USA 1995
Amnesty International: *50 years of Women's Rights* Amnesty International ACT 77/01/98
Amnesty International: *Human Rights are Women's Rights* Amnesty International ACT 77/01/95
Amnesty International: *Ten Years after Tiananmen* Amnesty International ASA 17/10/99
Amnesty International: *USA, Developments on the Death Penalty in 1995* Amnesty International
Amnesty International: *Juveniles and the Death Penalty:* Executions World-wide since 1985, AI Index: ACT 50/05/95
Amnesty International: *Death Sentences and Executions in 1996* Amnesty International AI Index: ACT 51/01/97
Amnesty International: *Breaking the Silence: Human Rights Violations Based on Sexual Orientation,* Amnesty International UK 1997
Bolt, Michael: *Man for all Seasons* Methuen 1996
Cloonan, Martin: *Massive Attack* Index on Censorship Issue Six 98
D'Entremont, Jim: *The Devil's Disciples* Index on Censorship Issue Six 98
Fenton, James: *Out of Danger* Penguin Books 1992
McCleddan, Jim: *The Guardian Guide to the Internet,* 1998
Mandela, Nelson: *Long Walk to Freedom* Abacus 1995
Manguel, Albert and Stephenson, Craig: *Dangerous Subjects,* Index on Censorship 6/96
Orwell, George: *1984,* Penguin Books 1949
Owen, Ursula: *Hate Speech,* Index on Censorship/1999
Petley, Julian: *Smashed Hits* Index on Censorship Issue Six 98
Rajendra, Cecil: *Refugees and Other Despairs* Choice Books 1980
Saghal, G., Yuva, N., Davies, I. (Ed.): *Refusing Holy Orders: Women and Fundamentalism in Britain* Virago 1992
Selwood, Sara: *Free Expressions* Amnesty International Art Pack AIUK 1991
The Global Liberty Campaign: Website: **www.gilc.org**
The Guardian Website: **www.newsunlimited.co.uk/freedom**

Up-to-date and detailed information on human rights concerns and campaigns in the UK and across the world is always available via the Amnesty International website at
www.amnesty.org.uk

FREEDOM!

Index

Photocopy Original © Hodder & Stoughton 2001